The Art of NETSUKE CARVING

The Art of

NETSUKE CARVING

by MASATOSHI
as told to
RAYMOND BUSHELL

KODANSHA INTERNATIONAL LTD.
Tokyo, New York and San Francisco

Distributed in the United States by Kodansha International/USA Ltd. through Harper & Row, Publishers, Inc., 10 East 53rd Street, New York, New York 10022. Published by Kodansha International Ltd., 12–21, Otowa 2-chome, Bunkyo-ku, Tokyo 112, and Kodansha International/USA Ltd., 10 East 53rd Street, New York, New York 10022 and 44 Montgomery Street, San Francisco, California 94104. Copyright in Japan 1981 by Kodansha International. All rights reserved. Printed in Japan.

LCC 81–80659
ISBN 0–87011–480–8
JBC 3071–7896779–2361

First edition, 1981

CONTENTS

Introduction

Everything published about netsuke is written from the point of view of collectors and connoisseurs. They make a solid contribution to our understanding of the subject: classifying types, identifying materials, differentiating techniques, characterizing carvers, and establishing criteria of quality. Yet for all the value of their writing they leave a wide area blank, and, as a consequence, our appreciation suffers. First, we know nothing about netsuke from the viewpoint of the craftsmen who made them. In other fields, the artists themselves wrote a great deal about their art, their attitudes and aims, their media and techniques. Second, we know nothing about the netsuke carvers as living human beings and about the circumstances that animated their creations. Instances abound in other fields—for example, the painter who revealed his contempt in his portrait of the supercilious duke, or the composer who had to grovel for the stipend he was promised for his quartet. There are no such tidbits of human interest to enrich our appreciation of netsuke. Our netsuke satisfy us aesthetically but leave our desire to know something of the people who carved them and of the surrounding circumstances unsatisfied.

In *The Art of Netsuke Carving*, Masatoshi enables us for the first time to see the subject from the viewpoint of the carver himself. He recounts his training, the influences that molded his craftsmanship; his tools, how he makes and uses them; his materials, how he selects them for quality and suitability; his carving, the various techniques he employs for particular results and effects; why he polishes his netsuke so meticulously; his coloring, why he stains some materials and not others; where he finds his ideas for his subjects; how he decides his treatments; and how he works out his designs. All this is an area in the total netsuke picture that has been left blank. Masatoshi fills in the blank comprehensively. Now, for the first time, we have an authentic catalogue of the major part of the lifework of a carver that compares with those we have for so many painters and sculptors of the Western tradition.

Many of the tantalizing questions that beset us find their responses in Masatoshi's book. How many years did a carver spend as an apprentice? How many as an assistant? How many netsuke did he make in his lifetime? How much time did he spend on a single netsuke? Whom did he carve for? Did he choose subjects and treatments for himself or for his customer? Did he copy other carvers? How varied a range of styles and techniques did he adopt? Why did he change styles? Did apprentices and assistants do some of his work? Where did he get his ideas? Why did he change his *gō*, his *kakihan*, his style of signing? These are normal questions for the collector to ask, but they are questions that only a carver like Masatoshi can answer.

Masatoshi was taught by his father, Kuya; Kuya was apprenticed to his uncle Toshiaki, who was born in 1841, toward the end of the Edo Period. Toshiaki, for his part, was taught by an older family member who was born earlier in the nineteenth century; and so on. In an unbroken line, Edo attitudes, practices, and traditions have been handed down to Masatoshi virtually intact. We cannot recover the past and unrecorded lives of the carvers of old, but Masatoshi gives us a window through which we can view the Edo carvers as he, Masatoshi, embodies them. From Masatoshi's training and experience we can generalize, we can infer and deduce with reasonable accuracy, and we can apply his attitudes by analogy to the rank and file of the Edo carvers. Besides, Masatoshi seasons his descriptions of the netsuke that are illustrated in these pages with observations that imbue them with human interest.

Masatoshi's story is described "as told to." But the impression this phrase conveys is misleading. It was not a facile recounting and recording. I elicited and extracted. I interrogated, badgered, and prodded. I insisted. Masatoshi gave up the information reluctantly. Revealing his methods and techniques runs counter to his training, to the code of his craft, to the tradition of *isshi sōden*—family secrets handed down inviolate from father to son. Reinforcing this reluctance was his natural reticence and reclusiveness. For example, he has always declined to let me watch him work. Why then did he accede? For almost thirty years now we have been bound together in a congenial relationship, I as his sponsor and he as my protégé. I passionately urged him to publish his story as a service to netsuke, and finally I wore down his resistance with the constant reminder that he had no one to succeed him.

I have been charged with hoarding the works of Masatoshi. Thoughtful collectors have said that I do him a disservice by shielding his netsuke from public sale. To the charge of acquisitiveness I must plead guilty, particularly as concerns Masatoshi. But my motives have not been mercenary, and I do have something to offer in mitigation if not in exoneration. First let me note that, without acquisitiveness, collections would not exist and that I have given Masatoshi some public exposure through books, articles, and an exhibition. For the first half of the many years that I have been acquiring Masatoshi's netsuke I paid substantially more than their market value, and so even had I wished to dispose of them I could only have done so at a loss. When the market for Masatoshi suddenly soared I was already aware of the unusual character of our relationship, the remarkable development of his talents, the advantage of having the bulk of his lifetime work at one time and in one place, and, most of all, the extraordinary opportunity to learn about netsuke from his viewpoint and present the carver's story of his craft.

I cannot say precisely when I first conceived the idea for this book, but a passive period of gestation began a few years after my meeting with

Masatoshi in 1952. The active labor pains that resulted in this book-birth began about five years ago with an initial drawing of Masatoshi's answers to my questions. Since then, these sessions have continued regularly. I elicited the facts of his life and work, organized the material, and wrote it down. Masatoshi's book has assumed for me almost as much importance as his netsuke.

I am grateful to Mikoshiba Misao for her double duty as interpreter and translator. I am grateful to Masatoshi for his double duty as autobiographer and carver.

Raymond Bushell

EDITOR'S NOTE

Names of Japanese are given in the Japanese order, that is, family name first, given name second. Artists and carvers, however, are normally known by the art name they most commonly use rather than by the name they inherited at birth. Masatoshi's family and given names are Nakamura Tokisada, and, although Masatoshi occasionally uses his given name, Tokisada, as an art name, he is known by his "principal" art name, Masatoshi.

All names and technical terms are explained in the Glossary. The netsuke are listed individually in the Index.

I. Life and Training

If my dear mother had not died when she did, I would have been a cook instead of a carver. She died of a seizure at the public bath, where she had taken my little brother and sister. When I saw her in death she had a small smile on her face. She was only forty-four. I had just completed my eight years of compulsory education and wanted to be a sailor, thinking how adventurous it would be to travel to foreign lands. But for reasons I never understood, my father had decided that I should be a cook. I adjusted to his decision by imagining myself working as a cook aboard ship. My mother's death changed all that. There were a younger brother and sister to look after, and, consequently, my father decided that I should follow him as a carver. I began my apprenticeship with my father as teacher. The year was 1931. I was sixteen.

Only in our relationship of father and son did my apprenticeship differ from the customary arrangement for learning a craft in the Edo Period. A craftsman who wanted his son to follow in his profession usually entrusted him to another craftsman. The boy would then go to live and work as a servant-apprentice in his master's home, where he would be given food and shelter. His life was expected to be harsh as an essential condition for proper training. Harshness for the craftsman was regarded in the same light as austerities for the priest—a quality that gave birth to singlemindedness of purpose, to sincerity, and to dedication. It was the need for this ingredient of harshness that militated against a craftsman teaching his own son. Sometimes, I wonder whether my work shows a certain mildness as a result of the warm and loving atmosphere in which I was trained. I wonder whether the ingredient of harshness is missing from my craftsmanship.

Life for many apprentices, however, whether apprenticed to craftsmen or to shopkeepers, was worse than harsh. Although still children, they had to earn their rice. They swept and cleaned, fetched and carried, and were on call at all hours, not only for the master and his wife but for his assistants too. The bitterest part was that they were often forced to work as menials for five or ten years before their masters condescended to begin their teaching. Meanwhile, they could not complain, because their master stood in the position of parent and their real parents were usually too poor to take them back. My father and his friends told stories of craftsmen who begrudged their apprentices the opportunity to learn the techniques of the craft because they feared the loss of free labor or the competition of an independent craftsman. Sometimes ambitious apprentices had to watch furtively and study surreptitiously to learn techniques, as though they were filching from their master's strongbox. Perhaps these were exceptional instances of cruel masters and victimized apprentices. At the opposite extreme was the paternal guidance and concern shown by a kind master like Morita Sōko in his dealings with Sosui and his other students. Selfish craftsmen did not hesitate to sign an apprentice's work as their own, while a Sōko helped with all the difficult parts before returning the piece to his student to finish and sign. The median nature of the master-apprentice relationship was harsh enough if it merely accorded with the hard times that prevailed among craftsmen and shopkeepers in the Edo Period.

As my father taught me and was my strongest influence, I want to say a little about him and about our family. Father was tiny and delicate boned, weighing barely forty kilograms (ninety pounds). Still, he was sinewy and resilient and enjoyed good health. He died in his eighty-first year, in 1961. Physically, I am much like him.

He was a typical *Edokko* (man of Tokyo), with the happy-go-lucky attitude toward fortune and misfortune summed up in the expressions *shinpai nai* (don't worry) and *shikata ga nai* (can't be helped). His livelihood alternately prospered and declined. He moved our residence more than twenty times. He was never agitated, even when the outlook was bleak. Even when we were living in two tiny rooms of six mats and three mats, we always had food. My father would say that, if we were willing to work, the god who gave us teeth would give us rice. When I was a child, father sometimes took me with him to deliver a carving to a customer and receive the payment. On the way home we invariably stopped off at a *nomiya* (wine shop) for something good to eat and drink. Father slept well even when he had no money, and when he had money he ordered *sake* and *sashimi*. I always felt that father should have lived in Edo times; he would have been right at home. Occasionally, in the Edo spirit, he would tell a tall tale or two or exaggerate some story absurdly.

Life was no harder for *netsuke-shi* than it was for most craftsmen and shopkeepers. It is well known that Kokusai, who originated the *kokusai-bori* technique of carving in stag-antler, had to eke out a living by working as a male geisha (*taikomochi*). One of my father's friends, an *okimono-shi* (carver of cabinet figures), operated a small stall that sold fermented beans. Another was a wood carver who sold green tea and seaweed as a sideline. Many *netsuke-shi* had to peddle or to carry on some petty business to make ends meet. I once knew a carver of ivory mask *netsuke* whose wife had to work alongside him all his married life in order to subsist. Many *netsuke-shi* were forced to quit, though in recent years the stringent conditions have improved for some carvers.

My father, whose *gō*—or more properly *gagō* (art name)—was Kuya, studied under his uncle, Shimamura Toshirō. The Shimamura family's hereditary profession was that of shrine and temple carver. They were carvers rather than carpenters; they carved decorative panels and friezes. Father claimed that the Shimamura family could trace its history back twenty-two generations. I cannot verify the accuracy of so ancient a lineage, but Buddhist records and family memorial tablets (*ihai*) confirm some four or five generations. One of our ancestors was Shimamura Entetsu, but I cannot determine how many generations there were between Entetsu and my great-grandfather, Shimamura Bunjirō. My father once showed me the chronicle of our family, but I am unable to find it.

The curse of the Shimamuras was their proclivity for fathering daughters but not sons, who could have carried on the family name. Generation after generation of Shimamuras was forced to adopt sons for marriage to its daughters. (When there are no natural sons, we preserve the family lineage and name by adopting sons to marry our daughters.) The curse appeared to have been lifted with the birth of three sons—in addition to two daughters, one of them my grandmother—to my great-grandfather, Bunjirō, but the tragic irony of this sudden abundance of male heirs was that it led to the extinction of the Shimamura line.

Since there were three sons, no one objected when two of them, the eldest and youngest, were adopted by heirless families. The middle son, Shimamura Toshirō, was a carver of ivory *okimono*. His *gō* was Toshiaki, and he enjoyed a reputation as a *meijin*, or master-hand: he is mentioned in the *Meijin monogatari* (An Account of Master Artists) by Matsumura Shōfu. He is especially dear to me because he was my father's teacher. As a young man, Toshiaki's ambition was to continue carving until he was fifty and then to devote himself to painting. When I was young, I too nurtured the same ambition, but in the end I never caught the painter's fire. Now it is only carving that stirs me.

The Shimamura jinx of no male heirs struck again with Toshiaki. Having no son, he adopted his best student, Yoshida Yoshiaki (whose *gō* was Hōmei) to marry his daughter and succeed him. But a bitter estrangement occurred, and Hōmei abandoned the Shimamuras, returned to his family, and left Toshiaki without a male heir. The Shimamura line was extinguished. (I am a descendant by blood of the Shimamuras, though my name and family were changed when my father was adopted.)

Toshiaki died in 1896 at the age of forty-two. The forty-second year in a man's life is a critical and dangerous year. It is, in fact, a *yakudoshi*, one of the "evil years" when disease, accident, natural calamity, or even death is most likely to occur. For men, the ages are twenty-five and forty-two; for women, nineteen and thirty-three. Forty-two is a fatal age because the numbers "four" and "two" together are read "*shi-ni*," which means "death" —but I don't know why the other ages are feared. In determining our *yakudoshi*, we must count in the traditional Japanese way with the years of birth and death included in the total and not in the modern method of counting with our first year ending on the first anniversary of our birth. When the traditional Japanese count is forty-two, the count of full years lived will be either forty or forty-one depending on the date of birth. My experience supports my belief in *yakudoshi*: my first wife died when I was forty-two.

Of my three great-uncles, only Toshiaki practiced carving. His brother Kanetarō, however, became famous as a *nikubori-shi* (tattoo artist), adopting the *gō* of Horikane. My father once told me that Horikane tattooed a design on the person of the Prince of Wales when he visited Japan. Horikane tattooed a dramatic scene on father's back representing the struggle of Minamoto Akugenta Yoshihira killing his uncle Yoshikata. He applied the design in simple lines, without recourse to the vignette, or shading, technique known as *bokashi*. Father used to blame his frequent colds on the tattoo. He believed that it was because of the tattoo that he had to go so often to the toilet in winter. In the West tattoos are common in design and crude in execution, but in Japan a *nikubori-shi* has the same status as a woodblock artist, and his designs are as striking as those in *ukiyo-e*. One tattoo may cover all of a man's back or even the whole body.

Toshiaki's eldest sister, Chise, was my grandmother. She married Sahara Shōzan, who—far from being a carver—became a doctor during the upheaval following the Meiji Restoration. He had joined the Shōgitai, a rebel band formed at Ueno, in Tokyo, to defend the old feudal order. The rebels were quickly defeated by the new government, and my grandfather was forced to flee to Nagasaki. While in exile, he studied medicine according to revolutionary Dutch principles. Dutch medicine and manuals were in sharp conflict with the traditional Chinese medicine that the Japanese doctors practiced. When the bodies of executed criminals were dissected, it was found that the Dutch charts of anatomy were accurate, while the ancient Chinese manuals showing "five viscera and six entrails" were fallacious. Chinese medical practices, however, had been followed for hundreds of years, while the new Dutch medicine was foreign and suspect. Even the Dutch language was ridiculed, because it was written sideways instead of down the page. When at last it was safe again, my grandfather returned to Tokyo, where he established himself as a physician in Western medicine. I believe he had a hard life. He died in 1882.

My father, the youngest of four children, was not yet one year old at the time. His correct name was Sahara Takakazu, but everybody called him Shinzō, the alternative reading of Takakazu, and finally he had to accept Shinzō as his *tsūshō* (calling name). He married into the Nakamura family, which adopted him as it lacked a male heir, and was entered into the Nakamura family register. At first, father used Kuya or Ittensai Kuya as his *gō*—Kuya, if the reserve for his signature was small, and Ittensai Kuya, if space permitted. About the year 1940, he received his *kaimyō* (Buddhist or posthumous name) from our family temple, the Daishōji, a Zen temple in Akabane, Tokyo. Part of his *kaimyō* was Musōin, which he changed arbitrarily to Musōan. From then on he signed himself Musōan Kuya and transferred his former *gō* of Ittensai to me, and I began on occasions to sign myself Ittensai Masatoshi. When I received my own *kaimyō*, I stopped using Ittensai.

I heard that father's elder brother Kojirō was a carver, but I can find no proof. No art name is shown for him on his memorial tablet in our family temple.

Father began his apprenticeship in *okimono* carving, with my great-uncle Toshiaki as his teacher. When Toshiaki died, father continued his training under Toshiaki's close friend Hashimoto Shingyoku, who was also an *okimono-shi* and whose specialty was the same as that of Toshiaki: the *bijin*, or beautiful woman, carved in graceful, flowing ivory. Father's relationship with Hashimoto was not the usual one of master and apprentice but that of teacher and student. He was not obliged to serve Hashimoto, and Hashimoto was not obliged to provide a home for him. Instead of living in Hashimoto's house, he visited him daily to study. Hashimoto, for his part, had undertaken to train father as payment for his debt of friendship to Toshiaki. I don't know the exact arrangement, but I'm sure that father assisted Hashimoto or paid for his training with small gifts or a little money now and then.

It was not until many years after he started working independently as an *okimono-shi* that father turned to carving netsuke. He learned the craft through his own efforts. It was a man named Sawada, the proprietor of a *fukuromono-ya* (purse and pouch shop) at Nihonbashi in the center of Tokyo, who urged him to carve netsuke. Sawada showed father many fine netsuke and explained their characteristics and their differences from *okimono*. He was inflexible and a perfectionist, paying for all of father's efforts but ruthlessly discarding those that fell below his standards. Father tried hard, but it took a long time before his work satisfied Sawada. I believe Sawada was very rich. Father often declared that he owed a great deal to Sawada.

Father used to carry a *bokutō* (wooden sword) made of cherry wood for his protection. So far as I know, he never once used it in anger. His friend Koizumi Segai, a spirited and witty man with whom he often drank *sake*, engraved a poem on father's *bokutō* in beautiful characters: "O bamboo leaves, / when you can bear no more, / shake off the snow that burdens you. Carved by Segai." Segai was probably the *netsuke-shi* who carved humorous netsuke (see *The Wonderful World of Netsuke*, Plate 12.) I was about ten at the time, and he appeared to be much older than father.

One of the more unlikely commissions father received was for a walking stick for William Sebald, the first American ambassador to Japan following the war. Father went to a lot of trouble, carefully selecting a length of white sandalwood (*byakudan*) with a natural grain that suggested tiger stripes and carving an ivory handle of a dragon to match the stick. It was a clever and original work. He was finally ready to present the cane when he learned that Ambassador Sebald had left Japan. Suddenly the situation was thoroughly confused: it was not clear who had ordered the cane, who was to present it, or who was to pay for it. The matter was finally disentangled, and the cane was eventually delivered to Mr. Sebald at his new post. Somehow, the story found its way into the pages of the *Tokyo Shimbun*'s edition of 15 February 1952 and the *Arakawa Shimbun*'s edition of 24 February 1952.

The newspaper articles said that father was a descendant of the legendary Hidari Jingorō, that he had wandered around France as an *akagetto* (a footloose country bumpkin), that he was a scholar of the philosophy underlying Buddhist sculpture, that he was awarded belts in *judō* and in *kendō*, and that he was eccentric and individualistic. I have no idea of the source for such fictions and exaggerations.

Father died on 14 December 1961. On the same day, 14 December, of the previous year he had announced, "I am dying, I will die tonight." He

1. Masatoshi's father; this photograph was taken in 1952, when Kuya was seventy-one years old.

was not joking. He said that he would drink *sake* and eat *sashimi* and be ready for the trip to *meido*, the world of the dead. Our family took his premonition seriously, and we catered to his wishes even though he appeared to be in high spirits. When he fell asleep that night, his death seemed quite remote. Precisely one year later to the day, he fell into a coma. At the moment he drew his last breath, I said, "Congratulations, father." The doctor said he died of apoplexy. I hope when my time comes I will die the same way, calmly and painlessly. But how can we ever know—will we live long, will we have a foreboding of death? Even to contemplate it is strange and somehow terrifying.

Father had seven children: five sons, of whom I am the second, and two daughters. All of them, except my younger sister and myself, met with a tragic end of one sort or another. My sister Miyako died when I was an infant, and two of my younger brothers, Wataru and Isao, died of the epidemic of Spanish flu that raged across Japan in 1918 and 1919. My elder brother, Teruaki, also died in tragic circumstances. At the time of his death, we were living in a house which we had rented from a certain Mr. Hisaki and his wife, who were childless. They grew to love Teruaki and asked to adopt him as their own son. My parents consented, and Teruaki went to live with the Hisakis. One day not so long after, father heard that Teruaki had been hurt while out riding his bicycle. In great alarm he rushed to the Hisakis, intending to bring Teruaki home with him. Mr. Hisaki told father not to be excited; the accident had only been a minor one; Teruaki was fully recovered and at that very moment was carrying a *mikoshi* (portable shrine) in a local Shintō festival. He insisted that father leave Teruaki alone, and father was obliged to agree. One month later, on 1 September 1923, the Great Kantō Earthquake struck, destroying the lives of over one hundred thousand people. Although I was only eight, father took me to search the devastated area many times, but we never found a single trace either of Teruaki or of the Hisakis and their house. We never learned whether they had been swallowed up by the earth or consumed by fire. Until the day he died, father regretted that he had not insisted on taking Teruaki back.

My younger brother Haruyoshi was brought up by my sister Midori and her husband. They provided him with a good home and affection, but for no reason we could discern he deserted them. Since then, we have had no contact with him at all. We believe he is a drifter and petty gangster.

Now to return to the account of my own training. First of all, I should say that my name is Nakamura Tokisada. I was born in Tokyo on the second of August in the fourth year of the Taishō Era, 1915, which was a Year of the Rabbit. I spent seven years training as an apprentice with my father until 1938, when, at the age of twenty-three, I graduated to the rank of assistant. From then on we worked together, while at the same time I carved netsuke to fill whatever orders I could get on my own. I served as father's assistant for four years, but in 1942, when I was twenty-seven and had already been married one year, my wife and I decided to move into our own house. The departure from my parent's home marked the beginning of my complete independence as a carver. I believe the seven years I spent as an apprentice and the four years as an assistant were about average for craftsmen in the Edo Period.

The first job father gave me as an apprentice was to take care of the tools. I had to keep them clean, scoured, and sharp. Even such menial work called for explanations and instructions, and I had to practice again and again before I got things right. Tasks looked easy when I saw father do them, but when I tried them myself I discovered the difficulties. For example, in "setting a saw" (*nokogiri no metate*) I had to attach a blank blade to the frame, cut triangular teeth of a certain size and shape into the blade, and then sharpen it. To do it right took long practice and experience.

Another job was to take care of the materials that father used in carving, polishing, and coloring, and to prepare them properly. Menial tasks are important as a means of familiarizing oneself with the feel and characteristics of all the paraphernalia used by the *netsuke-shi*. They are the first step in the development of the intimate understanding of materials and tools essential to good craftsmanship. The craftsman ultimately develops an intuition that tells him one material, one tool, or one method is better than another for a particular purpose.

My first job related to the actual carving was to saw blocks out of the materials, making sure that the blocks were of the size and shape that father required. At first I bungled and made clumsy errors like misjudging one of the dimensions or botching a right angle, and occasionally I even mangled a finger in the bargain.

Over the years I learned how to use and how to make tools, how to saw and file material into a rough semblance of the model, and how to shave a rough model into the design—the *netsuke-shi* does not say that he "carves" (*horu*) the material, he says that he "shaves" (*kezuru*) it. I learned, too, how to engrave patterns, how to undercut, how to use special tools to obtain subtle effects, how to inlay eyes, how to drill *himotoshi* for the cords to pass through, how to polish, and how to stain and color. I would need many large books to explain in detail all the practices, methods, and techniques I learned during my years as an apprentice.

As father was already fifty when I began my training, he was anxious to teach me all he knew as quickly as possible. Patiently and eagerly he answered my questions, until he was certain I understood. He showed me examples, he demonstrated techniques, he guided me in my practice, he corrected my mistakes, and he enlightened me with experiences from his own life and from the lives of other craftsmen. Father never discouraged my "whys" and "hows"; far from it—he answered them at length, a policy that was contrary to that of Edo master craftsmen with their apprentices.

The master craftsman traditionally discourages the apprentice who asks, "Why do you do this?" or "How do you do that?" He is likely to reply, "Don't ask me, ask my hand." The response is not necessarily intended as a rude rejection. The craftsman expects his apprentice to learn by watching and doing and not by discussing, for he himself will have learned by careful observation and countless repetitions. He knows from his own experience that if his apprentice watches and practices he will learn and that his questions of "how" and "why" will become superfluous as he gradually learns by doing. Eventually his constant practice will grow into an unthinking proficiency.

Another reason why the craftsman traditionally dislikes answering the questions of apprentices is that he has absorbed and assimilated the basic techniques into an automatic activity. He has forgotten his rules and principles—or, to be more precise, he has forgotten he knows them. He finds it awkward or difficult to remember and articulate them because he has been following them for so many years that he no longer thinks about them. For example, if someone asks me why I use a certain tool for a certain operation, the chances are I will only be able to answer him intelligibly after applying a considerable amount of thought to my response. It's much the same as answering questions about points of grammar to which I give no thought in speaking my native language.

I had served about three or four years of my apprenticeship before father allowed me to carve an entire netsuke by myself. The first netsuke I tried were boxwood masks of familiar characters like Otafuku and Daikoku, but they were only practice pieces and were quite poor. Father either discarded them or gave them away as presents to our family and friends. My next step was to carve masks in ivory, a much harder material than wood and one which I also found much harder to carve well. After working on ivory masks for some time I returned to wood, this time using some white sandalwood that father had procured. I was pleasantly surprised, after working in ivory, to find that the sandalwood carved easily. A year or so later I began to practice carving in-the-round (*marubori*) in both ivory and wood. I remember carving various figures, including Soga no Gorō and other Kabuki subjects, but I can't recall what happened to them.

I believe it was in the fifth or sixth year of my apprenticeship that father decided that some of my netsuke had commercial value, and these he offered for sale. He also decided which of them I should sign, though the choice of signature was left up to me. I recall signing Tokisada on occasion but more often Yūzan or Issai because the *kanji* had fewer strokes and were easier to carve. My work sold slowly, one piece at a time, and did not fetch much.

In those first efforts I made fundamental errors. I was so anxious to make my work impressive that I ignored the requirements of compactness, solidity, and simplicity, as a result of which my netsuke were often full of hooks, catches, and appendages. They were badly overdecorated and were fragile instead of being sturdy. Only gradually did I learn to curb my tendency to make a display of my techniques. Even today I sometimes find myself having to resist the temptation to indulge in display.

Carving my own netsuke, poor as they were, was a great stimulus to my desire to improve and to become a competent craftsman. When I began my apprenticeship, I scoffed a little at father's first admonition: "When you work you must not think, 'How much time should I spend on this?' or 'What price should I ask for that?' If you harbor such thoughts, you will cheapen your work." By the time I was independent, however, I was ready to take this advice to heart.

One of the first netsuke I carved after I finished my apprenticeship was for a private order. I designed a cormorant fisherman and etched a repeat pattern of some sort on the fisherman's hood. Owing to my inexperience I finished with a blank area too small for another repeat of the pattern. I filled in the area with three dots, hoping my error would not attract attention. My customer arrived accompanied by his son, a university student, who examined the piece intently. To my horror, the first thing the son wanted to know was the meaning of the three dots. I thought I had been found out and tried to make a joke of it, telling him that the dots indicated the rank of the fisherman. Far from realizing that something was amiss, the student praised me effusively for my conscientious study and attention to detail. I was stunned and lost the courage to confess the truth. Even after so many years have elapsed, I am embarrassed whenever I think about that episode.

While I tried to emulate father and adopted many of his subjects, my style is not the same as his. He enjoyed carving in special ways that called for a high order of technical and mechanical skill. He had a penchant for marquetry (*yosegi*)—the fitting together of a variety of woods of different shapes—and for hinged-work (*chōtsugai*) models that swing open in various ways. For example, he carved a netsuke of the head of the monster Shutendōji, whose maw opened on a hinge to reveal Yorimitsu and his four followers climbing Devil Mountain, where Shutendōji had his abode, to slay him. The figures were as small as rice grains, yet father managed to delineate their armor, helmets, gauntlets, and straw sandals in detail. I never approached father's mechanical mastery, but during my training I constantly strove to attain his technical proficiency. My efforts then make it easier for me now to cope with the difficulties different models present.

Father worked only at night, when supper was finished and the family was ready for bed. I too fell into this nocturnal pattern quite naturally and have maintained it all my life. The quiet and tranquility of night is conducive to concentration and maximum effort. My routine is to begin work at about nine at night and to continue for some seven hours until dawn, and then to sleep until early afternoon. I spend the afternoon attending to personal affairs and relaxing. In the interests of a normal family life, I reversed my schedule once or twice and tried to carve in the daytime. The attempts were failures, and I realized I could never make a satisfactory netsuke in daylight. Daylight may be good for health, but it is bad for carving. I gave it up with relief and returned to my nocturnal paradise.

I married in 1941, when I was twenty-six. Traditionally, twenty-five or twenty-six is considered the ideal age for a man to marry, and twenty-three or twenty-four for a woman. Before I met the woman who was to become my wife, I had already rejected three other candidates proposed by a *nakōdo* (matchmaker). The first was only nineteen, the daughter of a shopkeeper of purses. She seemed in poor health, and, as a matter of fact, she died one year later. The second prospect came from a large family with a host of brothers and sisters. They lived near me and ran a general store. The family was afflicted with tuberculosis, and one after another they died, including the proposed daughter—all save the youngest daughter, who is now married and still lives in the neighborhood. Whenever I go walking, I make a point of passing her house. The third candidate was six months my senior. The various relationships in her family were remarkably complicated. She had a natural mother and a stepfather, but her brothers and sisters seemed to be the offspring of a succession of different mothers and fathers. We broke off. The stepfather was six years younger than his wife, and when his wife died, he married her younger sister. Fate is curious.

I met my wife, Fumi, through Watanabe, a curio dealer. Fumi, he told us, was the second daughter of his friend Miyamoto, who was also a curio dealer. Watanabe acted as go-between and arranged the *omiai*, or formal meeting. Fumi and I received good impressions of one another, and so a marriage was arranged.

We agreed that the amount of the betrothal payment to my wife's family should be 150 yen. As war was in the air, we paid 50 yen of the betrothal money in the form of government bonds, a required patriotic gesture, and we took other steps in the name of patriotic economizing such as getting married at home. I wore the national uniform of the conscript, and my wife, a modest black bridal kimono with a phoenix design. Her sister wore the same kimono when she married. Pictures of the two brides in the identical black kimono remind me of the austerities of the war years.

Unfortunately the relationship between my wife and my stepmother was very bad. By custom, when a wife comes to live in her husband's home, she must act as a servant to her mother-in-law. Although the custom is not so rigidly observed nowadays as it once was, the wife is still expected to work under her mother-in-law's direction. There is even an old saying that if a husband loves his wife he spoils his mother's servant. Some antipathy between wife and mother-in-law is expected, but in the case of my family it turned into open hostility and became unbearable, so that I could no longer concentrate on my carving. We decided that we should leave my father's house, and so we moved into a small rented apartment. Our removal had the incidental result of finalizing my independence as a *netsuke-shi*. The day after we moved, the first air raids on Tokyo took place.

At about this time, father received an excellent commission—it was quite a windfall for those hard times—to build two pagodas in white sandalwood, one of three tiers, the other of five. The smaller was to be thirty centimeters (one foot) high, the larger, thirty-six centimeters. Father and I worked together, beginning the carving in September 1942 and finishing five months later. When I look at our photographs of the pagodas, I am amazed that we were able to complete them so quickly. They were delivered to Kōbe, where they were later destroyed by fire.

In 1944 I joined the infantry but was discharged due to a heart murmur, my symptoms being strange noises emanating from my chest, a sense of oppression when I bathed in hot water, and shaking knees which almost folded when I walked fast. At that time it was unpatriotic to work as a carver, and, besides, there was no one to buy carvings. I joined Hitachi Machinery as a lathe operator, a position for which I was absolutely unsuited but managed to hold, until I was conscripted by the navy and ordered to Yoko-suka. I waited around at the naval base for several days while I was herded from here to there like a horse or a cow. I was finally scheduled to go to Yamanashi Prefecture as a farm laborer. It seemed strange to me that a naval conscript should be assigned to the mountains. Not long after, a second medical examination revealed my heart condition, and I was discharged for a second time. I returned to my job with Hitachi Machinery but quit as soon as the war ended in August 1945. My condition was diagnosed as beriberi heart. It took a year or two to cure the disease, but I have not been troubled with it since. My father was also forced to quit carving during the war. He waited for peace as a caretaker in a shoe factory. We both returned to carving promptly with the end of the war.

But what a change I found from prewar days! Ivory was no longer being imported. It was either completely unavailable or else extremely difficult to locate. I searched from shop to shop and from dealer to dealer, wherever I might hope to scrounge a remnant of ivory. When I could find them, I used billiard balls and *samisen* plectrums. The practices prevailing among shopkeepers for buying netsuke had also been badly dislocated. Inflation was rampant, and values and prices chaotic. I had to rely on dealers to buy my work, since private orders were rare or nonexistent.

The dealers to whom I sold my netsuke during the immediate postwar years differed widely in their methods of doing business with me. Each in his own way is vivid in my memory. For example, Dealer A never bargained. As far as he was concerned, my price was reasonable and he paid it. I can picture him now, examining one of my netsuke appreciatively and gently polishing it with a strip of *momi* (red silk). He often asked me, however, to add some pattern or some detail to netsuke he had bought from other carvers. Sometimes he would even ask me to complete someone else's half-finished work and to inscribe some name like Hōzan, which I did.

Dealer B would give me three or four pieces of ivory, each just big enough for a single netsuke. He wrote down the weight of each piece and compared the weight of the finished netsuke. He wanted to be sure I didn't steal his ivory. He invariably bargained with great stubbornness and was not satisfied unless I reduced my price, even if by only a small amount.

Dealer C provided me with ivory of fine quality and allowed me to use it as I liked. He never bargained and never made any special requests.

Dealer D sometimes bargained, sometimes not, depending on his mood. However, he made me buy my ivory from him, and he deducted the cost of the ivory from the price of the netsuke.

Dealer E bargained relentlessly. Often he took the netsuke, promising to pay me the following day, after he had sold it in Yokohama. He often broke his promises or paid me only half the agreed amount. Finally I had to quit carving for him.

Dealer F forced me to hire a relative of his as my assistant. I was reluctant and resented having to do this, but it was his condition for buying my carvings, and I needed the work. I allowed the assistant to do some rough shaping and then went over his work afterward with my own knife, so that what he did had no effect whatsoever on the final result. But my pride would not permit me to sign one of my regular *gō* on a netsuke that someone else had touched, however insignificantly. On these netsuke I signed Mitsu-masa, a name which I had plucked out of the air. I carved the character for "*masa*" a bit differently from the "*masa*" in Masatoshi. Except for the "Mitsumasas," every netsuke I have ever made is entirely and exclusively my own work. From sawing out the initial block to giving it a final hand polishing, only my own hands and my own tools have touched it. The netsuke shown in Plates 1, 2, and 3 are signed Mitsumasa.

Some dealers would make me drink *sake* with them, hoping to put me in an easy mood for a sharp bargain, while others would pay me half in cash, half in ivory. That way I couldn't win, because they adjusted the price of their ivory to the price of my netsuke. In those days every netsuke I sold was an individual transaction requiring hard negotiations to settle the price. Sometimes I felt that I had two jobs not one, the first job being to make a good netsuke, the second to get the money for it. The situation continued in this degrading manner until 1952, when, as a result of our first meetings with foreign collectors, father and I gained a greater sense of security.

Father never kept records of the netsuke he carved. There was no particular reason; it was simply not his custom. I did not keep records either until 1952, when I began carving for foreign customers. From then on, I kept records of most of the netsuke I produced, and it is from these records that the dates of completion are taken for the netsuke illustrated in this book. I can give no better reason for recording my netsuke after 1952 than I can for not having done so before. I may have thought at first that it was necessary to keep some records because I was dealing with foreigners.

By now I have forgotten, or can only vaguely recall, the netsuke I carved before 1952. When I examine one I carved before then, I recognize it without doubt as my own work, but it's more than I can do to remember the date and circumstances.

Since 1952 I have signed my works with the following *gō*: Masatoshi, Ittensai Masatoshi, Jikishiin Masatoshi, Tokisada, Yūzan, and, occasionally, Shunzan. Masatoshi was my own choice for my *gō*. I took the character for "*masa*" from Hashimoto Gahō ("*masa*" is the alternative reading of "*ga*"), a famous Meiji painter whom I greatly admired, and for "*toshi*" from Toshiaki, my great-uncle who taught father. Masatoshi may have a pretentious ring to it, but it is my favorite *gō* and the one I use most often. From time to time I use my true name, Tokisada, as my *gō*. I am inclined to use Tokisada when I feel that the netsuke is a radical departure from my usual subject or style. This is the reason too—as far as I can remember —why I have on a few occasions used Shunzan as my *gō* (Plates 147, 188, and 213). The character for *"shun"* is the same as the character for *"toshi"* in "Masatoshi." As for my other *gō*, Yūzan, I used it because it is easy to carve and has a smart appearance. For a time I wavered between Masatoshi and Yūzan, but finally I decided on Masatoshi because of my deep affection for the name. I went on using father's *gō* Ittensai, which he transferred to me, from time to time with Masatoshi until I received my own *kaimyō*.

My *kaimyō* was conferred on me in 1961 by the chief priest of Daishōji, our family temple. The status of the *kaimyō* is roughly proportionate to the number of characters, a longer name generally signifying a higher grade, with the priest determining the grade of the *kaimyō* he confers. Even though a parishioner may make a large donation, it will not assure him a long *kaimyō*. In my case, the chief priest requested that I give a netsuke instead of cash. He determined my *kaimyō* himself without any suggestion from me. It is "Jikishiin Jikū Shintei Koji," a name which, in order to convey its full meaning and religious connotations, is best explained like this:

Jikishiin—"to aim at the moon without illusions."
Jikū—"time and space encompassing all."
Shintei—"a steady, quiet, peaceful universe."
Koji—"a man who has faith in Buddhism and teaches it to others."

To be honest I do not feel that I have such faith in Buddhism that I deserve the designation of "Koji."

Most people believe that a *kaimyō* ought not be conferred until after death, but this is a misunderstanding. A man should prepare for death while he is alive. The chief priest of Daishōji explains that a *kaimyō* is like a passport from this world to the next and from transitory time to eternal time. Having a *kaimyō* while still alive contributes to a feeling of security and peace, a preparedness for death.

I often combine my *kaimyō* and *gō* and sign Jikishiin Masatoshi, although I can only carve this combination when there is adequate space. Except for my affection and preference for Masatoshi, there has never been any particular significance to my choice of *gō*. My choice is often a matter of the mood of the moment and my reaction to the netsuke when it begins to emerge in a finished state. My choice of *gō* has no relationship whatsoever to the quality of the carving.

My only child is a daughter, Tamiko, born in 1946. When the time came for her to marry, I was prepared to defy the custom requiring her husband to be adopted into my family and let the Nakamura line die out. Many a good prospective marriage foundered because the husband-to-be refused to change his name and family. Fortunately, my son-in-law willingly entered my family register and took the Nakamura name to succeed me. He is an office worker and has no connection with carving and craftsmanship. I now have three grandchildren, two girls and one boy, and should any of my grandchildren show an aptitude for carving, I would be delighted to teach them as affectionately as my father taught me.

I have always been a loner, a hermit without a cave, content with my work and my family. My happiness is in my home and my workshop. I have never joined organizations or clubs for the promotion of ivory carving or for the discussion and study of methods and techniques. A few such associations are active in Tokyo, but I have declined to participate. The establishment of ivory carvers' associations began with the Meiji Restoration and the introduction of the Western style of teaching art in open classrooms, but my attitudes are rooted in the Edo Period, when instruction in the principles of a craft had to be earned in an intimate relationship with a master. Then, the tradition prevailed of *isshi sōden*, transmission from father to son (or to an adopted pupil) in order to guard special techniques and devices as family secrets. Admittedly, the secrecy sometimes resulted in the loss of unique methods. I have never taken a student and feel no regret about it.

My reclusive nature shows in other ways too. Mr. Bushell once asked me whether he could watch me work. Much as I wanted to please him, I had to refuse for the simple reason that I cannot work while anyone watches. Other eyes on my hands while I tried to carve would surely paralyze them. Some people may consider me a little peculiar, but I can't change my nature. My father was outgoing, expansive, and gregarious—all things that I am not. While I was still an apprentice, he promised one of his foreign customers that he would take me to their home to demonstrate netsuke carving. I could not refuse without causing father an irreparable loss of face. Reluctant, embarrassed, and angry, I quickly roughed out an ivory gourd—a slipshod job, just enough to demonstrate shaping, shaving into model, and polishing. I finished in two hours, gave it to them as a present, and resolved there and then that never again would I improvise a carving or exhibit myself.

Mr. Bushell once offered, as my sponsor, to give me a vacation abroad to Hongkong or Honolulu. I have never been abroad, so perhaps he thought I would be curious and pleased. I declined—to his surprise—and asked to go instead to Nagoya to spend a week with my daughter and grandchildren and on with them to Kyoto, a city I had never before visited.

In the chapters that follow, I deal with the various aspects of carving —tools, materials, techniques, polishing, coloring, subjects, and designs. I discuss these aspects in general terms, according to the principles that have guided me, and leave all special applications and explanations for the descriptions of the individual netsuke to which they apply. In those instances I think the illustrations will help to make the explanations clear.

II. Tools

The first thing I want to say is that I never use power tools of any kind. I avoid lathes, drills, cutters, buffers, and any instrument that is motor-driven. I was taught that all energy and power should emanate from me, the craftsman, and pass directly from my hands to my materials. In these days of time-saving devices, people tend to ridicule the idea of doing all the work by hand. They consider my ways outmoded and ask me why I don't use an electric saw to cut the basic blocks which I intend to carve. "It will save you time and labor," they tell me, as if I hadn't realized. My only answer lies in tradition, training, and pride. I am a craftsman and I have to do everything with my own hands. Any agency that intervenes between me and my material debases my work. I can tell just by looking that power tools do not cut, drill, shave, smooth, and polish as sensitively as I do with my hands. The loss, however slight, of registration and quality would not be worth the saving in time and labor.

The types of tools that I use day in, day out fall into five categories: saws (*nokogiri*); files (*yasuri* and *sharime*); chisels, both square (*aisuki*) and round (*marunomi*); drills, both straight (*kiri*) and spiral (*doriru*); and knives, both those with a cutting edge on the left (*hidariba*) and those with a cutting edge on the right (*migiba*). I also have occasion to use a few miscellaneous tools: an ordinary knife (*kogatana*), hammer (*tonkachi*), calipers (*nogisu*), ruler (*monosashi*), and vise (*manriki*).

While I work, I have on hand by actual count 5 saws, 55 files, 56 chisels, 26 drills, and 82 knives, making a total of 224 individual tools (Figure 3). More than half of these tools I use frequently, the others being duplicate spares or extras. Many of my tools have thin shafts and delicate cutting edges. When a tool snaps or chips or when repeated sharpenings reduce it to a state where it is no longer effective, rather than interrupt my work, I replace it with a reserve tool. Similarly, when a tool becomes dull, I sometimes take a few moments off to sharpen it with whetstone (*toishi*), but at other times I replace it with a spare, let the dull tools accumulate, and then sharpen them all together.

Once I have decided on my subject, size, and material, the saw is the first tool I use. Whether I am working with wood, ivory, horn, or antler, I use a saw first to cut out a block of the material and then to do the preliminary rough shaping of the block. I follow with heavy files and round chisels for the final stages of rough shaping. I buy the saw frames ready

2. Masatoshi at work sawing a tusk in his studio.

made and attach flexible blank steel bands to them myself. I also do the cutting, shaping, and sharpening of the teeth—a procedure known as *metate*, setting the saw. I always cut the teeth in a triangular shape (*sankakume*), but with different sizes for different bands. Figure 4 shows two of my saws, one with coarse teeth, the other with fine. Surprising though it may seem, I use the same saws regardless of the material and regardless of whether I am sawing with, against, or diagonally across the grain. Figure 5 shows a special, hard steel file which I use for serrating the steel bands of my saws. This type of file is called a *ha-yasuri*, literally a "leaf file," and is so named because of its extreme thinness.

My files can be divided into two distinct categories, *yasuri* and *sharime*. *Yasuri* (Figure 6), like the *ha-yasuri*, are used for shaping tools, while *sharime* (Figure 7) are used for shaping netsuke. *Yasuri* are made of hard steel, *sharime* of ordinary steel. I buy *yasuri* in various sizes and shapes— square, round, and triangular—and in various corrugations, ranging from coarse to fine, from the ready made stock of dealers in machine parts (*kōgu-ten*). I use the *yasuri* progressively from coarse to fine, as I shape and sharpen my tools, particularly my knives and chisels.

Sharime, on the other hand, have to be ordered specially, as I require them in shapes and with characteristics that are not stocked by a machine parts dealer. The ones I order have extremely high ridges and come from a specialized toolmaker in Tochigi, a town north of Tokyo. It usually takes him thirty to ninety days to fill my order. Even then, the ridges are shallower than I want and they soon lose their effectiveness. In the old days it was a different story and he furnished high-ridged files exactly as I ordered.

One thing *yasuri* and *sharime* have in common is the way I use them: in a thrusting motion always in the same direction, away from my body.

Chisels can be divided by shape into square chisels (*aisuki*) and round chisels (*marunomi*) (Figure 8). The shank, or shaft, of the square chisel is flat and the cutting edge is a straight line, while the shank of the round chisel is concave and the cutting edge is curved. Square chisels produce a flat surface, round chisels a curved surface, a rounded edge, or a groove. I use the heavier square chisels for chiseling off thick shavings and the heavier round chisels for hollowing.

None of my knives are ordinary, flat knives with one edge sharpened like those used in the kitchen—except, that is, for the *kogatana* (Figure 10). Far from it—they are knives with a solid, triangular, three-dimensional "blade." When they are lying flat on a table, the apex of the triangle points upward, the base is flat, and the cutting edge is on the left or the right, depending on the knife. The knife is called a *hidariba* if the cutting edge is on the left, and if on the right, a *migiba*. The *hidariba* is the tool I use most often of all. Of my eighty-two knives, seventy-two are *hidariba* and only ten are *migiba*. *Netsuke-shi* rarely use the term "knife"; instead, we specify *hidariba* or *migiba*. My knives cover a wide range of sizes and shapes—the standard shapes being straight and curved, with the curves varying from shallow to deep.

But there is a third type of *hidariba*, neither straight nor curved, which I devised myself for particular purposes. This *hidariba* has a sharp hook, making it especially well adapted for undercutting work, such as on the deep folds of a kimono, and for shaving otherwise inaccessible parts. Figure

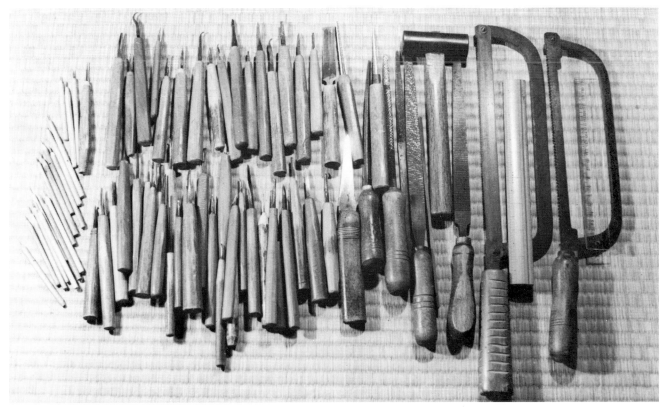

3. A selection of the many tools Masatoshi has on hand while carving a netsuke.

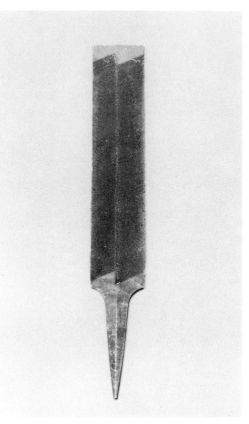

4. Two saws, one with coarse teeth (left) and the other with fine teeth.

5. *Ha-yasuri*, a file for serrating the steel bands of saws.

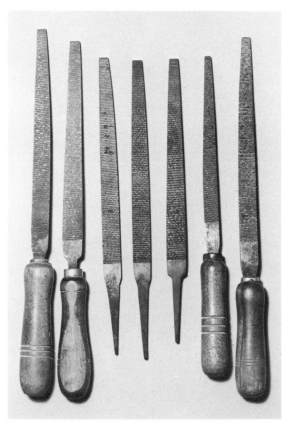

6. *Yasuri*, files for shaping tools.

7. *Sharime*, files for shaping netsuke.

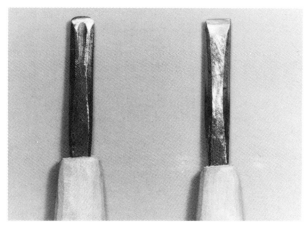

8. A round chisel (left) and a square chisel.

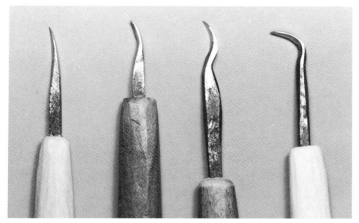

9. Straight, curved, and hooked *hidariba*, knives with their cutting edge on the left.

9 shows the three types of *hidariba*—straight, curved, and hooked. Besides these, I make the *migiba* in the same three shapes.

When I use a *hidariba*, I turn it on its sharp, left edge and scrape or shave the material away from me. Similarly, when I use a *migiba*, I turn it on its sharp, right edge and shave away from me. But with both *hidariba* and *migiba*, the edge opposite the cutting edge is also sharp—although not as sharp as the cutting edge—and I sometimes find it convenient to use the opposite edge instead of the main cutting edge, in order to avoid shaving against the grain. I use thin knives for shaving wood and thick ones for shaving ivory and horn. Thin knives break easily on ivory.

Drills or gimlets can be either straight, *kiri*, or spiral, in which case they are called *doriru*, a word derived from the English word "drill." Figure 11 shows a group of *kiri* and *doriru*. Sometimes I use hard, steel needles (*hari*) instead of straight drills.

My most frequent use for the *kogatana* is in shaping wooden handles for my tools. Whereas I buy stock handles for my large, heavy files and tools, I carve my own handles for my handmade tools out of magnolia wood (*hō-no-ki*). As for the hammer shown alongside the *kogatana* in Figure 10, I use it with a chisel to cut away the tough hair and rind of rhinoceros horn. I use the mallet together with a straight drill to raise pimples and warts according to the technique known as *ukibori* (see page 47).

Although I have no hard and fast rules governing my selection of tools for various operations, I invariably use a saw to cut my rectangular block from the material and a saw again, together with heavy files and chisels, for the rough shaping of the block. The next stage is to fashion the rough shape into my model, and for this I generally use *hidariba*, *migiba*, chisels, and drills. As my carving progresses from rough shape to final form, the tools I use also change progressively from heavy to medium to fine. I use my most delicate tools for such operations as undercutting, delineating the folds of garments, opening the *himotoshi*, engraving an inscription or signature, excavating the site for an inlay, and carving an eye socket. Other intricate work that requires the use of fine tools includes hairline engraving, carving faint reliefs and minute details, and simulating textures such as leather, stone, crepe, hair, and hide.

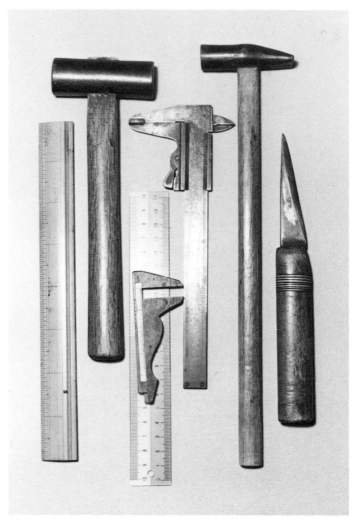

10. A ruler, a mallet, calipers, a hammer, and (right) a *kogatana*, flat knife.

While I have no fixed rules for my choice of tools, my selections are not haphazard. An intuition born of experience guides me, and the peculiarities of the particular material I am working on also influence my decisions. Generally, however, I use a straight *hidariba* for inscriptions, a hooked *hidariba* for undercutting, a straight drill to bore the openings of the *himotoshi*, a round chisel to enlarge them, and a *hidariba* or curved chisel for the channel that joins them (Figure 12). For faint relief and pattern carving (*moyōbori*), I tend to use round chisels, hooked *hidariba*, and straight drills or needles (Figure 13).

The technique for producing textures such as leather, stone, and crepe is called *arashi*, or roughening the surface. My principal tools for this technique are delicate round chisels, although I also use straight drills. In order to produce a realistic textural surface, a certain elasticity in my tools is important. I obtain this springiness and resilience by cutting notches in the shanks of my round chisels. Once the chisels have these notches, I can use them to shave by staccato or stuttering nicks, in contrast to a steady glide, as I excise chips of the material in a regular pattern.

I forge most of my own tools myself—my knives, my chisels, and my straight drills—but not so the saws, files, and spiral drills. The local blacksmith (*kajiya*) supplies me with metal blanks, which he shapes in duplication

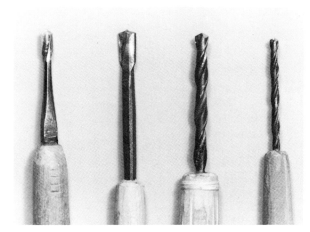

11. Drills and gimlets, both straight (left) and spiral.

12. A straight drill, a round chisel, a *hidariba*, and two curved chisels—all of them tools for opening the *himotoshi*.

13. A group of some of the more delicate tools—including round chisels, hooked *hidariba*, straight drills, and needles—used for hairline engraving.

of special wooden models I carve for him. This I do so that he knows exactly what the tools I need look like. Once I have received the blanks, I file them until they are the precise shapes I want. Now they are ready for forging. I prefer a forging fire of pinewood (*matsu*) charcoal, but pinewood has become impossible to obtain. Even the oakwood (*nara*) charcoal that I use as a second choice is becoming scarce.

The blacksmith's blanks are of relatively soft steel, which is why I have to harden them by forging (heating in fire) and tempering (cooling in water). This is a precarious procedure, because if I harden my tools too much, they chip or shatter when I put them to use, but if I do not harden them enough, they bend under the pressure of carving. I must temper them to the exact hardness I need, something which is extremely difficult to do, especially with thin, delicate tools. Forging and tempering are the most oppressive of all the chores associated with my craft. This is particularly true in hot weather, as I have to forge and temper in my small, enclosed workroom. Tools are prone to rust in hot, humid weather, and they require constant attention.

An incident from the days when I was still assisting my father brings home the difficulty of successfully forging tools. One of my father's close friends, Suzuki Mannosuke, was an *okimono-shi*. He used often to come round to our house, drink a lot of *sake*, and praise the pickles I prepared. My father once showed him an ivory carving I had made of a figure in a kimono, on which I had simulated the texture of silk crepe. The technique, a delicate one called *chirimen arashi* (silk crepe texture), requires the use of a special tool. Suzuki asked me to show him the tool and to explain how I made it. I described in detail the forging and tempering and told him that hardening the metal was much more difficult than shaping it. I described how the increasing temperature of the fire causes the color of the metal to change from blue to purple to light brown to white. The moment the color turns to light brown is the instant to temper the metal by plunging it into water. The color changes succeed one another with great rapidity as the metal heats in the fire or cools when it is withdrawn, and the light brown color is as fleeting as the light of a firefly. This is particularly true of delicate, thin tools. I explained that after tempering and cooling I attach to the shaft a wooden handle that suits my grip and sharpen the cutting edge with whetstone—and the tool is ready for use.

The next time Suzuki visited, he said that in over twenty attempts he had not succeeded once, and he implored me to give him one of the *arashi* tools I had made for myself. The fact is that making tools is a great headache. Even under the best conditions for firing and tempering, I average only two or three satisfactory tools out of every ten attempts. Because he was my father's friend, an elder, and because he entreated me so urgently, I could not refuse, but my inner reluctance was a measure of just how burdensome it is to make satisfactory tools.

III. Materials

Elephant ivory (*zōge*) is my favorite material. Just as human teeth do, ivory varies in size, shape, color, hardness, and luster. When selecting ivory, the visual qualities I look for are a pinkish or creamy color, a small fine grain, a moist oily appearance, a deep luster, and a glowing texture. When most of these characteristics are present, it is almost certain that the ivory will be of good quality. In terms of hardness, the best ivory ranges from medium to extremely hard. Soft ivory is difficult to carve in sensitive detail, tends to be clayey, and cannot normally be polished to a fine luster. For this reason, soft ivory is often used for religious figures, on which a high polish is not befitting.

There are no absolute rules for determining the quality of ivory. Hard ivory with good visual qualities, a small grain, and fine color and luster may prove to be dry or clingy, resisting the carver's efforts to register sensitive details. On the whole, however, hard ivory sells at a premium— hardness and weight being the dealer's principal criteria in pricing his stock. In estimating quality, even the most experienced dealers make mistakes, since visual criteria can sometimes be misleading. I prefer, therefore, to check for myself, and occasionally a dealer allows me to make a few scrapings with my knife, even though he normally varnishes the exposed cross-section to prevent it from cracking.

But the ultimate test of quality is in the carving: is the ivory responsive to the knife? The expression used by the *netsuke-shi* is, "Does it obey the knife?" Is it resilient? Does it register crisply? There is, however, a further hazard—one that cannot be confronted until the last stages in producing a netsuke—and that is: does the ivory take a polish? For if ivory does not polish well, the end product will be unsatisfactory. Except for the question of polishing, I know the quality of the ivory by the time I finish with my saws and files and begin with my chisels and knives. On those occasions when I have made a mistake in selecting ivory, the dealer has allowed me to return the unused portion and choose another.

The netsuke of a *Cat and Rat* (Plate 279) is an instance of ivory material that proved disappointing. The ivory looked good but it turned out to be clayey and would not polish well. I returned the unused part to the dealer and chose another piece. *The Double-headed Monster* (Plate 98) provides another example of disappointing material. The grain was large, but that was not the problem. The defect that marred the final product lay in the hardness, which was uneven. However patiently and persistently I polished, I could not flatten the surface. It remained uneven. It being impossible to color a wavy surface uniformly, the upshot of it was those unsightly stripes particularly visible on the monster's neck.

I am disheartened with poor material. Nothing goes well, and the final result is unsatisfactory. On the other hand, when my material is sensitive and responsive, my knives seem to sing and move along of their own accord. I feel exhilarated, sure in the knowledge that my netsuke will be a good one.

Mr. Bushell once brought me from Hongkong a tusk which a Chinese friend of his had guaranteed to be of exceptional quality. It turned out, on the contrary, to be coarse. I didn't want to hurt his feelings by complaining, but when he criticized the netsuke I made, I was compelled to tell him the truth. He said it was better to waste ivory than to waste netsuke, and he asked me to discard the tusk. We both learned a lesson: he, not to select ivory for me; and me, not to use inferior material. Since Mr. Bushell first became my sponsor, I have sought only the best materials—though occasional mistakes are unavoidable.

I never buy the whole tusk. Instead, I buy the desirable parts of a desirable tusk. Diagram A shows the main divisions of the elephant tusk, although dealers distinguish numerous subdivisions and particular characteristics for their grading and pricing. The parts I prefer are the tip (*marusaki*), the second quarter (*marumuku*), and sometimes part of the third quarter (*bachi-tori*). The tip and the second quarter usually have a finer grain and texture than the third quarter. The root (*gara*) is used for brush stands, vases, and chopsticks. The choicer and smaller the part of the tusk selected, the higher the premium that must be paid. A piece just large enough for a single netsuke taken from the core of the tip or second quarter would be most expensive.

A. The main divisions of an elephant's tusk.

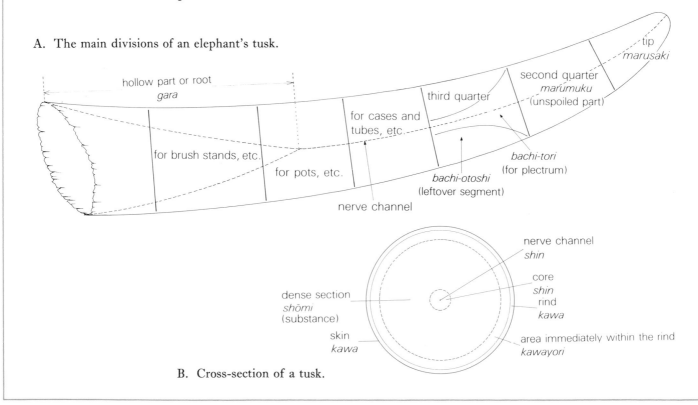

B. Cross-section of a tusk.

The cross-section of an elephant's tusk reveals four basic layers (Diagram B). These are: the surface skin or "bark"; the rind, which is very porous and, as a rule, darkest in shade; the area between the rind and the core, usually the densest section of the tusk; and the core, which includes the central nerve channel. The core is the section of the tusk with the finest and most regular grain. While the core is less dense than other sections, it is not porous like the rind.

The hard, fine-grained material that Kaigyokusai prized was the tusk of the Burmese, Thai, or Cambodian elephant. This kind of ivory, known as *tōkata* or *annankiji* (literally, "Annamese grain"), is pinkish in color, small, even, and fine grained, oily, lustrous, and live. For Kaigyokusai, *tōkata* was only the beginning of the process of discrimination and elimination. From the best *tōkata*, he selected the tip or the second quarter; from the tip, he chose the core; and from the core, the part in which the nerve channel was negligible or filled in by nature—in which case it is known as a *nemuri-shin* (sleeping core).

Usually the nerve channel is hollow but can be integrated or disguised in the design. Otherwise, it must be plugged with an ivory pin or filled in with ivory dust and a special fish glue known as *nikawa*. I used a core section which included the nerve channel for the *Billiken* doll (Plate 346) with an ivory pin to plug the hole. It was not an eyesore, as the channel was parallel to the *himotoshi*. Where, however, the shape of the composition permits—as, for example, in the *Blade of Grass* (Plate 78)—I have used a fine core section absolutely free of nerve channel and other blemishes.

I managed to acquire the tip and second quarter of a *tōkata* tusk directly from the importer in 1979, when the Burmese Government held its first ivory sale in thirty-five years. It was pinkish in color, glowing with oily luster, and showed only the faintest of grains. I used it for the netsuke shown in Plates 66 and 114, and for a set of the *rakan* (disciples of Buddha) that I began more than a year ago. As superb as I found this Burmese ivory, I consider some of the best African material to be its equal in quality. The carvings illustrated in Plates 48 and 60 provide examples of splendid "African *tōkata*," while those shown in Plates 67 and 218 are examples of rare "grainless" ivory (*yōkankiji*).

Guided by the characteristics of ivory, I can often tell how the carving lay in the tusk. Old carvers took advantage of the porousness of the rind and of its naturally darker hue. They carved the backs of their standing figures from the rind and the faces and arms from the lighter layer that lies inside the rind. The rind, being porous, absorbs more color and darkens more, whether from stain or smoke. This is the reason why many old netsuke are dark at the back and light on the facing side. The core, too, absorbs color to a greater extent than the denser area between the core and rind, though not as much as the rind; the core is the part of the tusk which usually shows the faintest and finest grain. Another clue to how a netsuke would lie in the tusk is the position of the nerve channel, which, although little more than one millimeter in diameter, can normally be detected unless it is a sleeping channel. The carver eventually covers the tiny hole with a separate ivory pin, or he fills it with ivory dust and glue, unless he is able to eliminate it entirely in his design. There are still other indicators of the position of the netsuke relative to the tusk.

I always try to design my netsuke so as to take advantage of the color and coloring characteristics of the ivory I am using; those shown in Plates 42, 57, and 77 are good examples of how I can manage to do this.

Whale-tooth (*kujira no ha*) is harder and denser than ivory. Sawing and shaving are a little more laborious, but in general the carving characteristics are the same. I use the same tools for carving whale-tooth as I do for ivory and the same polishing and staining agents.

Whale-tooth—or, more exactly, the tooth of a sperm whale—even a very large tooth, is large enough for only one netsuke. This is because of the thickness of the rind. I usually avoid using the rind because it is much softer than the inner part (*shin*) of the tooth. Soft parts do not carve well, nor do they polish well. Unlike elephant tusk, the rind of the whale-tooth is lighter in color, while the inner part is darker. As well as being soft and light, there is also more of it, and this means that, once I have cut away the rind, I am sometimes left with less material than I would wish. The birds illustrated in Plates 46 and 52 are cases in point. Rather than reduce the size of the netsuke, I sometimes allow my carving to extend a little way into the rind. The natural color variation between the rind and the inner part shows where I have done this. In some cases I use the color contrast deliberately to enhance my design (see Plate 45).

Whale-tooth suffers quite frequently from blemishes (*yamai*), which take the form of flecks or balls of yellowish dentine. *Yamai* are rarely found in elephant ivory. Before buying any, I examine whales' teeth carefully by feeling the walls of the trumpet-shaped hollow at the root of the tooth, and I discard all those that have lavalike excrescenses. These external flaws indicate that blemishes are likely to be found hidden underneath. Unfortunately the reverse does not follow: a perfectly smooth root hollow may be accompanied by a proliferation of internal blemishes. Even after discarding nineteen out of twenty whales' teeth because of tumors on the surface, I cannot predict that the twentieth will be free of dentine blemishes when I carve it.

I never know when I'm going to come upon one of these dentine flecks —it may be exposed with the next scrape of my knife. No matter how far along I have got in my carving, these unsightly blemishes may turn up, ruining the netsuke and forcing me to discard it; the *Prehistoric Fish* (Plate 176) was an exception. I have no choice, however, when these flecks and balls are loose, leaving a surface with ugly pits here and there. When, on the other hand, the flecks are few and are solidly attached, my decision about what to do with the netsuke depends on whether or not the yellow specks spoil the design (see Plate 52). Whale-tooth does, however, have some advantages, one of them being that the nerve channel is invariably sleeping or nonexistent and therefore presents no hazard to carving. One considerable superiority of whale-tooth over ivory is its luminosity. Occasionally I shade whale-tooth lightly with stain or smoke, but usually I prefer its natural color, which is almost translucent.

Unlike ivory and whale-tooth, both of which have a soft rind, hippopotamus tooth (*kaba no ha*) has an enamel coat about three or four millimeters thick which is extremely hard. Cutting it soon dulls my saws and files. Once through the enamel, however, hippopotamus tooth has about the same hardness and density as whale-tooth and carves much like whale-tooth and ivory do, although, because it is that bit denser, it takes a little longer to color than ivory. The whitish spots on the left hand and elbow of the *Long-tongued Brat* (Plate 335) are the enamel. The color of hippo tooth is a uniform, dull white. This is why I invariably stain the material: to relieve the blanched whiteness.

A peculiarity of hippo tooth is the finely ridged character of the core. It is a sequence of narrow ridges that the most persistent grinding and polishing fails to flatten. These hairline grooves fade naturally into flatness toward the rind. An examination of the *Java Sparrow* (Plate 40) shows that the bird's left side is finely ridged and the right side flat—the difference due entirely to the bird's position in the tooth.

The upper tusks of the hippo are straight, the lower pair curved like scimitars, but, when it comes to carving them, there is no particular difference, and the choice between upper and lower tusk depends entirely on availability.

Among the woods, ebony (*kokutan*) is my favorite, with boxwood a close second. Genuine ebony, however, is scarce; it is imported from Nigeria in small quantities and is difficult to obtain. A substitute wood from a tree grown in Indonesia is classed as ebony but is of inferior quality (see Plate 79). True ebony is jet black in color with only an occasional dark brownish streak and is extremely heavy and dense. It is supremely "obedient" to my knife. And what's more, it polishes to a high luster. It would be impossible to improve on the natural color of ebony, and so I never stain it. I have heard that ebony is prone to chip or split, but I have not found this to be the case. The rule for selecting choice ebony is simple: the blacker the color, the better the quality. As I carve ebony the dust blackens my hands and legs and even the area around my bench. All the ebony netsuke illustrated are carved out of the best material (see, in particular, Plates 59, 202, and 332).

I usually buy my woods in the timber merchants' district near Tokyo's Sumida River, known—appropriately enough—as Kiba, "place of woods." Many timber merchants have been established there for generations, selling lumber of all types including rare and imported woods. There I find Chinese woods (*karaki*), white sandalwood (*byakudan*), teak (*chīku*), quince (*karin*), aloeswood (*jinkō*), black persimmon (*kurogaki*), and rosewood (*shitan*), as well as domestic and imported boxwood.

I prefer domestic to imported boxwood. Foreign boxwood is larger in diameter than domestic boxwood, but it is less oily, less elastic, and lighter in weight. I prefer boxwood that retains some oiliness even after the water content is dried out. Oiliness is necessary for a brilliant polish. The *Camel* (Plate 276) is an example of imported boxwood of good quality.

Boxwood (*tsuge*) is the all-time traditional favorite of the *netsuke-shi*. It is dense, hard, tight grained, and fine textured, and it registers details and polishes brilliantly. Indeed, I like it almost as much as I do ebony. Its failing is the large number of tiny knots that can appear unexpectedly at the next shaving of the knife. This is the reason that we find so few old boxwood netsuke finished in their natural color, even though boxwood's natural color is a range of lovely tawny yellows and blonds. Just as I finish all my ebony netsuke in their natural brilliant black color, so too would I like to finish my boxwoods in their own natural color, but often I am thwarted by tiny blemishes. Take, for instance, the *Fox* (Plate 271): the natural color was an attractive yellowish brown which I had intended to enhance with polishing when, at practically my last shaving, a knothole appeared, small and shallow, but nevertheless a visible blemish. I had no satisfactory alternative but to fill it with pulverized boxwood from the same block of wood, mixed with *nikawa*. I colored the piece in a standard medium brown.

Ordinary boxwood sawdust is too coarse for filling blemishes. What I have to do, therefore, is cut a tissue-thin shaving, pulverize it, and mix the powder with *nikawa*. Three knotholes appeared on the back of his head in my last few shavings of the *Macrocephalic Bakemono* (Plate 330). Had the blemishes occurred on his face, I might have had to discard the piece. Under the circumstances I avoided a wasted effort by filling the knotholes with boxwood powder. The blemishes were well concealed when I stained the netsuke with *yashadama* (a traditional dye obtained from birch cones).

Whenever the material is immaculate and unblemished, I try to preserve the natural tawny color of boxwood. When this is the case, I rely on polishing alone to bring out the beautiful luster and grain of the natural wood. The netsuke illustrated in Plates 130, 133, and 257 are examples of boxwood in its natural state. Nevertheless, I sometimes take netsuke carved from a naturally yellow boxwood and dip them in a cold, weak solution of *yashadama*. This imparts a satiny finish but has practically no effect on the tone of the natural wood. The main purpose of the bath is to color polishing powders that lodge in crevices and are difficult to remove by ordinary brushing (see Plates 134, 142, 191, 244, and 308).

I buy some of my finest wood not from the dealers and importers in Kiba but from specialty shops whose stock-in-trade is based on a particular wood. For example, combs are made of boxwood, and the shops that deal in combs traditionally use the choicest of choice boxwood. The owner of a comb shop once furnished me with a particularly fine block of boxwood that came from Mikura Island, one of the Seven Isles of Izu. I used it to carve the *Monkey* (Plate 257). The quality was extraordinary, and I was able to carve the monkey's coat with perfect uniformity. To equal advantage I once bought a type of red sandalwood known as *kōki* from a *samisen* maker who uses only the finest specimens of this mysterious wood to make the necks of his instruments (see Plate 116 for an example and description of *kōki*). A personal relationship is essential before the shopkeeper will part with some of his precious material. I acquired the superb boxwood I used for the *sumō* wrestlers in Plate 133 from the head of a carvers' association in Ise who is friendly with Mr. Bushell.

Some woods are rough, thick grained (*me no arai*), and porous (*kihō no ōi*), among them teak, rosewood, and red sandalwood. These coarse, porous woods must be thoroughly dried and seasoned before I begin to carve, otherwise they are prone to crack. They are unsuitable for minute carving and delicate relief. The other side of the coin, however, is that their rough texture is the very quality that makes them eminently suitable for particular subjects. Thus I chose teak for the *Abstract Bird* (Plate 41), to simulate clay in two burial figurines (Plates 216 and 217), and to give a weathered look to the *Scarecrow* (Plate 219). I chose rosewood for the *Bat* (Plate 200) and red sandalwood for the owl caricature (Plate 208).

I find stag-antler (*kazuno* or *shika no tsuno*) a good choice for humorous subjects and caricatures (see, for example, Plates 53 and 168). The material itself is often eccentric in shape with unpredictable soft patches and pimpled, corrugated surfaces. The problem with stag-antler is to find a block of material of sufficient bulk and solidity for a good netsuke. The main stem attached to the cranium is often solid (see Plate 264) as are the junctures where the antler's various tines join. The material for the netsuke shown in Plates 210 and 353 came from abroad and was exceptional in both size and charactcristics.

Experience has taught me that rhinoceros horn (*saikaku*) is a difficult material to work. That part of the horn which is attached to the skull shows two colors, a translucent light shade and a grayish black. The lighter area is nearer the rind, the darker area nearer the core, but as the base of the horn narrows toward the tip, the lighter area disappears and the color becomes a uniform grayish black. The material at the base of the horn is the toughest and the most difficult to carve, especially the lighter part, yet it is this area that polishes best. Before I can begin sawing a block of rhinoceros horn, I have to use hammer and chisel to strip away the tough skin and hair particularly at the base.

The carving of minutiae and surface detail in rhino is a task quite beyond me. I design the material in gross form and let the details go, aiming at attractive shapes and a fine finish. I polish rhino fastidiously to enhance the natural color and concentrate on form and movement because I cannot rely on decoration and embellishment. I am at a loss to explain the remarkable relief carving the Chinese craftsmen of old succeeded in applying to their rhinoceros horn cups. I can only imagine that they had some secret process for rendering the material pliable and sensitive. I regard rhino horn as ideal material for certain exotic subjects for which no other material is quite as suitable—for example, the subjects of Plates 94, 95, 231, and 270.

I use tortoise shell (*bekkō*) mainly for inlaid eyes. Various shades can be obtained by spreading lacquer or colored *nikawa* at the base of the eye socket before inlaying eyes of transparent tortoise shell. This is the traditional method used by Edo Period carvers like Toyomasa—though their eyes are often mistakenly identified as yellow horn.

Sometimes I choose tortoise shell as my material for a whole netsuke. It has no grain and no layers and is softer than boxwood and ivory. It is easy to carve, despite a characteristic rubbery response to the pressure of my tools, which begin to feel as if they are dancing and bouncing along on the tortoise shell. It is not possible to do minute carving in this material. I discuss the problem of fusing tortoise shell for carving in-the-round in the descriptions of Plates 106, 107, 180, and 181.

I have mentioned only those materials that I use frequently. Other materials that I use infrequently or experimentally are identified and some are discussed in the descriptions of the individual netsuke. I list them here for convenience:

Amber: Plates 80, 155.
Black persimmon: Plate 206.
Boar tusk: Plate 132.
Buffalo horn: Plate 212.
Hornbill ivory: Plates 149, 153, 154.
Kōki: Plate 116.
Lignum vitae: Plates 201, 298.
Negoro lacquer: Plate 173.
Red sandalwood: Plates 208, 292, 322.
Rosewood: Plate 200.
Teak: Plates 41, 216, 217, 219, 287.
Tiger fangs: Plate 157.
Tooth, land animal: Plates 54, 349.
Tooth, marine: Plate 69.
Umoregi (semipetrified wood): Plates 64, 163.
Unidentified: Plate 158.
Walrus tusk: Plate 184.

IV. Carving and Techniques

There are seven distinct stages in the carving of a netsuke. The first two stages, in which only saws are used, are preliminary and are called *kijidori*. In the first stage of *kijidori*, a rectangular block of the desired dimensions is cut out of the material; while in the second stage, unwanted edges, corners, and segments are sawn off—for example, the right and left corners of a block intended for the head and shoulders of a figure.

The third stage is known either as *arazuki* or as *arabori* and involves carving the block into a rough semblance or outline of the shape of the netsuke. It is, in other words, carving in the gross sense. I use heavy and medium files and large chisels in *arazuki* but no knives or fine tools.

The fourth stage, *kezuri*, is the process of shaving and scraping to reduce the rough outline to proper proportions and shape. *Kezuri* can be further divided into an initial and a final phase. The initial phase involves all the work necessary to carve the subject into its proper shape—whether it is the flamboyant pose of an actor, the body of an animal with long, curving tail, or a beauty wrapped in the folds of a kimono—and includes all the objects or attributes that are part of the design, as well as the opening and channeling of the *himotoshi* and the engraving of inscriptions. For the initial phase of *kezuri*, I use straight, curved, and hooked *hidariba* and *migiba*, square and round chisels, and drills.

The final phase of *kezuri* is to prepare all the surfaces for the carving of delicate relief patterns and textures. For this I use a sequence of sandpapers —those made in the United States are best—from rough brown to fine black emery paper. When the surfaces are as smooth as glass, the *kezuri* stage is finished.

The fifth stage, *moyōbori*, involves the engraving of surface and relief patterns, the hair of humans, the fur and hides of animals, hairline carving (*kebori*), and surface roughening (*arashi*) to simulate various textures. The tools for *moyōbori* are the most delicate straight and curved *hidariba*, round chisels, drills, and needles.

The sixth stage is *migaki*, polishing, which I will describe in detail in the following chapter. My last step in polishing is to use *ibotarō*, a type of vegetable wax. I impregnate a cloth with melted *ibotarō* and run it over the netsuke to impart a final sheen. I sometimes finish by dabbing my naked fingers with *ibotarō* and giving the netsuke a series of parting caresses.

The seventh and final stage is *irotsuke*, staining or coloring, and this I will explain in chapter six. I never apply color, however, in the case of ebony and certain other materials for which polishing is all that is necessary to emphasize their natural luster. Figures 14 to 34 show these seven stages of progress in the carving of an ivory netsuke.

One of the basic techniques of netsuke carving is to avoid cutting against the grain. The direction of the grain—whether the material be wood, ivory, or horn—is from the root toward the tip. The expression "against the grain," however, has a different meaning for a *netsuke-shi* than it does for the ordinary carpenter. When I cut or shave at right angles to the direction of the grain, I am not going against the grain, although a Western carpenter would use a crosscut saw. For me, going "against the grain" means shaving a netsuke diagonally downward toward the root. The *netsuke-shi* calls going against the grain "*sakame*."

The effect of shaving *sakame* (against the grain) is to make the area coarse and rough. Fine, sensitive carving is impossible on a *sakame* surface, nor can such a surface be polished flat or colored evenly. Unlike a smooth surface, a *sakame* surface soon discolors as it accumulates dust from the air and from handling. My knives protest when they have to carve against the grain: they protest with their voices, making a grating or rasping sound. But when I carve with the grain, the sound they make is even and pleasant. There is a difference, too, in the shavings. When I am carving ivory with the grain, the shavings are tissue-thin and curl like tiny ribbons, but when against, the shavings break and crumble. Similarly, when I am carving wood with the grain, the shavings are thin and uniform, but when against, they become dangerously thick, and I risk chipping some detail of my netsuke—a risk which I am loath to take when the carving has reached a delicate stage.

A *sakame* surface must be corrected. Correcting a *sakame* surface with sandpaper is unsatisfactory. It is harder to be precise with sandpaper than it is with a knife, and, besides, the risk of breakage is greater under the pressure of sandpapering. I generally rectify a *sakame* surface by going over the area with a few shavings with the grain. In order to avoid carving against the grain—so far as it is possible—I am constantly turning my material so that my knives and chisels are moving with the grain. Sometimes, the material I am using is as much in motion as my tools.

I obtain the smoothest surface on any part of the netsuke by carving in a single direction only. I do, however, sometimes change direction if it makes the carving easier—although, of course, always going with the grain. Even so, a change of direction reduces the surface smoothness to some degree, and, in order to return the surface to perfect smoothness again, I usually shave the area a few times in the original direction. I stick to this practice in every single part of the netsuke, because, if any roughness remains after my knife work is finished, the netsuke will not color evenly.

In carving a repeat pattern—the feathers of a bird, the nodules on a turtle's carapace, or the floral design of a kimono—I follow the principle of starting from the center and working outward. By doing this, I avoid running the risk of having to crowd the pattern or spread it out. I learned the wisdom of this method early in my career when a cormorant I carved finished with a conspicuous bald spot on its head instead of feathers (see page 19), Amateurishly, I had started the feather pattern at the edge and was repeating it as I moved toward the center. The principle of moving from the center outward has another advantage, one which may be readily understood by taking the example of a turtle's carapace. The central nodules are the largest and most pronounced, and so when these are carved first, they act as a gauge or standard for the sizing and spacing of the rest of the nodules, which should gradually become smaller toward the edge of the shell.

When I carve a minuscule repeat pattern or relief design, absolute steadiness and control are essential. Otherwise, the engraving will lose neatness, regularity, and uniformity. The smallest disturbance, even a slight sound, destroys my concentration. A troubling thought that enters my mind unbidden may cause my breathing to deepen, transmitting tension to my hand and spoiling my work. When I am engrossed in a delicate pattern, I try to regulate my breathing in a shallow steady rhythm. Even when my control is perfect, I must complete each segment of the design without interruption before moving on to the next. The reason for this is the natural variation of my hand between one work period and another.

I owe the development of my technique for inlaying embellishments, particularly eyes, to my experience in repairing old netsuke. I noted the frequency with which inlaid eyes in animals and humans fell out and discovered there were two reasons for this, besides the obvious one of the inlays being too shallow. First, I realized that the hole for the eye was generally cone shaped, either with the apex at the deepest point in the hole or with the sides tapering to a narrow base. Second, I discovered that the eye itself was invariably secured with sealing wax (*fūrō*). A cone-shaped inlay with a pointed apex or narrow base is not properly gripped by the material, with the result that the jarring and attrition of daily use and time loosen the inlay, which then drops out as the sealing wax dries and loses adhesiveness.

My own method of inlaying is more secure. I etch the shape of the eye or other inlay on the material and then drive a square-tipped drill into this outlined area to a secure depth. For example, I excavated the sockets for the warts of the frog in Plate 291 to a depth of three millimeters. I enlarge the excavation by straightening the walls until they are absolutely perpendicular to the flat base. Thus the socket for the inlay is as wide at the bottom as it is at the surface. My next step is to shave the material to be inlaid to the exact dimensions of the socket. Once I am satisfied that the bottom of the inlay is as flat as the bottom of the excavation, that the sides of the inlay are absolutely perpendicular, and, finally, that there is no play—no air space—between inlay and socket, I apply epoxy resin to all contact surfaces on the inlay and on the material and insert the one into the other. Whether its shape is rectangular, round, or oval, the inlay fits the socket precisely, the materials adhering to one another on all sides and bases. It is solidly gripped and glued and should last as long as the netsuke.

I never shape the eye until the inlay is firmly fixed in its socket. Instead, I leave an excess of material—whether tortoise shell or the black coral known as *umimatsu*—above the surface of the netsuke to be shaped and polished afterward.

I have originated a technique for making eyes that follow the viewer how-

From Block of Ivory to Completed Netsuke: The Stages Involved in Fashioning a Netsuke

14. *Tōkata* ivory . . .

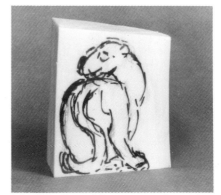

15. Pencil markings, a rough guide . . .

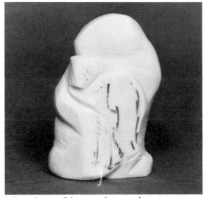

16. *Arazuki*, rough carving . . .   17   18

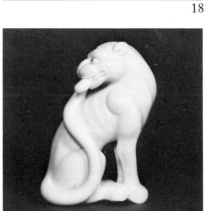

19. *Kezuri*, the shaving and scraping of the material into shape . . .   20   21

22   23   24. After *kezuri* . . .

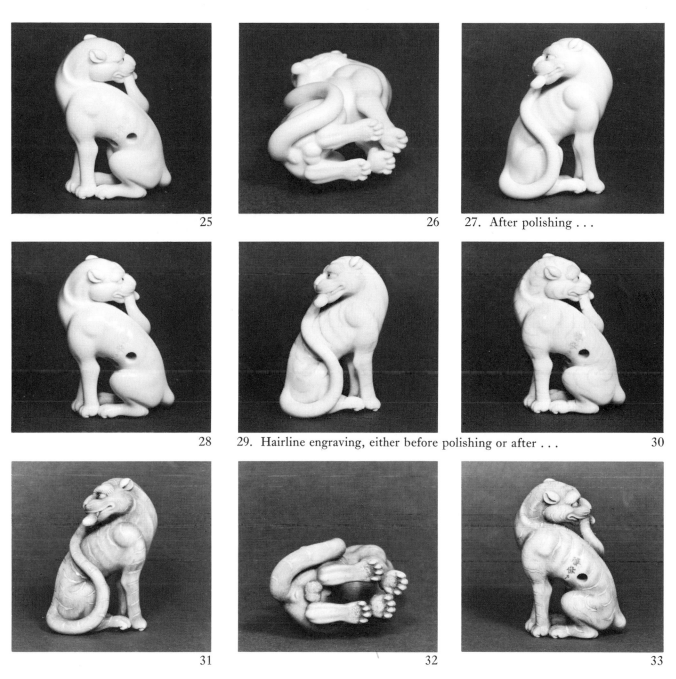

25

26

27. After polishing . . .

28

29. Hairline engraving, either before polishing or after . . .

30

31

32

33

31–34. After the coloring, a tiger with stripes and a finished netsuke.

34

ever the netsuke is moved or from whatever angle the viewer regards it. The eyes appear to move up and down and right and left as though they had a life of their own. This quality is called *happōnirami*, literally "staring in the eight directions." In order to obtain this effect, I choose a material which is transparent—light yellowish tortoise shell being the best in my experience. (We call it *shiro-bekkō*, white tortoise shell, but in fact the color is a transparent yellowish shade rather than white.) The essential point is that the material for the pupil is inlaid into the bottom of the tortoise shell; there is no way to make an eye that follows if the pupil is inlaid from the top. I hollow out the bottom of the tortoise shell, deepen the hole until it is about half the length of the tortoise shell itself, make it the right shape for the pupil, and then fill it with lampblack (*yuen*). Finally I shape the surface of the eye, making it more spherical and less flat than I would a normal eye inlay. This tends to magnify the pupil and helps achieve the effect of following.

Perfect *happōnirami* is difficult to obtain. The relationships must be exact, the shape precise, and the material and clarity flawless. I have examined one or two old netsuke in which I feel certain the carver was striving for the effect, but the attempts were unsuccessful because one or another of the elements was faulty. The *Domestic Duck* (Plate 45) is the first of the netsuke illustrated with eyes that follow. Thereafter, all netsuke with *happōnirami* eyes have the words "eyes follow" appended to the description.

The term "*arashi*" literally means a "roughening up" of some surface or other. *Arashi* is a technique I use for treating the surface of my material to imitate various textures such as those of cloth, crepe, leather, hide, and stone. I use the smallest and most delicate of my knives, chisels, and needle drills to create these special effects. As with the engraving of lacy repeat patterns, I have to maintain absolute calm and control, and my senses of sight and touch must be kept at a very high pitch, in order for the *arashi* technique to be a success.

Taira no Kiyomori's coat in Plate 10 is an example of *chirimen arashi* (silk crepe roughening); the tobacco pouch of the temple guardian god in Plate 111 is an example of *kawashibo arashi* (leather roughening); while the monkey in Plate 256 provides an example of *ishime arashi* (stone roughening).

I make stripes, squares, and various patterns on kimono and other garments by delicately scoring or crosshatching—generally with a fine *hidariba*—to simulate the warp and weft of cloth. These scored areas absorb more color and turn darker than unmarked surfaces. This technique is called *nunome arashi* (cloth roughening). The garments of Kirare Otomi in Plate 8 provide an example of this technique.

My first step in making the *himotoshi* is to start boring with a gimlet. I open the two holes and widen them with a straight *hidariba* and continue burrowing until the holes meet. At this point, the channel is more or less V-shaped. Then, using a curved *hidariba* or round chisel, I widen and curve the channel into a "U" shape, not stopping until the channel is perfectly smooth and wider than the holes—except in the case of a large netsuke, where I sometimes carve one hole larger than the other to accommodate the knot. There are several advantages to a U-shaped *himotoshi* with a channel wider than the holes. The cords pass smoothly and easily through the channel without jamming, wedging, or tearing, as they are prone to do on the sharp point of a V-shaped channel. Furthermore, openings smaller than the channel hold the cords securely, diminishing the wear caused by constant friction. (See Diagram C on page 64.)

When repairing and examining old netsuke, I have found that some have sharp, pointed, V-shaped channels. Sometimes the arms of the "V" have been extended into the shape of an "X," as though the carvers were insensitive to the progress of their tools.

Trick netsuke are called *shikakemono*. They are often very clever, with levers that move remote parts, loose or extensible heads, protruding eyes and tongues, and jointed parts. I have tried making *shikakemono* but was not particularly successful. The trouble with trick netsuke is that the more complicated they are, the more easily they get out of order and the more difficult they are to repair. The tricks themselves are trivial, adding nothing to the netsuke's aesthetic appeal. The *Sway-Head Tiger* (Plate 294) is a little different. The netsuke is based on a papier-mâché toy of universal appeal to children. The head of the paper toy is so light and so delicately balanced that the slightest touch or movement of air sets it swaying and bobbing. I tried to capture the same balance and effect in wood by using a peg as an axis to balance on the one side the head and on the other side the neck, which extends into the body in perfect equilibrium and so gives the head an easy up and down motion. I camouflaged the two ends of the peg in the surface design of the tiger. In addition, I carved the tunnel for the peg with wide flares at either end, thereby affording the head free movement to right and left. The combination of the two motions allows the head to sway and bob easily and with a degree of naturalness.

My father taught me *ukibori*, the technique of raising features such as pimples and warts on fish, frogs, and lizards, veins on leaves, patterns on kimono, and inscriptions. In *ukibori* these features are raised without reducing the surrounding area by shaving, as in true relief. The pimples on the *Blowfish* (Plate 187) and the warts on the frog in Plate 307 are examples of *ukibori*. But *ukibori* is a technique which I use infrequently, as I prefer standard relief carving for raised features. A raised feature carved in standard relief is in the natural, durable grain of the wood. On the other hand, raised features in *ukibori* are in bloated wood, a little unnatural in appearance, and more susceptible to early wear. It is for this reason that *ukibori* is often effaced or partially worn away. Not that my own preference, however, diminishes my admiration for the perfection to which the great Iwami carvers elevated *ukibori*.

The tool for *ukibori* is a drill with a smooth, rounded, spherical point rather than the customary sharp point. Its function is to depress and squeeze, not to cut. I choose a drill of a size that matches the size I envision for each pimple, place it against the wood on the spot where I wish to raise a pimple, and strike the handle with a mallet. This action depresses the material without cutting, shaving, or excising it. I dimple the wood in this way at all the spots where I wish to raise pimples or warts. At this stage the area is pitted with indentations. Now I shave the area down to the level where the indentations are no longer visible and the surface is virtually flat, with nothing raised and nothing depressed. Although not apparent, the grain of the wood has been compressed at all the points which I struck with the round-pointed drill. The final operation is to moisten the area with a few drops of water. Natural forces do the rest. The pimples appear within five minutes—the compressed points having swollen and bloated into pimples, raised above the surrounding level. Lastly, I give the area a light polishing.

Pimples on a flat wood surface are the simplest application of the technique. Applying *ukibori* to a curved surface or to an edge, on the other hand, is a hazardous endeavor, because the shock of the mallet against the drill on a curved surface or edge can cause the wood to split or chip. This is the reason why I chose, for example, to carve the larger warts in standard relief on the sides of the frog in Plate 308.

Depressing wood to make leaf veins, patterns, and *kanji* is a much more difficult business than it is to make pimples. It requires supreme control and precision—even considerable strength—to depress hard woods in the shape of veins, patterns, and inscriptions. After studying Iwami *ukibori*, my hunch is that they must have perfected secret methods for applying the technique.

My astonishment at the achievements of the Iwami *netsuke-shi* using the *ukibori* technique in ivory is even greater. Tomiharu's ridges on the snail and his raised characters are examples of *ukibori* in ivory (see *Collectors' Netsuke*, Figures 52 and 53). The process for ivory is utterly different from that for wood. In the netsuke shown in Plate 354, I experimented with ivory *ukibori*, choosing as my subject two touching circles representing peace and harmony. The character "*wa*," appearing on one circle, stands for the words "*heiwa*" (peace) and "*chōwa*" (harmony); my signature is on the other circle. The steps I took to raise the characters are these:

1. Wrote the characters in *sumi* (black ink).
2. Traced the *sumi* with lacquer and dried the lacquer.
3. Immersed the piece in sulfuric acid (*ryūsan*), a process which caused the surface to turn caramel color and sticky.
4. Washed away that part of the ivory that had become loose or had actually liquefied.
5. Brushed the piece and polished it.

The sulfuric acid had eroded the ivory surface but had had no effect on the lacquered characters. This resulted in the characters being raised above the level of the surrounding ground. The pronounced fingerprint pattern as well as the deep caramel color are the direct results, not of carving nor of coloring, but of the lacquering and the dipping in acid. The swirls do not follow the arcs or natural grain of the ivory. This may be the basic method Tomiharu used to raise the ridges on his ivory snail.

There are other techniques which I have not seriously tried to use and in which I have little interest. Among them are *kagobori*, the carving of baskets and cages; *kurinuki*, hollowed and perforated carvings like *ryūsa* or figures in a clam shell; and *manjū*, relief carving (Diagram D). Practically all my output is *marubori*, carving in-the-round, and *katabori*, figure carving.

V. Polishing

Polishing (*migaki*) and coloring or staining (*irotsuke*) are distinct operations, although people tend to confuse them and think that when I polish I am also staining. This misconception may be the result of the advertising of commercial preparations that stain, polish, and preserve with one application. The various abrasives I use for polishing have no effect whatsoever on the color either of wood or of ivory. I never use formulas or patent preparations in my polishing, only neutral materials and my own two hands.

Then again, some people have asked me whether I have a secret formula or magical application. How otherwise, they ask, could I give such a deep, rich polish to wood and such a fine, lustrous gloss to ivory? The answer—far from having any connection with secret formulas—has more to do with plain hard work. I spend about twelve hours patiently polishing every netsuke I make.

When I am through with the carving, when I have shaved the netsuke into its final form, when I am satisfied with figures, faces, expressions, and clothes, when, therefore, there is nothing more to be done with tools, that is the time I begin polishing. The purpose of polishing is to remove the scrapes and marks left by tools, to efface the scratches of the previous abrasive as I proceed with finer and finer polishing agents, to eliminate oils, resins, and fingerprints, to make the surface smooth, to bring out the natural luster of the material, and to impart a gloss to the texture. A completely smooth surface is essential for the application of a uniform color. An uneven surface means uneven coloring. Oils, resins, and fingerprints counteract the adherence of color.

No matter what the material—whether wood, ivory, rhinoceros horn, stag-antler, amber, or tortoise shell—my polishing technique is the same. I follow six steps in polishing a netsuke, using a coarse abrasive for the first step and a progressively finer abrasive on each of the subsequent five steps. I expect each abrasive in turn to remove the marks remaining from the use of the previous one. Here is a description of each of the six steps, the polishing agents I use, and the approximate amount of time I spend.

1. Coarse brown sandpaper. (One hour)
2. Fine, black emery paper. Polishing with sandpaper and emery paper removes scrapes and marks left by the various tools. (Two hours)
3. Leaves of the *muku* tree (*Aphananthe aspera*). Old *muku* leaves are brown and curled (Figure 35). Before they are suitable for use on wood, I

moisten them (without drenching them) and press them flat by uncurling them under a cloth. I usually sit on the cloth while I get on with other work. The old brown leaves are best for overall polishing of large areas, while young *muku* leaves, which are grayish green in color, are more suitable for polishing details such as facial features and relief patterns. When polishing ivory, it is not enough merely to moisten the leaves. They must be soaked in water for about thirty minutes. The *muku* leaf polishing removes the faint scratches left by the sandpapers. (Three to four hours)

4. *Gokuzuihi* is a fine grit powder of an off-white color. A patient polishing with *gokuzuihi* eliminates the marks left by the *muku* leaves and dilutes oils and resins. (Four hours)

5. *To-no-ko* is an orangy yellow polishing powder of extreme fineness. I use it dry to polish woods, because, if wet, it roughens the delicate texture of wood grain. In the case of ivory and horn, however, I use it moist for the preliminary polishing and dry for the final one; being less absorbent, the textures of ivory and horn are not roughened by wet *to-no-ko*, as happens with wood. On the other hand, when smeared moist, *to-no-ko* makes faint scratches invisible, and I am forced to polish blind. With the final dry polishing, however, I can eliminate these faint scratches, which I missed when the *to-no-ko* was wet. The *to-no-ko* polishings efface the faintest blemishes and remove oils, resins, and fingerprints. Sometimes I use burnt stag-antler powder (*tsunoko*) instead of *to-no-ko*. When burnt, the residue of stag-antler is a black powder, incredibly fine and soft. (One hour)

6. *Ibotarō*, a wax which imparts a fine gloss, is made from the secretion of an insect that infests the *ibota* plant. It is classed as a vegetable or tree wax to distinguish it from bee's wax. I impregnate a cloth with melted *ibotarō* and use it to rub the netsuke. (Thirty minutes)

As can be seen from this brief explanation, polishing is a long process, one that requires patience and perseverance. Last of all, if I am pleased with a netsuke, I like to end up by polishing it with my bare hands. I feel as though I were caressing one of my children.

Netsuke with areas that are difficult to reach or details that are recessed pose particular problems for polishing. Such areas tend to be missed in ordinary polishing. Protected, obstructed, or otherwise inaccessible features are likely to escape the effects of the *muku* leaves and the *gokuzuihi* powder. In such cases I sharpen a willow-wood chopstick, wrap a *muku* leaf around it, and polish the inaccessible parts with a drilling or vibrating motion. There is a reason for selecting the wood of the willow tree (*yanagi*) for this purpose: willow is uniform in hardness—even the annual rings are no harder than the spaces between—and the wood itself is elastic and resilient. I follow the *muku* leaves with a wax polishing, still using the sharpened willow chopstick, around the tip of which I now wrap a fine cloth evenly impregnated with *ibotarō*.

My use of a willow chopstick is a violation of my father's strict practice. He cut his own branch from a willow tree and shaped it himself into the sharp pointed sliver he wanted for his polishing.

There is one exception to my principle that I must finish with my tools and my carving before I start polishing. In the case of delicate surface patterns and minuscule details, polishing can obscure or spoil a crisp effect, and therefore I sometimes carve small details, surface patterns, faint reliefs, and textures after polishing a netsuke. The alternative is to polish such areas gingerly and lightly in order to avoid effacing them. The hat tassels and the decorations on Benkei's costume in Plate 12 are examples of details which I carved subsequent to the polishing. So too is the hairline carving on the tiger, as shown in Figures 29 and 30.

Sometimes, I must polish again following the application of color. Since my usual practice is to dip the entire netsuke into the dye instead of applying the dye with a brush, the result is a uniform shade over the entire figure. But in many cases I want the hands and face a lighter shade so that they look more natural. What I do then is polish out some of the color on the parts to be lightened (see Plates 13 and 23). If I wish to remove all traces of color, I sometimes have to peel or shave the area.

35. Leaves of the *muku* tree, used moist for polishing wood netsuke and soaked for ivory; the leaves on the left are old, shriveled, and brown; those on the right, young and grayish green.

VI. Coloring

Ibushi (fumigation) with burning incense is one of the methods I use to color ivory netsuke. The hot smoke penetrates ivory, coloring it permanently but unevenly. Although I frequently turn the netsuke over with chopsticks, the incense smoke does not affect the various parts of the ivory equally, nor are the various parts equally absorbent. These variations result in an amberlike coloration that fades and deepens until it takes on a shading that resembles the patina of old age. The quality of *ibushi* color is similar to that of Buddhist images that have stood for centuries with incense slowly burning at their feet.

Ibushi is particularly suitable for coloring ivory subjects such as birds and animals where I deliberately seek a strong two-tone effect. In these cases I carve the netsuke so that the rind of the tusk becomes the part of the netsuke which I want darker than the rest. The rind—being porous and, usually, naturally darker—absorbs more color and darkens more than other areas (see Plate 43, where the bird's wings are dark, the body light). On the other hand, absolutely uniform incense coloration is difficult to attain and involves choosing a section of ivory that is uniformly dense and successfully exposing all surfaces equally to the incense smoke. The *Seahorse* (Plate 166), cut from the central core, is a rare example of uniform incense coloring.

The difficulty of controlling the absorption of smoke and, therefore, of securing a perfectly uniform coloration is one of the disadvantages of *ibushi* and militates against the use of incense smoke when I require a uniform shade. A more serious disadvantage is the accentuation of tiny surface cracks and flaws by the deposit of resins and residues from the smoke. An almost imperceptible crack may be emphasized as though viewed through a magnifying glass. I suspect that I may have inadvertently contributed to this danger in my younger days by placing my netsuke too close to the heat of the burning incense. I can think of no other explanation for the appearance of cracks which I did not notice while carving but which I discovered subsequent to smoking the piece. Once this had happened a few times, I took great care about keeping my netsuke further away from the incense and allowing more time for the netsuke to absorb the smoke.

I follow incense smoking with three steps that are important for the appearance of the netsuke. First, I use an application of ethyl alcohol to dissolve the tars and resins deposited by the incense. Some residues will remain in the crevices of etched patterns, pitted surfaces, and recesses and will continue to glint darkly. Secondly, I rub the residues with a deerskin that I have impregnated with "clean" house or shelf dust (*hokori*). The effect is to dull the residues and to extinguish the glint of incense deposits that the ethyl alcohol has failed to remove, while allowing patterns such as fish scales to stand out (see Plate 199). Sometimes I dull the glint of resins and residues with *sumi* instead of dust. Each has its particular advantage: dust imparts an antique appearance and the suggestion of patination, while with *sumi* I can attain greater color control and color variation. Lastly, I finish by repolishing the piece with vegetable wax (see Plate 159). All this applies only to ivory, as I never color with incense smoke netsuke made of wood.

There are certain materials which I never color at all: ebony, black persimmon, *kōki*, and *umoregi* among woods, as well as rhinoceros horn, buffalo horn, black coral, tortoise shell, and amber. Nature bestowed on these materials beautiful colorations and textures, which meticulous polishing enhances but coloring would only spoil.

The coloring agent of which I make the greatest use is *yashabushi*, popularly known as *yashadama* or simply *yasha*. It is a versatile and easily regulated dye, which I apply to both ivory and wood. *Yashadama* is a tree cone similar to the familiar pine cone (see Figure 36). I make the dye by infusing a few cones in boiling water in an earthenware pot; I pour off the liquid and set

36. Berries of the *yashabushi* tree, from which the dye is produced.

it aside, add fresh water to the cones, and boil them a second time; again I pour off the liquid; lastly, I mix the two infusions together and give them a long final boil. By the time half the liquid has evaporated, the dye is ready for use.

The older the infusion of *yashadama* the better. For example, I first started using the infusion I use today more than fifteen years ago. From time to time I make a little more of the infusion to add to the old—enough to keep the volume constant. (Strange to say, the same system is practiced by the *unagi* [eel] restaurants, whose renowned sauces were begun by their ancestors a hundred years or so ago.) Newly made *yashadama* is poor in color, and soon molds and forms a crust. I seal my *yashadama* in a small tub with a plastic cover to ensure that no crust forms.

I use *yashadama* very cautiously. I have learned to eliminate oils, resins, sweat, and fingerprints from all surfaces of the netsuke before applying the dye. If I overlook a faint fingerprint, for example, the *yashadama* will emphasize it in bold relief. The danger of leaving an unnoticed fingerprint is greatest in the humid summer months.

I embark on the coloring of a netsuke only after I have finished the polishing. The procedure I use for coloring with *yashadama* is as follows:

1. I wash my hands with *to-no-ko* to remove all traces of sweat and oils.

2. I wash the netsuke in running water while brushing it with a brush of badger hair charged with *to-no-ko*.

3. Using chopsticks to avoid having to touch it, I hold the netsuke under running water to wash away vestiges of *to-no-ko* powder.

4. I immerse the netsuke in a weak solution of glacial acetic acid (*sakusan*) for about one minute. The acetic acid acts as a fixative to increase the adherence of the *yashadama* stain.

5. I wash the netsuke in running water again, this time to remove the acetic acid.

6. I dry the netsuke thoroughly.

7. If the netsuke is ivory, I immerse it in a hot, though not boiling, infusion of *yashadama*. In the case of a wood netsuke, I use a cold infusion of *yashadama*. Wood being more absorbent than ivory, a hot infusion would coarsen its texture.

8. I wash the netsuke in cold water to remove fibers and residues left by the solution.

9. Another wash in hot water helps ivory netsuke to dry more quickly.

10. I dry the netsuke with a cotton cloth and use a willow stick wrapped with cotton to remove moisture from recessed areas.

11. Finally I dry the netsuke in the heat of an electric bulb.

As I said, *yashadama* is a versatile dye and one that I can adjust to a deep brown, a light brown, a yellowish brown, or so faint a stain that the effect on the natural color is practically imperceptible. The shade depends on the thickness of the solution, the temperature of the solution, and the length of time the netsuke is submerged. *Yashadama* is less penetrating than *ibushi*; it is a surface stain, while *ibushi* enters into the pores.

Yashadama can be made to produce a much greater range of colors if it is used as a primer and *sumi* applied over it. I never apply *sumi* without first undercoating with *yashadama*, because, if applied directly to the material, *sumi* is prone to dissolve on contact with moisture, especially when it is thinly applied. I make my *sumi* solution by rubbing an ink stick in a little water just as though I were preparing black ink for writing or painting. I make it in three strengths: thin, medium, and thick. The principle—derived from the practice of *sumi-e*, black ink painting—is to apply it thin for the initial coating, proceeding to medium and thick, until the intensity of blackness desired is reached. This gradual application assures an even coating. It is poor practice to begin with medium or thick. After application it is possible to reduce the intensity of blackness by diluting the coating with wet cotton, but this reverse procedure is less easy to control.

Sumi in solution adheres well without assistance since *nikawa* glue is a prime component of the *sumi* block. I apply *sumi* cold; heating it would make it too thick. The effectiveness of *sumi* on *yashadama* in representing hair and eyebrows may be seen in the netsuke illustrated in the sections on Kabuki and *ukiyo-e* subjects. The hair and eyebrows of the actors are as thick and lustrous as they would be if they had been lacquered. But the advantages of *sumi* over lacquer for hair and eyebrows are compelling. *Sumi* is thin and allows each strand of hair to lie individually and naturally (see Plates 21, 230), while lacquer forms a thick layer that obliterates individual hairs and coats the coiffure like a paint (Plate 33).

Examples of the polychrome effects obtainable by using *yashadama* and *sumi* in combination are the light greenish tinge of the bamboo leaves in Plates 188 and 189, the metallic bronze surface of the animal in Plate 96, the lustrous black coiffure of *Tōran Sennin* (Plate 123), the purplish brown of *Kirare yosa* (Plate 7), the light brown of *Taira no Kiyomori* (Plate 10), and the grayish black of the child actor in Plate 26. The range of color effects can be judged from the figures represented in Plates 34 and 38, where strong colors separate man and woman. By combining a wide choice of colors with the textural effects of *arashi*, I can increase my range of subtle and realistic treatments substantially. Great as the range may be, the equipment comprises only a few tools and a couple of dyes.

Yashadama on its own has other less spectacular uses. Hippopotamus tooth is a fine material, but its natural color is a dull white. A bath in a thin *yashadama* solution replaces this unattractive whiteness with a more lively tinge. The natural color of boxwood, on the other hand, is supremely attractive, but no matter how anxious I am to preserve its color, I must polish it with *gokuzuihi* and *to-no-ko*. The microscopic grains of these fine powders imbed themselves in the pores of the boxwood and resist removal, however persistently I try to brush them away. So, instead, I immerse the netsuke briefly in thin, cold *yashadama*, and this colors the particles of polishing powders without appreciably affecting the natural texture of the wood. It also imparts a satiny finish. The carvings illustrated in Plates 134 and 191 are examples of boxwood netsuke that I dipped in cold *yashadama* without the color being affected.

Netsuke-shi were certainly not ignorant of the attractive golden color and fine texture of natural boxwood. Yet the old carvers stained most boxwood netsuke a medium to dark brown. They preferred the darker, deeper color. The thick, warm patination that one finds in old boxwood netsuke is due in part to the application of dense dyes, since we know that, in the absence of coloring agents, untreated wood produces comparatively little patination. (Another reason for coloring boxwood with a dark stain was mentioned in chapter three: the prevalence of minuscule knotholes that must be filled with pulverized boxwood dust.)

The effects of *yashadama*, *ibushi*, and other coloring agents on stag-antler are greater than on ivory or wood because stag-antler is more porous and hence more absorbent.

I sometimes use gamboge for staining and coloring. My procedure for making and applying infusions of gamboge, which is made from the berries of the *kuchinashi* (gardenia), is the same as for *yashadama*. I began my gamboge solution about ten years ago. I can buy *kuchinashi* berries only once a year, when they are harvested. I soak them in water for three or four days. The tincture turns a reddish yellow.

The difference between *yashadama* and gamboge is in the color. *Yashadama* is brown, gamboge is yellow. I apply gamboge in those cases where I require a yellowish tone—for example, the *Heron* (Plate 49) and *Nupperabō* (Plate 319) among ivory netsuke and the figure in Plate 244 among wood netsuke.

I use potassium permanganate (*kamangan-san*) when I want to stain boxwood a deeper and darker shade than I can obtain with *yashadama*. I first apply a solution of dichromic acid (*jūkurōmu-san*) with a brush. The acid acts as a bond, increases the penetration of the dye so that it reaches minute details and recessed areas, and makes the potassium permanganate colorfast. I prepare the solution in three strengths—thin, medium, and thick—and control the intensity of the color by regulating the thickness of the solution and the number of the applications. I apply the solution cold, as a hot application might spoil the texture of the wood. Just as I do not apply *ibushi* to woods, so I never apply potassium permanganate to ivory.

Occasionally I use silver nitrate (*shōsangin*) for special effects that I cannot secure in any other way. The toys illustrated in Plates 297 and 299 and the leathery, almost metallic hides of the *Blowfish* (Plate 187) and of the *Salamander* (Plate 196) called for the use of silver nitrate. Silver nitrate is tricky to apply—I use a thin stick of willow wood—and difficult to control. It tends to ooze and is colorless, making it difficult for me to see what I am doing; on exposure to air, it gains color gradually, changing from light to dark as it dries. I always smoke my applications of silver nitrate with incense. Smoking mellows the metallic quality of the silver, changing the shade to a silvery black which blends better with the material.

When silver nitrate oozes and flows over into other parts of the carving, it creates a stain which is impossible to remove. The chemical penetrates so deeply that even shaving the area is ineffectual because the stain simply reappears at the lower level.

When I have need of particular shades that I cannot approximate with a combination of *yashadama* and *sumi*, I mix the colors I need in powder form with water. I first brush the area with acetic acid as a fixative and then apply the water color. Examples of special colors made in this way are the green and purple of the Noh dancer in Plate 33 and Sukeroku's purple headband in Plate 30.

My father taught me how to use chemicals such as silver nitrate, potassium permanganate, and acids. They are traditional materials in the workshop of the *netsuke-shi*.

When I have need for basic colors like reds, greens, blacks, and gold (in netsuke representing toys and dolls, for example), I mix colored powders either with raw filtered lacquer or with *nikawa*. I sometimes use the same color in lacquer and in *nikawa* on the one netsuke. Lacquer forms a tougher coating than *nikawa*. On a large area exposed to wear, a lacquer color is preferable, but on a recessed, protected, or insignificant area, I prefer *nikawa*. The advantage of *nikawa* is that it is less brilliant and more mellow than lacquer, and this mellowness is not affected by polishing. Lacquer, on the other hand, becomes more and more vivid as I polish and handle the netsuke. The texture of lacquer is very fine; that of *nikawa* tends to be a little grainy. Lacquer blankets like a thick coat of paint; *nikawa* covers like a thin film. To subdue the unwanted brilliance of lacquer colors, I sometimes resort to a practice called *tsuyakeshi*: I rub *gokuzuihi* or rough magnolia charcoal on the shiny surface to make it matt.

For gold details and gold separation lines, I mix *keshifun* (the finest gold powder) with moistened *nikawa* and apply it with a thin brush. But to avoid gaudiness, I use gold very sparingly. I still use the *keshifun* I bought from a dealer in Fukushima Prefecture fifteen years ago. The separation lines on the inkstone in Plate 286 and the treasure ball in Plate 114 are examples of gold *nikawa*.

When I use gold lacquer (for example, on the hat in Plate 352), I first coat the area with filtered raw lacquer (*ki-urushi*). Then using a soft badger-hair brush charged with *keshifun*, I apply it to the lacquer. I dry the netsuke in a makeshift drying cabinet (*muro*) in my workroom, as I do with all applications of lacquer.

I make my own black lacquer by kneading lampblack into filtered raw lacquer. I inherited the lampblack I use, which is of exceptional quality, from my father. Lampblack is the material used in the manufacture of ink sticks. I add lampblack to the lacquer until the mixture has reached the right density of black. In making shades of red and green, I normally direct the master of the lacquer shop (*urushiya*) as he mixes the powders until I have the shades I want. He filters the mixture through handmade Yoshino paper into *sake* cups that I have brought along for the purpose.

I make my own *nikawa* colors using *nikawa* I buy in gelatin form from the pharmacy. I add a little water as I knead colored powders or lampblack into the liquefied *nikawa*.

It is not necessary to use a primer or fixative in applying lacquer or *nikawa* to a wood or ivory surface. I use a brush as applicator. As in the case of other coloring agents, it is essential first to remove all vestiges of oils, resins, residues, and fingerprints. If lacquer and *nikawa* are to adhere perfectly, an immaculate surface is essential.

VII. Subjects and Sources

My favorite subject matter is the everyday life, activities, and beliefs of the people of Edo, both the place and the period. These are the subjects I carved as I learned the craft from my father. I feel comfortable with the Edo Period and I find joy in representing the world through Edo eyes. When I am vaguely wondering what subject to carve next, I usually linger for a moment or two on an Edo townsman, craftsman, merchant, or housewife engrossed in some typically down-to-earth activity. Indeed, I can think of no aspect of Edo life that I would not happily express in a netsuke.

When I visit museums and exhibitions and when I examine prints, paintings, and carvings, it is usually the depictions of ordinary people involved in everyday activities that capture my attention. And all the time, I wonder how this or that Edo figure or scene could best be interpreted as a netsuke.

I also have a strong partiality for subjects that are grotesque and ludicrous. As well as this natural predilection, I relish the freedom to render the bizarre and absurd in any form my imagination conjures up. Conventional subjects do not permit the same license and scope.

In my workroom I have a good library of Edo history and folklore, richly illustrated. When I am not working, I enjoy nothing better than to flick at random through the pages of these books, picking up hints from old legends, marveling at drawings of fighting men, strange beasts, and stranger saints, or being struck anew by the uncanny realism of an illustration of a bird, a fish, or a four-legged animal. Often it is an old netsuke that excites my admiration.

I have made a list of many of the books that serve constantly to replenish my store of ideas for netsuke. (See Bibliography on page 229. Asterisks appearing alongside entries denote those books that are referred to in the text or in the descriptions to the individual netsuke. When an illustration in one of these books served as a model or design for one of my netsuke, I have usually noted the fact in the corresponding description.)

When I first met Mr. Bushell he urged me to carve new subjects, to experiment with various materials, and to try other treatments. Although a carver and the son of a carver, I had had few opportunities to examine old netsuke. So I started studying both the netsuke in his collection and those he had borrowed from other collections. I learned a great deal from examining old netsuke, not only about their beauty and strength but also, on occasion, about their technical deficiencies. I studied catalogues and books richly illustrated with old netsuke. My eyes gradually opened to new possibilities, to a range of subject matter, and to a variety of styles far beyond what I had learned from my father. I realized then that my technical abilities were well developed but that my artistic horizons were circumscribed.

It wasn't only by studying old netsuke and illustrations in books that I broadened my horizons. I attended Kabuki performances regularly and occasionally went to see Noh and Bunraku. I went, too, to exhibitions of sculpture of all types, and I became an occasional visitor to Tokyo's zoo, where I studied the birds and animals, and to the acquarium for the fish. I struggled with simple designs and forms in an attempt to overcome my tendency toward elaboration. To this end, I studied toys and dolls, masks and *haniwa* burial figurines in order to understand the simplicity and subtlety of their sculptural forms.

Mr. Bushell has often suggested subjects for me, but otherwise he has left me free to practice my craft as I choose, and while he has always reviewed my finished work—sometimes unfavorably—my independence has never been affected.

Good subjects sometimes enter my mind unbidden and in such abundance that I cannot cope with them all at the same time—and some, unfortunately, vanish beyond recall. At other times I strain and struggle; I pore through my books and try to recollect forgotten images, but still I fail to develop a single viable idea. These stalemates and deadends are the most frustrating times of my life.

These remarks about subjects and sources are general. Whenever my memory serves me well enough, I relate in the descriptions of each netsuke the specific source or the circumstances that generated the idea for its creation.

VIII. Designs and Models

Once I have a subject, treatment, and design fixed in my mind, I have to decide on the size of the netsuke and the material I am going to use. It is my feeling about the subject that suggests the treatment, and it is my treatment that determines the material and size that are best suited. Occasionally, however, the material itself is of a sufficiently unusual character that it suggests the subject, and I then make my decisions in reverse order, as, for example, in the case of the stag-antler *Owl* (Plate 210).

The first thing I do with my block of material is to mark it with pencil as a guide for the rough carving. These marks are called *atari* (see Figure 15 on page 44). I never make clay models (*nendo genkei*) or drawings (*shita-e*), no matter how complicated the design. I rely purely on my mental image and on *atari* markings as reminders and guides. Occasionally I draw a pattern on paper before caving it to be sure it is satisfactory. But I have always believed that my creative energy is dissipated if I expend it on a model or drawing. I also believe that my first effort at carving a netsuke is the best one, that my first effort is imbued with a special spirit that permeates it but that will be lost if I try to repeat my first attempt. It is for this reason that I rarely repeat a model.

When I myself decide to repeat a carving, it is because I feel that a change in size, a different material, or some modification in the design will lead to an improvement. When I repeat a model at Mr. Bushell's suggestion, I do so with misgivings and usually with the conviction that my first model will remain the better one. My attitude of "one model—one netsuke" is a departure from that of traditional *netsuke-shi*, who often made many copies or variants of the same models.

Just as I don't like to copy my own models, neither do I like to copy the models of others. My copies of Kaigyokusai's crane (Plate 48) and of Kokusai's owl (Plate 211) are exceptions. I undertook them as technical exercises. In other cases I followed the original model closely, but I tried at the same time to improve on it and made many changes (see Plates 66 and 238). I have sometimes included the word "*sha*" (copy) with my signature where I have copied only a basic idea but have not copied in the strict technical sense. My desire to improve an old model has led me into a quandary occasionally as I studied the design with awe and wondered whether my changes would be improvements or detractions. In everything I carve I try to be both scrupulous and original.

Most of my designs have no models for them at all: they are the products of my imagination; they are originals. In the case of common subjects, however, such as mandarin ducks, which I have seen by the hundreds in museums, menageries, and rivers, the subject cannot be original, but the treatment is always my own.

In carving people and animals, the head is the most important element of the design. All other elements—anatomy, size, pose, and the relationships of the various parts—lead on from the shape and position of the head. The head is the first part of the design that I carve in detail, and on my success with the head depends the success of the netsuke. The eyes, in turn, are the most important element in the head, and after the eyes, the mouth. Eyes and mouth are features that move and give life to a carving, and it is their expressiveness or lack of it that determines whether the netsuke is alive or dead. Nose, forehead, and chin are relatively immobile and so are less important to the vitality of the netsuke. Once I feel that the shape and position of the head are right, that the eyes are clear and alert, and that the mouth is ready to open and talk, then I am happy and confident as I embark on the next stage of my carving, knowing that the entire body will emerge in good shape.

In carving a netsuke with more than one figure—for example, the *Rakan and Lion* (Plate 116)—I carve both heads completely before I attend to the bodies. Obviously the positions of the heads are based on my design for the relationship of their bodies. When the heads emerge satisfactorily, I am elated, and I can be sure that the bodies will interact and accord as I planned.

My carving has evolved through several distinct phases. At first I was youthful and enthusiastic and proud of my technique. It was a joy to carve and to display my talent and virtuosity. I carved all the way through the material. I perforated and undercut with abandon and did as much carving on the inside as on the outside, piling detail on elaborate detail and reaching inaccessible parts with faint reliefs and minute patterns. I used varied and brilliant colors. Now, thirty or forty years later, it is clear to me that designs like those of the netsuke shown in Plates 109, 110, and 117 do not make functional netsuke: they are too fragile. I can't help but marvel, however, at the control and the technical dexterity I displayed in my younger days. I was a master of the mechanics of carving, but I still had much to learn of the restraint of an artist. Nevertheless, the training in techniques and skills that I received from my father is the basis of any quality that there may be in my work today.

My father's approach to carving remained deeply affected by his background and training as an *okimono-shi*. Ideals of simplicity, sturdiness, and compactness do not apply to *okimono* as they do to netsuke. I never questioned the influence my father exerted on me, and I might have continued for the rest of my life carving complicated and unrestrained designs for my netsuke. Dealers and customers readily accepted them. It was Mr. Bushell who suggested that I adopt a more traditional approach to the design of my subjects and that I begin by modifying Kabuki subjects in a more conservative style. So it was that I started attending performances regularly and with growing enthusiasm at the Kabuki-za theater in Tokyo.

Climactic moments are captured in Kabuki by the *mie*, when all movement stops and the actor freezes in an exaggerated pose. I modified my portrayal of the *mie*—contorted bodies and tense, outstretched hands are good dramatics but poor netsuke—by bringing arms and legs closer to the body, by reducing the element of exaggeration in the postures, and by compressing swords, buckets, umbrellas, flowers, and suchlike into protected areas. I tried to do this without compromising the color and richness of Kabuki. My Kabuki subjects could still be criticized for being fragile, but they have no hooks or extensions and the designs are somewhat protected through their compactness and smoothness.

Again, it was Mr. Bushell who urged me to carve animals in addition to people, to use woods and other materials in addition to ivory, to simplify my subjects, and to follow tradition with sturdy, rounded designs. But he also encouraged me to express myself as an artist as well as a craftsman, to maintain originality, and to adhere to my ideals. For a long time I had trouble reconciling what seemed to me to be conflicting goals. I was perplexed and my work floundered. On one netsuke I would revert to elaboration, and then on the next effort I would leapfrog to simplification. I recognized some merit in Mr. Bushell's suggestions, but I was uncertain where they should stop and my own ideas take over. There were many painful misunderstandings, not the least of which were due to language.

My transitions from one subject or one style to another—for example, from actors to animals or from elaboration to simplification—were a series of crises. More than once I considered relinquishing the security of my strange sponsor for the more familiar and less demanding world of bargaining with dealers. In the end, I didn't alter my style all at once, but reacted piecemeal to a series of awakenings. I adapted gradually, even reluctantly, as I came to realize some changes to be for the better, but without ever abandoning my own principles and methods. My dilemmas and quandaries faded as I gradually arrived at a balance between my style of craftsmanship and the ideal form of orthodox netsuke toward which I was now striving.

Before 1960 I had never carved an animal. From then on, I plunged into themes new to me as I became increasingly attracted by traditional netsuke subjects. I went to the zoo and watched the movements and expressions of beasts and birds, and I visited the aquarium to study the fish. I became absorbed with the design problems involved in representing a freely moving animal, a tiger for example, into a rounded body with ears, paws, and tail compactly wrapped, without any loss in realism and character.

Birds and fish are streamlined by nature for easy passage through air and water. They lend themselves quite readily to further simplification and abstraction. I simplify almost all my designs of birds and fish, although I often distort and exaggerate them as well. I avoid relief carving except to suggest feathers or scales. Along the road to simplification, I adopted certain principles to guide me, principles which not only limit the extent of abstraction in my design but also serve to concentrate my mind on aiming first at the creation of a beautiful netsuke and only secondly at carving an identifiable species. In simplifying, I feel free to strip away layer after layer and to eliminate detail after detail without concerning myself about the species.

Nevertheless, the *Abstract Bird* (Plate 41) is one of very few that does not belong to a specific species. When I can do so without compromising the appeal of a model, I prefer to retain the essential identifying character of the bird. I work hard to make a good netsuke and I want it to be understood by everybody; the effort I expend in carving a netsuke is wasted if people have to ask what it is. In addition, I disapprove of modernistic netsuke that could just as well be fish as fowl for all anyone can tell by looking at them.

As I eliminate features and details in a constant drive for greater simplification, I am confronted at some stage with the decision of where to stop. The principle that guides me in this decision is not the particular degree of abstraction I have reached but whether I have arrived at a point where the netsuke is a complete, well-designed, and attractive creation in its own right.

My ideal in terms of abstraction is the crab by Ono Ryōmin illustrated in *Netsuke Familiar and Unfamiliar* (Figure 636). The design is an original one; it is fascinating and attractive; and it is recognizable as a crab despite the extreme simplification.

There are also principles that guide me in transforming toy and doll designs into netsuke (see Plates 286–301). Traditional toys and dolls are simple and cheap. They are made of clay, cloth, straw, and soft wood (mechanical toys are a modern development). Many toys have smooth, round designs, and therefore already have perfect shapes for a functional netsuke. But if I merely copy a toy, substituting ivory or boxwood for clay or straw, I will not have made a netsuke. Worse still, I will have copied without improving.

When I adapt a toy's design for a netsuke, I must treat it as a carving. I must transfigure it. Naturally I make it in netsuke size and add *himotoshi*, but carving is the operation that distinguishes the netsuke from the toy. Different parts of a toy are separated and distinguished by color. With a netsuke, the parts must be separated and distinguished by carving. Thin parts must be thickened and rounded, as, for example, the sleeves of the samurai's flunky in Plate 290. Elevations and depressions must be incorporated, and patterns and lines have to be engraved. For color I do not use the ordinary paints of the toy maker but the lacquer and *nikawa* colors of the *netsuke-shi*.

When I want to simulate the appearance of an old netsuke I treat it with a heavy smoking in incense, which turns ivory a deep amber reminiscent of the patina of old age (see chapter six). But this isn't all I do. Occasionally I have polished more vigorously—practically a grinding—those places which would have been subject to wear and erosion in ordinary use, having first carefully determined where these areas would be. This depends on where the *himotoshi* are placed and on how the netsuke would have been carried. I used occasionally to carve nicks (*kizu*) deliberately to simulate the damages frequently seen in old netsuke, but I stopped doing this long ago. Now, in order to convey the warm feeling of an old netsuke, I relay entirely on the coloration imparted by incense smoke under controlled conditions.

The *himotoshi* is every bit as important to the success of a netsuke as other aspects of the design. I make my decisions about the *himotoshi* when

I plan the design in my mind before I start carving. There are two distinct considerations regarding the holes: placement and carving.

First, let me describe what is involved in the placing. I position the holes so that the netsuke—whether of man or animal—sits, stands, or balances naturally and so that the best side faces outward. I regard as defective a netsuke that wobbles or rocks or fails to balance instead of sitting or standing firmly, as I do a netsuke with a front that fails to face outward. The argument that modifications necessary for proper balance and facing would have spoiled the design is an excuse for shoddy craftsmanship—unless, however, the netsuke is an old one, in which case wear and tear and not the carver's poor design may be to blame.

The secret of balancing and facing is more a matter of the placement of the exit hole than of the knot hole (see Diagram C), though the relationship of the two is also important. It is the exit hole which marks the center of the netsuke's gravity and bears the weight of the *sagemono*, and it is therefore the exit hole which determines whether the figure will "stand" head up at the *obi* or—if it's an animal—ride naturally and face outward.

I expect my netsuke to pass two tests for balance and facing. On a flat surface like a table, they should be able to sit without wobbling or stand without falling. When they are worn with *inrō* or pouch, they should face outward and stand right side up in the case of a person or sit or ride naturally

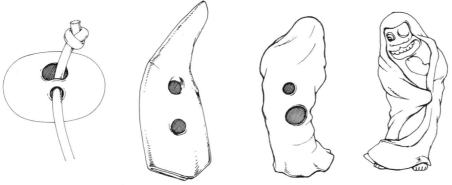

C. *Himotoshi*: the smaller of the two holes is the exit hole, the larger of the two, the knot hole; the knot itself either sits inside the hole or rests just outside as here.

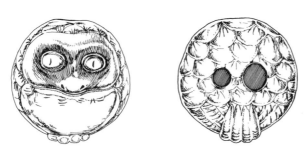

D. A *manjū* netsuke, showing the *himotoshi*.

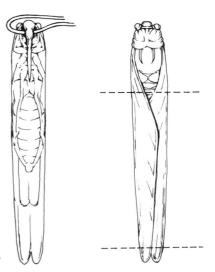

E. A *sashi* netsuke.

in the case of an animal. I don't like to see an animal that dangles by a loop of the tail or a figure that dangles by the crook of the elbow, though I sympathize with the motives of some carvers who prefer dangling netsuke to bodies scarred by holes. I actually overcame my aversion to this expedient in a few particular instances (see Plates 218 and 228). I also dislike the practice of centering the *himotoshi* at the front of the animal, causing the facing side to rest against the kimono and to be hidden from view, a practice which was prevalent among the Ise and Nagoya carvers. Perhaps it was the style there.

The second consideration affecting the holes of the *himotoshi* is the carving. The aesthetics of the *himotoshi* are as important as the balance. I try to carve the holes so that they form as minor a blemish as possible. I do this by attempting to conceal or camouflage them in the design. In some cases I emulate Kaigyokusai and avoid drilling holes altogether by designing a natural separation of the limb of an animal from its body or a stem from the leaf for running the cords. In other cases I imitate the old craftsmen who concealed the knot hole in a hollow sleeve. These techniques for nullifying the mutilating effect of holes are difficult to work into some designs without compromising the balance or facing. I know of no other type of carving where the craftsman must cope with the handicap of a deliberate defacement, even as he strives for perfection.

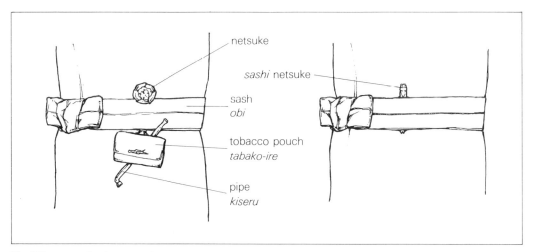

F. The netsuke is a toggle, acting as a catch on the sash of a kimono.

IX. Miscellany

When I was still young and inexperienced, I lacquered a thin, flat board from which I cut small rectangles for inlaying on my netsuke, and on these lacquered labels I carved my signature. My father, however, advised me against this practice, pointing out that inlaid labels are impermanent, easily removed, and just as easily replaced by another label with someone else's signature. Ever since then, I have quit using labels with the one exception of the *Abstract Bird* (Plate 41). Carved signatures are safest; they cannot be removed. We see many netsuke with missing signature labels and many netsuke with labels that appear newer than the netsuke themselves, breeding a plausible suspicion of substitution.

For a few years after I left my father's employ, I used red lacquer or red *nikawa* on my carved signatures. But I discarded this practice fairly early in my career. When I see one of my netsuke with a red *mei* (signature), I know it is an early work. The *Whippoorwill* (Plate 52) is a later exception.

I did not design my own *kakihan* (carved seal). It was designed by a friend of my father who was an official of the National Kakihan Association (*Kokusui kaō kai*). The design is based on three characters, "*toki*" and "*sada*" from my name and "*toshi*" from my *gō*. It was registered on a propitious day in October 1945 (see Figure 37). The design is rather complex, with the result that I carve it infrequently and, when I do, I simplify it a little (see the signature examples on page 70). When I carve a *kakihan* with my name, I never add words like "*tō*" or "*saku*," both of which mean "carved by." The *kakihan* is my identification; to indicate with "*tō*" or "*saku*" that I carved the piece is superfluous and poor form.

There is no significance, only whim, in the styles of writing I employ in carving my signatures. I carve Masatoshi in almost square *kaisho* characters with a slight cursiveness. But Tokisada I sign in running hand (*sōsho*) characters with moderate cursiveness (see signature examples).

I once saw a catalogue of an exhibition of netsuke held in a museum in San Francisco in 1940. I recognized one of the six netsuke illustrated as my carving of Kagemasa Gongorō, the hero of the Kabuki play *Shibaraku*. My name was given as Gashun, which is the alternative reading for Masatoshi. It was an exhilarating moment when I realized that a netsuke of mine had been exhibited in the United States.

I once heard a story about an old painter who was ashamed of much of the work he had done when he was young. He searched out his early

37. The certificate confirming Masatoshi's *kakihan* (right); on the left are the characters for Nakamura Tokisada and the date—a propitious day in October 1945.

paintings and bought back those that he regarded as unsatisfactory and destroyed them ruthlessly. Whether or not this story is true, I understand the painter's feelings. I myself have made netsuke which I would like to destroy. Some I made under duress from a dealer and others are simply bad. They were all produced when I was young, and none are illustrated in this book. On the other hand, I have an inordinate love for a few of my netsuke. Although I made them to sell, I was loath to part with them. The truth is I would like to have them back.

Almost every carver has an incident to relate about how his material split or broke while he was working on it—usually after many days of conscientious labor. I had this experience while I was sawing my material but not while I was carving it—until recently, when it happened to me while I was carving an ivory figure of a girl performing the Tekomai, a festival dance. I had finished the head and begun on the body when I was startled by a loud, sharp report. When I looked at the material, I saw a wide split running from the body through the head. I had to discard it.

My experience was not nearly so depressing as one that befell my father while he was carving an ivory *okimono* forty centimeters (sixteen inches) tall. The subject, from a Kabuki comedy, represented the chambermaid Iwafuji beating the samurai Onoe with her sandal. He had almost completed the figures when a deep fissure appeared, ruining the whole carving. It was a great loss of material, time, and labor. Care must be exercised with materials, especially in winter, when the air is dry and warmed by heaters.

Two materials caused a great deal of misery in my father's house. My stepmother was allergic to lacquer, and whenever we used it, she would suffer intensely from lacquer poisoning. Even though she avoided our workshop when we were using lacquer, she would itch, burn, swell, and take to bed with nausea. When my father sawed boxwood, he would be seized with sneezing fits and his eyes would stream with tears for hours on end. Even covering his nose and mouth with a surgeon's mask was no help. I was fortunate from the beginning, never suffering the slightest discomfort from lacquer, boxwood, or any other material.

Many people believe that it takes more time to carve a small netsuke because of its minuscule features and patterns than it does a normal-sized one. In fact, the opposite is true. A netsuke twice as large takes roughly twice as long to carve. Similarly, an *okimono* twenty-five centimeters (ten inches) high requires at least seven or eight times the time and labor of an average netsuke.

Do I carve real life faces in my netsuke? I don't know why, but I never have. Perhaps the faces of family, friends, and neighbors lack the expression, weirdness, or character I need. Once when she was five or six, I used my daughter's face, but that was for a pipe ordered by a seaman.

From time to time I am shown a netsuke and asked to judge whether it has been colored or whether the color is natural. When netsuke are antique and well handled, it can be difficult to tell whether or not the color of the material is natural. This is the case where the ivory or wood is stained very lightly, if at all. What I do then is look deep into the *himotoshi* or at some deeply recessed part, where a coloring agent would normally thicken and be unaffected by wear. It is in these areas that any difference in color with the main body of the netsuke should show.

On other occasions when I am shown a netsuke, I am asked to give an opinion on whether it is old or new. Generally I have no trouble in distinguishing a new carving from an old one, but sometimes the indications of age are cleverly imitated and it isn't easy to determine the matter. I do not like to declare authoritatively that a piece is new when my judgement is based only on my intuition—though I have ample confidence in my "sixth sense" (which is, as I interpret it, the ability to discern with the eye certain things that the mind cannot put into words). Once I have a feeling about a netsuke, I search for some tangible evidence, however minute, to support my intuition. An example that springs to mind is that of an ivory netsuke of a tiger with unequal holes. My instinct told me it was an imitation of an eighteenth-century model, but I wanted to find tangible proof. And when I looked at the *himotoshi*, I began to see grounds for my suspicion: the knot hole was well worn but the exit hole was relatively fresh. The wear was contrary to the effects of normal use. The knotted end of the cord is almost stationary—it moves little; it is at the exit hole that the cords move about and wear the edges down with friction. Here was the evidence of carving to imitate genuine wear, and it was the carver's mistake that confirmed me in my suspicion.

Another difficult case was that of a stag-antler bird. The carver had done an excellent job of making the piece appear thoroughly old, but he had made one fundamental mistake: he had chosen a risky material. Stag-antler is porous, and it is almost impossible to remove from pores and recesses the microscopic dust of the material and of the polishing powders. Only time removes all traces of dust and powders. Meanwhile specks of fresh dust or powder on the stag-antler were a telltale.

I usually detect a new netsuke by sight, but sometimes it is my nose that provides the confirmation. Any netsuke that has been stained by incense smoke retains its smoky scent for a long time, often for years, especially if it is kept wrapped up or lying in a box.

I have also been asked to determine whether the eyes inlaid in an old netsuke are made of black tortoise shell or *umimatsu*. When first inlaid, *umimatsu*—even in so tiny a speck of material as an eye—can be distinguished from black tortoise shell. The textures are different, *umimatsu* having a slight roughness compared with the smoothness of tortoise shell. But as the netsuke ages, as patination develops, and as wear and handling smooth and tone surfaces, the difference in the textures tends to become less and less perceptible. At this stage, in many cases, I cannot be positive about my identification.

How much time do I spend on each netsuke? And how many have I carved altogether in my life? The longest I have ever spent on one netsuke is about forty-five days and the shortest about twelve days, with my average being about three to four weeks. I consistently carve about fifteen or sixteen in a year. As for the total number of netsuke, I believe I've carved about 650 pieces since the end of my apprenticeship in 1938. The figure is based on my annual output through 1980 and on my records. It accords with an estimate made by Mr. Bushell based on a count of those in his collection and those he knows to be in other collections.

Very few *netsuke-shi*, if any indeed, have had the opportunity I have had of viewing at one time and in one place all the principal netsuke that they produced during their lifetime. Spread on a table for this book is my life's work—from clumsy apprentice to experienced craftsman. I am a little awed by the dexterous craftsmanship of my youth. My eyes and fingers may no longer assure such fine-tuned control and coordination, but I have compensated, I hope, by a serenity of spirit, a confidence in my goals, and a maturity of artistic judgement.

Before old age sets in, some artists observe a minor tradition of climaxing their maturity with an ambitious undertaking, the hallmark of their careers. I am presently carving such a "principal work" using Burmese *tōkata*. When it is completed it will represent the Sixteen Rakan and their animal companions. Those of the *rakan* I have already finished are reproduced on the cover of this book.

38. A human face is hidden among the warts of this frog (see Plate 307); the features of the face were carved, those of the frog were raised by *ukibori*.

Signature Examples

Masatoshi 1a	1b	1c	1d	1e
Masatoshi and *kakihan* 2a	2b	2c	Masatoshi *tō* 3a	3b
3c	3d	3e	Masatoshi *saku* 4	Masatoshi *koku* 5a
5b	Masatoshi *sha* 6a	6b	6c	6d

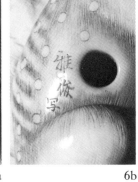
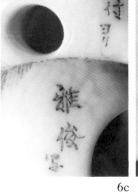

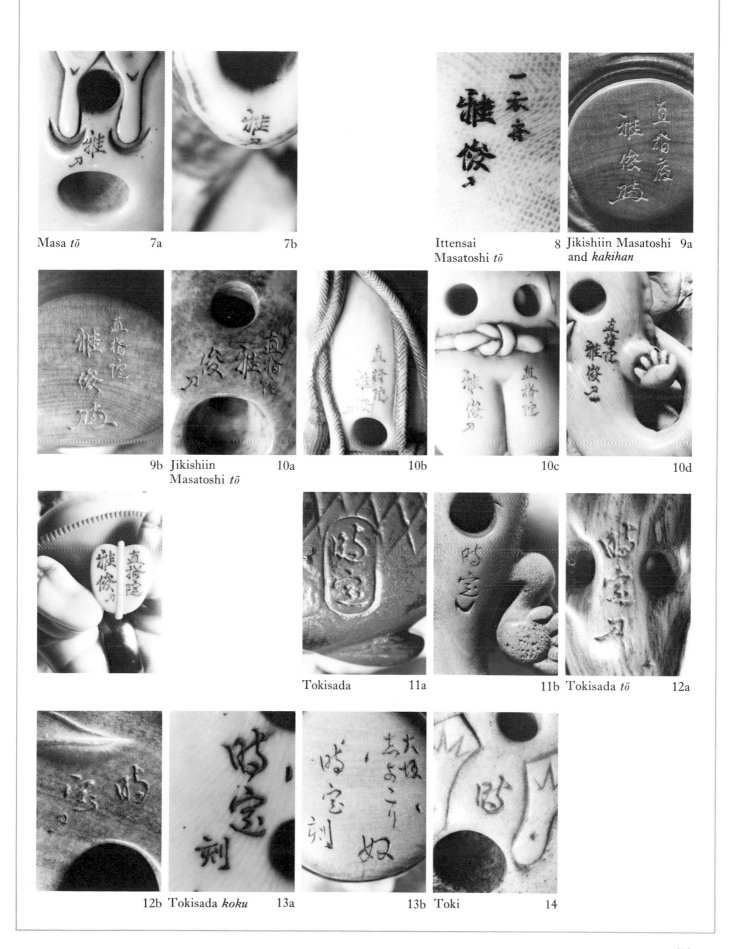

Masa *tō*   7a   7b   Ittensai   8   Jikishiin Masatoshi   9a

Masatoshi *tō*   and *kakihan*

9b   Jikishiin   10a   10b   10c   10d

     Masatoshi *tō*

Tokisada   11a   11b   Tokisada *tō*   12a

12b   Tokisada *koku*   13a   13b   Toki   14

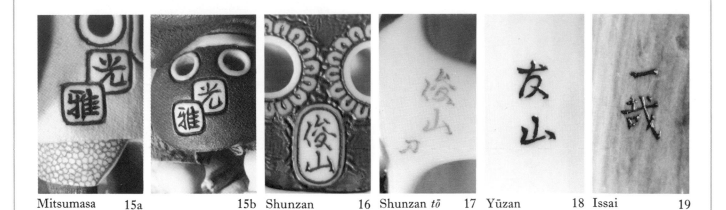

Mitsumasa 15a 15b Shunzan 16 Shunzan *tō* 17 Yūzan 18 Issai 19

The illustrations of netsuke are nearly all thirty percent larger than life size. A few large netsuke are shown at life size or less than life size; where applicable, the difference between the size of the illustration and the size of the actual netsuke is specified in the description.

I took all the transparencies with a Mamiyaflex RB 67 using Ektachrome tungsten film.

Raymond Bushell

1. Early Work

1

2

3

4

2. Kabuki

5

6

7

8

9

10

11

12

13

14

15

KABUKI

16

17

18

19

20

21

KABUKI

22

23

24

25

26

27

28

29

31

32

30

33

KABUKI

34

35

36

37

38

39

KABUKI

3. Birds

40

41

42

44a

43

44b

45

46

47

48

49

50

51

52

53

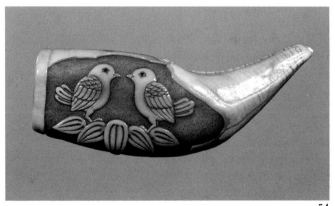

54

55

BIRDS

56

57

58

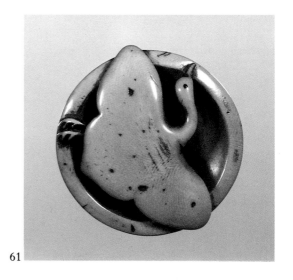

59

60

61

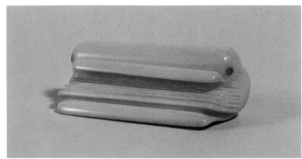

62

63

65

64

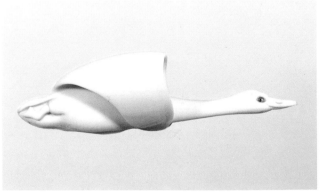

66

67

BIRDS

4. Insects

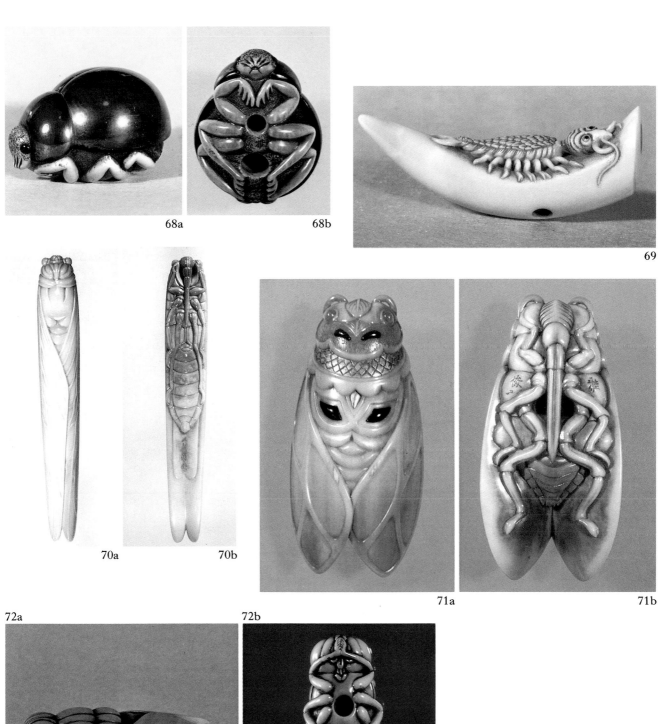

68a

68b

69

70a

70b

71a

71b

72a

72b

74a   73a   75a   73b   76a

74b   75b   77a   76b   77b

INSECTS

5. Botanical Subjects

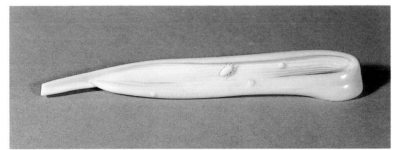

78

79

80a

80b

6. Supernatural Animals

81

82

83

84

85

86

87

88

89

90

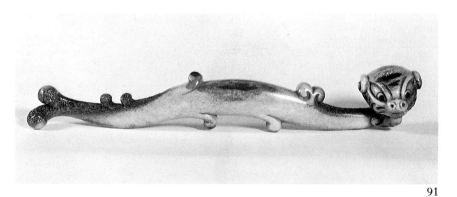

91

92

SUPERNATURAL ANIMALS

93

94

95

96

97

98

SUPERNATURAL ANIMALS

99

100

101

102

104a

103

104b

7. Turtles and Crabs

105

106

107

108a   108b

 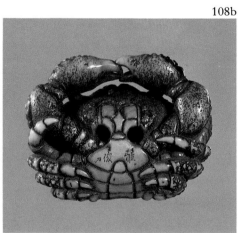

8. Gods and Sages

109

110

111

112

113

114

115

116

117

118

GODS AND SAGES

119

120

121

122

123

9. Customs, Festivals, Ceremonies

124

125

126

127

128

10. People

129

131

130

132

133

134

135

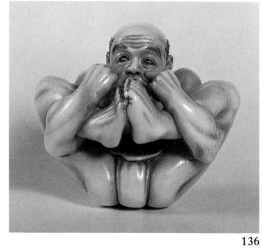

136

137

138

139

PEOPLE

140

141

142

144

145

143

PEOPLE

11. Masks and Heads

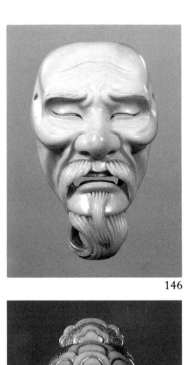

146

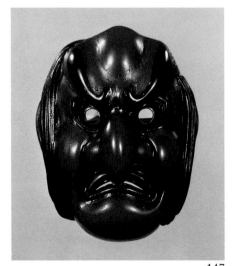

147

148

149

150

151

152

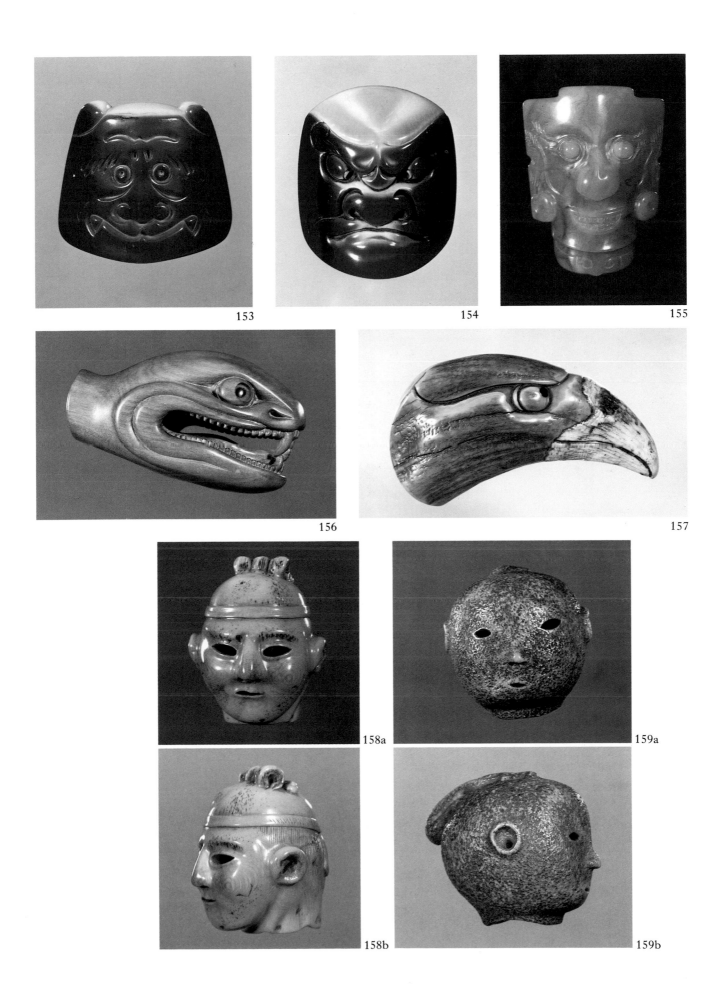

153

154

155

156

157

158a

159a

158b

159b

MASKS AND HEADS

160

161a

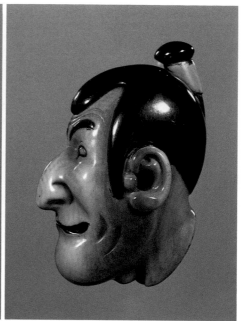

161b

162

163

164

MASKS AND HEADS

12. Fish

165

166

167

168

169

170

171

172

174

173

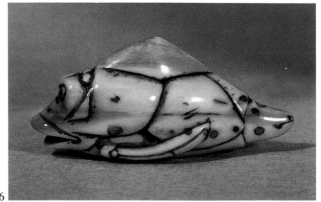

175

176

FISH

177

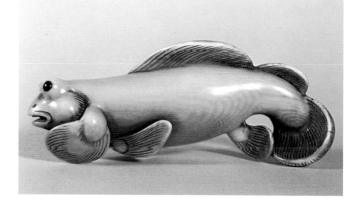

179

178

180

181

182

FISH

183

185

184

186

187

188

189

FISH

13. Lizards, Snakes, Bats, Owls

190

191

193

192

194

195

196

198

197

199

200

201

LIZARDS, SNAKES, BATS, OWLS

202

203

205a

204

205b

LIZARDS, SNAKES, BATS, OWLS

206

207

208

209

210

211

LIZARDS, SNAKES, BATS, OWLS

14. Objects

212

213

214

215

216

217

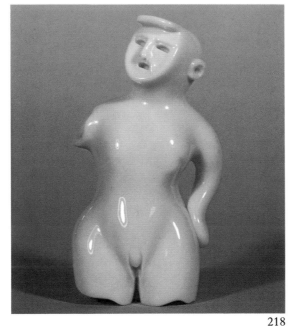

218

219

220

OBJECTS

15. Subjects from Ukiyo-e

221

222

223

224

225

226

227

228

229

230

SUBJECTS FROM UKIYO-E

16. Legends and Myths

231

232

233

234

235

236

237

238

239

240

241

242

LEGENDS AND MYTHS

243

211

245

246

247

248

LEGENDS AND MYTHS

249

250

251a

251b

252

253

LEGENDS AND MYTHS

17. Animals

254

255

256

257

259

258

260

261

262

263

264

265

ANIMALS

266

267

268

269

270

271

ANIMALS

273

274

272

275

276

277

278

ANIMALS

279

280

281

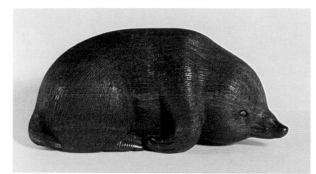

282

283

284

285

18. Toys and Dolls

286

287

288

289

290

291

292

293

294

295

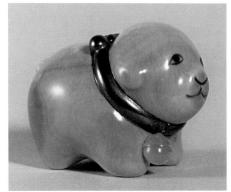

296

TOYS AND DOLLS

297

298a

298b

299

300

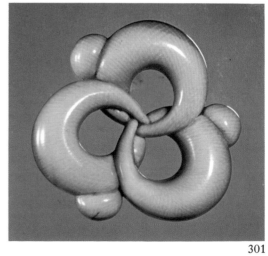

301

TOYS AND DOLLS

19. Frogs

302

303

304

305

306

307

308

309

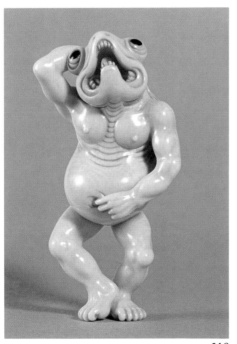

310

311

FROGS

20. Weird Beings

312

313

314

315

316

317

318

319

320

321

322

323

WEIRD BEINGS

324

325

326

327

328a

328b

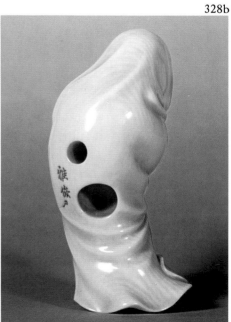

WEIRD BEINGS

329

330

331

332

333

334

WEIRD BEINGS

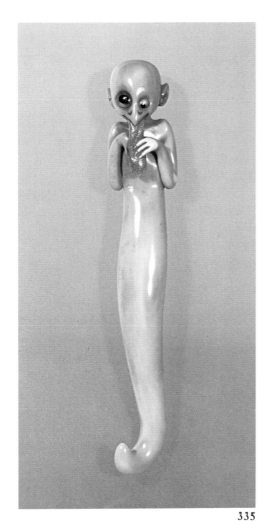

335

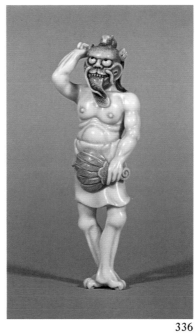

336

337

338

340

339

WEIRD BEINGS

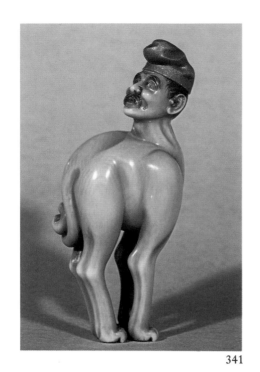

341

342

343

344

345

WEIRD BEINGS

21. Miscellanea

346

347

348

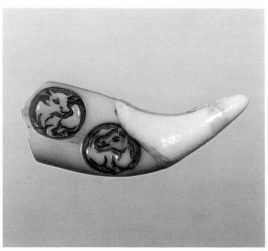

349

350

351

352

353

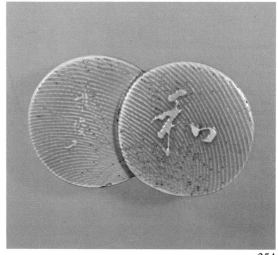

354

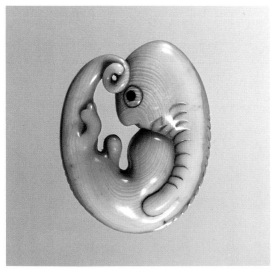

355

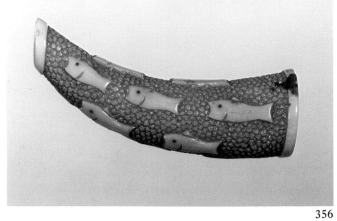

356

MISCELLANEA

Descriptions of Color Plates

1. Early Work

1 Demon
Oni

The demon (*oni*) carries a huge pipe case and tobacco pouch on his back with a netsuke representing the Sacred Mushroom (*reishi*). He wears leopard-spot pants. This is one of my earliest netsuke. By coincidence, Mr. Bushell bought it in Kyoto six years before we first met. Although I carved it, I have no recollection of the circumstances. I believe that it must have been just before or just after World War II. It is signed Mitsumasa, so I know it is a netsuke for which I had a helper (see page 22). The same failure of recollection applies to Plates 2 and 3, which I also signed Mitsumasa.

SIGNED: Mitsumasa, in two square reserves.
MATERIAL: ivory.
BASIC COLOR: *yashadama*; blue lacquer—pipe case, pouch; brown lacquer—hip pad; *sumi*—hair, eyes, leopard spots, scarf, markings.
COMPLETED: before 1946.

2 Traveler
Tabibito

I carved an ordinary townsman of the Edo Period dressed for traveling. He wears a short coat (*michiyuki*) and straw sandals. He carries a rush hat for protection against the sun and his provisions in a pair of bundles connected by straps (*furiwake-nimotsu*) and balanced over his shoulder. His hair is in the style typical of the Edo commoner.

The *yashadama* stain is strongest on the traveler's coat and weakest on his face and hands. I scored the surface of his coat to increase the absorption of color but polished away most of the stain on his hands and face. I crosshatched his leggings with the technique known as *nunome arashi*, fabric roughening (see page 46).

SIGNED: Mitsumasa, in two square reserves.
MATERIAL: ivory.
BASIC COLOR: *yashadama*; *sumi*—hair, eyebrows, eyes, markings on kimono, stockings, sandals, hat, packages.
COMPLETED: before 1952.

3 Polishing a Sword Guard
Tsuba-migaki

An artisan (*shokunin*) of the Edo Period, a polisher of metals, is buffing a huge sword guard (*tsuba*) that serves as the signboard (*kanban*) of a shop. The relief design on the sword guard is of a dragon grasping the Tide Jewel in his claws.

SIGNED: Mitsumasa, in two square reserves.
MATERIAL: ivory.
BASIC COLOR: *yashadama*; *sumi*—hair, eyebrows, kimono pattern, dragon's scales; gold *nikawa*—Tide Jewel, dragon's eyes.
COMPLETED: before 1952.

4 Neck Wrestlers
Kubi-hiki

The men, samurai lackeys (*chūgen*), are neck-wrestling. The same daimyō employs them both, as shown by the identical family crest (*mon*) on their kimono. The older man has a stripe on his coat indicating that he holds a higher rank than his opponent, and, although the frailer of the two, he is winning. In fact, he is taking an unfair advantage by bracing himself with his hands against his knees instead of keeping his arms folded, as does his opponent. The younger man does not dare complain.

My father originated this subject. The two men and the scarf around their necks are carved from a solid block of ivory.

SIGNED: Masatoshi, in red in an oval reserve.
MATERIAL: ivory.
BASIC COLOR: *yashadama*; *sumi*—hair, eyebrows, pupils, *obi*, kimono border.
COMPLETED: before 1952.
ILLUSTRATED: *Arts of Asia*, July/August 1973.
Sumo World, January 1980.

2. Kabuki

5 Sashichi

Sashichi is the protagonist of a Kabuki play of the *enkirimono* group, dramas that turn on the rupture of a relationship, for example, between betrothed lovers. Sashichi is a firefighter, the hero of a daredevil profession, who is lionized by the citizens of fire-prone Edo. He exchanges pledges of enduring love with Koito, a popular courtesan, who afterward decides to end their relationship.

Too late, he finds her letter explaining why she had to sever their ties. Her foster mother had shown her a document preserved by her real mother in their umbilical cord proving that Koito is the daughter of the samurai who murdered Sashichi's father and against whom Sashichi has sworn revenge. Torn between her love for Sashichi and her duty to her father, Koito resolves to abandon her lover and commit suicide.

I portrayed Sashichi in a transport of jealous rage, clutching the kitchen knife with which he stabbed Koito to death. I carved the text of Koito's farewell letter in legible characters which accord with the spoken version of the stage play.

SIGNED: Masatoshi *tō*.
MATERIAL: ivory.
BASIC COLOR: *yashadama*; black lacquer—socks, underpants; *sumi*—hair, eyebrows, knife, shirt, patterns on towel and kimono, characters on letter.
COMPLETED: July 1956.

6 Jihei

Shinjū ten no Amijima (The Double Love Suicide at Amijima) is a Kabuki play based on a real-life incident that occurred in Ōsaka in the early eighteenth century. Jihei, a merchant and family man, falls in love with Koharu, a geisha, who returns his passion. Jihei's wife and family badger and torment Koharu in order to force her to end the romance.

Nagged relentlessly and stigmatized on all sides, the desperate lovers pretend to repudiate their written pledges of love so as to placate family and friends. They end their unhappy existence in a double suicide at the temple of Amijima.

I carved the merchant Jihei as he sets out to meet his love at a teahouse. The pattern on his kimono is a hailstone checkerboard pattern, and that of his head-covering, one of geese and pampas grass.

SIGNED: Masatoshi, in an oval reserve.
MATERIAL: ivory.
BASIC COLOR: *yashadama*; *sumi*—hair, eyebrows, patterns on kimono, *obi*, and towel, sword scabbard; gold *nikawa*—sword guard.
COMPLETED: February 1956.

7 *Kirare yosa*

Kirare yosa (Scarred Yosa) is a play of the *sewamono* type, a play in which the actors use the common language and wear the ordinary clothes of the period. Yosa is the handsome heir of a wealthy family, but he is attracted to a life of gambling, drinking, and dissipation. When his dissoluteness proves incorrigible, his despairing family disowns him.

Yosa has an affair with a geisha named Otomi, heedless of the fact that she is the mistress of a gangster chief. The gangster takes revenge on Yosa by mutilating him with thirty-four knife cuts. Penniless, disowned, and disfigured, Yosa takes up a life of petty blackmail in league with a rogue named Kōmori—because of the bat (*kōmori*) tattooed on his cheek—who suspects that Otomi has a murky past and will make an easy prey for blackmail.

I carved Yosa at the instant he looks up from his smoking tray (*tabako-bon*) and recognizes Otomi, whom he thought had drowned herself. Yosa's emotions, so long suppressed, burst out in a torrent of outrage. For what reason, he wants to know, did he suffer disfigurement and degradation? In the most scathing terms he excoriates Otomi, accusing her of callousness and betrayal. His speech of denunciation is one of the high points of the drama.

SIGNED: Masatoshi.
MATERIAL: ivory.
BASIC COLOR: *yashadama*; *sumi*—hair, eyebrows, eyes, mouth, scars, kimono, *obi*; black lacquer—smoking tray.
COMPLETED: July 1954.

8 Kirare otomi

Kirare otomi is a parody with a female twist on the earlier play, of which Kirare Yosa is the protagonist (Plate 7). In that play the gangster disfigures Yosa when he discovers Yosa's liaison with his girl friend Otomi, but in this play it is Otomi whom he mutilates.

Later, Otomi learns that the gangster has grown rich on the profits of his brothel. She embarrasses him before his patrons by applying for a job as one of his whores despite her hideous disfigurement. She is actually practicing extortion on him, and he is forced to buy her silence with two hundred gold coins.

She gives the money to Yosa, her true lover, so that he can ransom his family's heirloom, a celebrated sword which he had pawned, and eradicate his disgrace. I carved Otomi as she counts the gold pieces into her purse.

SIGNED: Masatoshi *tō*.

MATERIAL: ivory.

BASIC COLOR: *yashadama*; *sumi*—hair, eyes, scars, patterns on kimono and garments; red *nikawa*—lips.

COMPLETED: December 1957.

9 Chōbei

In the Kabuki play *The Last Days of Chōbei of Ban-zuiin*, Chōbei is a *machiyakko*, a courageous man of the people who protects commoners against bullying samurai.

Chōbei insults Jūrōzaemon, a ranking samurai, and so, when Jūrōzaemon invites him to a party, Chōbei suspects treachery. Although he knows his life is at stake he prefers to accept than to show fear. At dinner a servant spills *sake* on him in a carefully staged "accident." Jūrōzaemon invites him to bathe and, with his henchmen, attacks him while he is in the bath and stripped of weapons. I carved Chōbei

as he grasps a wooden ladle to defend himself. His defense against his enemies' steel lances is valiant but vain. The following morning, as Chōbei had instructed her the previous night, his wife appears at Jūrōzaemon's house carrying a burial tub to collect her husband's remains. The murderers are astounded at Chōbei's courage.

The play is based on historical fact. The real Chōbei was lured into taking a bath which was heated from the outside. Jūrōzaemon's servants added fuel until the water boiled, forcing Chōbei to leap away from the protection of the metal tub. Thereupon, his attackers, thrusting their lances between the wooden slats of the bathhouse, speared him to death.

SIGNED: Masatoshi *tō*.

MATERIAL: ivory.

BASIC COLOR: *yashadama*; *sumi*—hair, eyebrows, eyes, kimono pattern.

COMPLETED: November 1954.

10 Taira no Kiyomori

Taira no Kiyomori was the medieval leader of the Taira clan. Through unscrupulous ambition and ruthless action, he established himself as the solitary despot over the country. His exploits are related in romances, the most famous of which is the *Heike monogatari*, and enacted in a host of Kabuki plays, in which his rule is invariably depicted as being marked by tyranny, extravagance, and suspicion. I carved Kiyomori as he orders preparations for battle.

SIGNED: Masatoshi.

MATERIAL: ivory.

BASIC COLOR: *yashadama*; *sumi*—pupils; gold *nikawa*—armor.

COMPLETED: August 1965.

11 Taira no Shigemori

Shigemori was a contrast in character to his tempestuous father, Kiyomori (Plate 10). Shigemori was gentle, calm, and considerate, loved by one and all, yet his father despised him for his seeming lack of masculinity and daring. An incident in the palace proved how wrong his father was.

A huge reptile appeared suddenly and terrorized the servants. Without a moment's hesitation, Shigemori attacked it and cut it to pieces. The episode is not in fact performed in the theater, but I carved Shigemori and the serpent as I imagined the scene if it were staged and performed in Kabuki.

SIGNED: Masatoshi.

MATERIAL: ivory.

BASIC COLOR: *yashadama*; *sumi*—hair, eyebrows, beard, mustache, kimono pattern, snake scales; gold *nikawa*—standing hat.

COMPLETED: March 1955.

12 The Subscription List
Kanjin-chō

A barrier has been set up at Ataka for the purpose of capturing Minamoto no Yoshitsune. Religious camouflage is Benkei's ruse for conducting his lord, Yoshitsune, safely past the vigilant Togashi, the captain of the barrier guard. He disguises himself as a mountain priest (*yamabushi*) and his lord as his common porter. Togashi is suspicious and challenges Benkei to read the Subscription List, *Kanjin-chō* (the name of the play). Arrest and execution are at stake. With great presence of mind and verbal ingenuity, Benkei extemporizes, exhorting donations for the restoration of Tōdaiji, the famous temple in Nara. He employs arcane and ecclesiastical language. The guard notices that the list is blank, but so great is his admiration for Benkei's courage and cleverness that he pretends to be deceived, exercising the generosity of a samurai to an enemy. Unbearable tension built by alternating hopes of success and fears of discovery is broken as Benkei and Yoshitsune are allowed to pass.

I carved Benkei as he reads the subscription list.

SIGNED: Masatoshi, in red in an oval reserve.

MATERIAL: ivory.

BASIC COLOR: *yashadama*; *sumi*—hair, eyebrows, pupil, coat, kimono patterns, prayer-bead tassels, cap; gold *nikawa*—sword guard, special decora-

tions for mountain priests (see page 51).

COMPLETED: January 1953.

ILLUSTRATED: *Arts of Asia*, July/August 1973.

13 Kakiemon

The play *Master Craftsman Kakiemon* is one of the group known as New Kabuki. It deals with the trials and tragedies that befell Kakiemon, the potter who produced the classic porcelain of Arita that bears his name. I carved Kakiemon staring intently at a persimmon tree as he ponders the problem of reproducing the magnificent color and texture of the fruit in his glazes. The crest partially visible on his sleeve is the character for persimmon, *kaki*. After fifteen years of adversity the potter succeeded in producing his unique "Kakiemon red."

SIGNED: Masatoshi *tō*.

MATERIAL: ivory.

BASIC COLOR: *yashadama*; *sumi*—hair, eyebrows, pupils, coat, jacket, kimono.

COMPLETED: April 1973.

14 Tokube

Tenjiku Tokube was a real person who lived in the early Edo Period, an adventurous merchant who made many trips to India. Tales about him were embellished into legends and finally dramatized in a Kabuki play, *Exotic Tales of Tokube in India.*

Tokube is surrounded by enemies who want to capture him. He thwarts them by "frog magic," at which he is adept. He bursts mysteriously from a monstrous papier-mâché frog, as thick, black smoke pours from its maw. The pyrotechnical effect on the stage is spectacular.

It is at this climactic moment that I represented Tokube. I carved his hands in the symbolic position of a wizard working his magic. I crossed his eyes and turned down his mouth at one corner to accentuate his weirdness. His companion, the frog, is a monster. It has teeth and spouts flames. Its eyes are misshapen, the pupils inlaid with red hornbill ivory (*hōnen*).

SIGNED: Masatoshi *tō*.
MATERIAL: ivory.
FROG'S PUPILS: hornbill ivory.
BASIC COLOR: *yashadama*; *sumi*—hat, hair, eyebrows, pupils, kimono, frog's warty back; red *nikawa*—frog's mouth.
COMPLETED: May 1973.
ILLUSTRATED: *The Kotto*, No. 3.

15 Nikki Danjō

Meiboku Sendai hagi (The Disputed Succession) is a classic Kabuki loyalty play based on an historical theme, a plot in 1660 against the daimyō of Sendai. While the daimyō is in Edo, a group of disgruntled retainers plot to murder his infant son and seize power. Masaoka, the faithful nurse who has charge of the infant, thwarts the attempt to poison him by substituting her own child and feeding him the poisoned cakes. One of the plotters is so overcome by admiration for Masaoka's loyalty and her sacrifice that he confesses and gives her a list of the conspirators. Suddenly, a colossal rat appears and seizes the incriminating document in his jaws. One of the faithful retainers hurls an iron-ribbed war fan at the rat, wounding it in the head. The rat vanishes in a smoke cloud, and Nikki Danjō, the leader of the conspirators, suddenly appears in the animal's stead.

I carved Nikki Danjō at the instant he replaces the rat. His hands and fingers are arranged in the conventional configuration that symbolizes the master magician. He holds the list of conspirators in his teeth just as did the rat, and his forehead bears a wound at the very spot where the iron fan struck the animal.

SIGNED: Masatoshi, in an oval reserve.
MATERIAL: ivory.
BASIC COLOR: *yashadama*; *sumi*—hair, eyebrows, scroll, make-up (*kumadori*), kimono; gold *nikawa*—sword hilt.
COMPLETED: September 1958.

16 Kamiyui Shinza

Kamiyui (Hairdresser) Shinza is the evil protagonist of this play. From the gossip of his patrons, he learns that Okuma is in love with Chūshichi under hopeless circumstances and that in desperation she is pressing her lover to elope and commit double suicide. Shinza urges Chūshichi to pretend to elope in order to save Okuma from suicide. He assists the lovers to escape, but he has his own evil, greedy plan. He separates them by a trick and makes it appear that Chūshichi was abducting Okuma and that he was rescuing her from Chūshichi.

He holds Okuma hostage, expecting to be paid in gold for his "trouble" before he returns her to her family. Several characters generously offer to intercede with Shinza but ironically each in turn discloses his cynical interest in profiting from her family's distress. Finally, Chōbei, a popular hero, employs a clever ruse to maneuver Shinza into a position where he must accept a pittance in lieu of his demand or face the police.

I carved Hairdresser Shinza carrying the implements of his trade.

SIGNED: Masatoshi *tō*.
MATERIAL: ivory.
BASIC COLOR: *yashadama*; *sumi*—hair, eyebrows, pupils, mouth, kimono.
COMPLETED: February 1958.

17 Belly-cutting *Seppuku*

The *seppuku* (belly-cutting) scene is from the story of *The Forty-Seven Rōnin*. Enya Hangan is ordered to commit *seppuku* as punishment for his assault on Moronao. Moronao's henchman, who is present as a witness, berates Enya for procrastinating with the ceremony. Enya stalls, waiting for the arrival of his chief retainer, Yuranosuke, whom he intends to give instructions for a vendetta against Moronao. He responds to the taunts of his enemy wordlessly and dramatically by dropping his formal kimono (*kamishimo*) to reveal that he is already wearing the traditional white garment of death.

I portrayed Enya Hangan holding the dirk of his death wrapped in paper, his face contorted not with fear but with frustration over the delayed arrival of Yuranosuke.

Enya Hangan breaks the protracted tension when he shouts the name of Yuranosuke as his retainer enters the chamber, and at the same time drives home the dagger for the first cut. After whispering a few instructions to Yuranosuke, he draws the dagger across his belly and twists it upward.

SIGNED: Masatoshi.
MATERIAL: ivory.
BASIC COLOR: *yashadama*; *sumi*—hair, eyebrows, pupils, mouth.
COMPLETED: December 1953.

18 Sagisaka Bannai

The Journey of the Bridegroom is a dance interlude performed to provide light relief from the drama of *The Forty-Seven Rōnin* (Plate 17). Kanpei, one of Enya Hangan's retainers, is betrothed to Okaru, lady-in-waiting to his lord's wife. It is early spring and the lovers are journeying to visit Okaru's parents. On the way they are accosted by Sagisaka Bannai, one of Moronao's henchmen. He is a ridiculous, cowardly villain, a comic figure whose antics ease the tension of the main theme. A mock fight follows in dance form, the actors using blossoming cherry branches in place of swords. Kanpei beats Bannai soundly, and Bannai slowly slinks away. The lovers continue their journey.

I carved Sagisaka Bannai as he struts about before the duel.

SIGNED: Masatoshi.
MATERIAL: ivory.
BASIC COLOR: *yashadama*; *sumi*—hair, eyebrows, pupils, mouth, make-up, kimono pattern; gold *nikawa*—sword guard and hilt.
COMPLETED: April 1971.

19 Soga no Gorō

The story of *The Soga Brothers' Revenge* is told in many versions and episodes in Noh and Bunraku as well as Kabuki. The brothers were children when their father was murdered. Eighteen years later they avenged his death by killing the murderer, who, in the meantime, had become a powerful daimyō. As the Soga brothers gave formal notice of their vendetta and did not adopt any underhand methods in their attack, they were treated honorably and not as common criminals as were the forty-seven *rōnin*.

A tense episode in the drama is the struggle between Soga no Gorō and his friend Asahina, who prevents him from launching a premature and foolhardy attack. Asahina is a powerful man and in the struggle tears off part of Gorō's suit of armor. I portrayed Soga no Gorō in a dance version of the episode. He dances in *aragoto* style, an exaggerated bravado manner, holding the armor over his head on the point of his sword.

SIGNED: Masatoshi, in an oval reserve.
MATERIAL: ivory.
BASIC COLOR: *yashadama*; black lacquer — hat, scabbard; *sumi*—hair, make-up, sword hilt, kimono pattern; gold *nikawa*—armor, sword ornament; red *nikawa*—tassels on swords.
COMPLETED: April 1971.

20 Igami no Gonta

Yoshitsune's Thousand Cherry Trees is a Kabuki play based on loyalties in the death struggle between hostile clans, the Taira and the Minamoto. "One thousand" signifies a great number, and "cherry trees" signifies loyal samurai, thus the figurative sense of the title is "Yoshitsune's Army of Loyal Samurai."

Yazaemon is loyal to the Taira clan. He is hiding in his fish shop Koremori, the defeated general of the clan, disguised as an apprentice. Yazaemon's son, Igami no Gonta, treacherously sides with the victorious Minamoto, who are searching the village for Koremori.

In extreme agitation Yazaemon enters carrying the head of a fallen Taira warrior, which he hopes to pass off as the head of Koremori. He hides the head in a rice tub. The Minamoto enter the shop searching for Koremori. Igami no Gonta delivers a tub containing a head and produces a woman and small boy gagged and bound, saying they are Koremori's wife and son. As Igami no Gonta had previously furnished military intelligence to the Minamoto, the inspection of the head is perfunctory, and the head readily accepted as Koremori's. Yazaemon, certain that his son has indeed handed over the head of Koremori, is overcome with revulsion at his son's treachery and stabs him. As Igami slowly bleeds to death, he tells his father that he had repented of his unfilial disloyalty and that they were his own wife and son he had sacrificed. With his last breath he summons Koremori with his wife and child.

I portrayed Igami no Gonta as he produces the rice tub containing the supposed head of Koremori.

SIGNED: Masatoshi *tō*.
MATERIAL: ivory.
BASIC COLOR: *yashadama*; *sumi*—hair, make-up, *obi*.
COMPLETED: December 1955.
ILLUSTRATED: *Collectors' Netsuke*, Figure 341.

21 Abe Yasuna

Abe Yasuna is the main character of a dance play (*shosagoto*), *The Arrowroot Leaf*. Yasuna's beloved Sakaki dies, and Yasuna goes insane with grief. He clings to her kimono and wanders the countryside aimlessly. In the dance Yasuna alternates between happiness as he remembers her alive and sorrow when he realizes that she is dead. The portrayal of mad-

ness through dance is a difficult performance. The accompaniment to the dance is principally vocal, a style called *kiyomoto*, high pitched and emotional.

I carved Yasuna as he dances holding Sakaki's kimono folded across his arm. I etched the pattern of plum blossoms and pine leaves on the inside as well as on the outside of her kimono. I tried to give Yasuna an expression of insane grief.

SIGNED: Masatoshi.
MATERIAL: ivory.
BASIC COLOR: *yashadama*; *sumi*—hair, make-up, patterns on kimono; gold *nikawa*—crescent pattern on Yasuna's kimono.
COMPLETED: February 1955.

22 Kisen Hōshi

Kisen Hōshi (Priest Kisen) is one of the "Six Great Poets" of the ninth century. The priest-poet visits the Kiyomizu Temple in Kyoto to enjoy the cherry blossoms, which are in full bloom. Attracted by the beauty of Okaji, a young teashop waitress, and carried away by the gay spirit of the occasion, the priest successively dances alone, then with Okaji, and finally with a group of priests.

I tried to capture the priest's pure ecstasy in my portrayal.

SIGNED: Masatoshi.
MATERIAL: ivory.
BASIC COLOR: *yashadama*; *sumi*—make-up, apron, gourd stem.
COMPLETED: October 1955.

23 Kōchiyama Sōshun

Kōchiyama Sōshun is a petty swindler and extortionist whose favorite ploy is to pose as a priest. He learns that the daimyō of Matsue is enamored of Namiji, the daimyō's own young servant. In his efforts to seduce her, the daimyō prevents her from leaving the castle despite the pleas of Namiji's widowed mother. Kōchiyama, posing as the high priest Dokai, pays the lustful daimyō a call and refuses all refreshments stating that he will accept only *yamabuki* (yellow rose) tea. The daimyō correctly interprets this symbolic demand to mean that the pseudo-priest wants gold under threat of exposing his licentious ways. Although the daimyō realizes that Kōchiyama is an imposter, he is nevertheless forced to pay blackmail and release Namiji.

I represented Kōchiyama as he tries to conceal the mole that is an open clue to his true identity.

SIGNED: Masatoshi, in an oval reserve.
MATERIAL: ivory.
BASIC COLOR: *yashadama*; *sumi*—make-up, neck sash; gold *nikawa*—fan; red *nikawa*—prayer beads.
COMPLETED: September 1957.

24 *Osome hisamatsu*

The play *Osome hisamatsu* is performed less for its dramatic content than as a showpiece for the female impersonator (*onnagata*) and especially for the technique of changing costumes with lightning speed (*hayagawari*). In *hayagawari* a performer plays two or more roles, making instant kimono changes so skillfully that the audience is unaware that it is the same actor reappearing in an entirely different role. In *Osome hisamatsu* there are seven roles with lightning costume changes handled by the one female impersonator. The roles cover almost all possible types of impersonation: ordinary girl, lady-in-waiting, geisha, woman criminal, elderly matron, crazed woman, and young boy.

I carved the *onnagata* playing the role of Oroku, a hard, criminal type of woman.

SIGNED: Masatoshi, in an oval reserve.
MATERIAL: ivory.
BASIC COLOR: *yashadama*; *sumi*—hair, make-up, coat, kimono, *obi*.
COMPLETED: April 1973.

25 Izaemon

In *Tales of the Licensed Quarter*, Izaemon is the typical Kabuki hero, concealing his skill as a warrior behind a facade of effeminacy, and Yūgiri is the prototype of all stage courtesans, beautiful and loyal. Izaemon is rich and pampered, while Yūgiri is popular and celebrated. They are in love, but their relationship is dashed when Izaemon's mother disinherits him for his shameless liaison. Yūgiri falls ill following the birth of their child, and her wealthy patron plans to adopt the child as his own. Izaemon is heartbroken and helpless. The play ends happily when Izaemon's mother relents and restores him to his place in the family, and Yūgiri recovers her health. The lovers are reconciled; Izaemon ransoms Yūgiri from her bordello, and a wedding feast is prepared.

I represented Izaemon in despair when he is turned out of his home with nothing but a rush hat and a paper kimono.

SIGNED: Masatoshi *koku*.
MATERIAL: ivory.
BASIC COLOR: *yashadama*; *sumi*—hair, make-up, kimono patterns, sword hilt; black lacquer—scabbard; gold *nikawa*—sword guard.
COMPLETED: April 1957.

26 Children's Kabuki
Kodomo kabuki

The child actors in children's Kabuki range in age from eight to fourteen. They are generally born to the Kabuki stage as the children of dedicated actors.

I carved a boy actor who plays the part of a daredevil firefighter and acrobatic scaffold climber (*tobi*). He dances a spirited lion dance (*kioijishi*) at a shrine festival. The design on his short jacket is the stylized curled-hair pattern of the *shishi* (mythical lion). The red character on his collar is read *"matsuri,"* meaning "festival."

SIGNED: Masatoshi.
MATERIAL: ivory.
BASIC COLOR: *yashadama*; *sumi*—hair, coat pattern, undergarment; red *nikawa*—characters on collar and pouch.
COMPLETED: July 1965.

27 The Faithful Samurai
Nao Zamurai

Kataoka Naojirō is a *rōnin* sarcastically nicknamed Nao Zamurai (Faithful Samurai). He is a petty criminal, a member of the gang headed by Kōchiyama Sōshun (Plate 23). The police are closing in on him; it is winter and he is cold and hungry. He is outside a noodle shop anxious to enter and warm himself with a bowl of noodles but wary of police traps. A blind masseur in the noodle shop tells Nao Zamurai that his beloved Michitose of the Oguchiro House in the Yoshiwara is pining away for him. He knows he must flee Edo without delay but he wonders whether he dare risk a visit to the licensed quarter to see his love for the last time.

I represented Nao Zamurai outside the noodle shop, a fugitive in a quandary over his next move.

SIGNED: Masatoshi, one character on each clog.
MATERIAL: ivory.
BASIC COLOR: *yashadama*; *sumi*—hair, make-up, patterns on towel, jacket, kimono, umbrella; gold *nikawa*—coin.
COMPLETED: November 1954.

28 Kurobei

Kurobei is released from prison, where he had been sent for attacking a samurai. One of his cronies tells him that he has quit brawling and that whenever he feels in danger of losing his temper he folds his hands and recites a prayer to Amida. He hangs a rosary from his ear as a constant reminder of the need to keep himself under control. Kurobei resolves to follow his friend's example.

Kotoura is a courtesan in love with one of Kurobei's companions. Kurobei's father-in-law, Giheiji, has her in his power and is returning her to a samurai she scorns and from whom she escaped when they meet Kurobei. Kurobei tries to take Kotoura away, but Giheiji berates and insults Kurobei, demanding compensation for supporting his wife and child while he was in prison. Kurobei makes a supreme effort to control his temper despite his father-in-law's taunts and insults. When he can stand it no longer, he draws and runs his father-in-law through. The police surround Kurobei, but he manages to escape by swimming across a river.

I portrayed Kurobei as he draws to kill Giheiji.

SIGNED: Masatoshi.
MATERIAL: ivory.
BASIC COLOR: *yashadama*; *sumi*—hair, tattoo, *obi*.
COMPLETED: April 1954.
ILLUSTRATED: *Collectors' Netsuke*, Figure 346. Catalogue, Raymond Bushell Collection, Tokyo.

29 Benten Kozō

A gang of thieves decide on a maneuver to fleece the Hamamatsuya, a drapery shop. Benten Kozō enters impersonating a lady of rank and accompanied by a confederate posing as her retainer. The two pretend to steal a length of fabric and entrap the shop's manager into making a false accusation. A row ensues and the shop's owner, Kobei, is forced to pay a large sum as consolation money to Benten Kozō. At this moment another confederate, posing as a samurai, enters the shop, hears the story, and exposes Benten Kozō and his accomplice as tattooed ruffians and frauds. He insists on beheading them both on the spot. Kobei is horrified at the loss to his business and reputation if their heads were to be struck off, since they had actually stolen nothing. Again he must hand over fabrics and gold coins, this time to pacify the violent samurai. The gang, known as the White

Wave, have had a profitable day.

I carved Benten Kozō exposing his cherry blossom tattoo as he makes a bold, bombastic speech.

SIGNED: Masatoshi, in an oval reserve.
MATERIAL: ivory.
BASIC COLOR: *yashadama*; *sumi*—hair, make-up, tattoo, kimono, cloth; red *nikawa*—lips; gold *nikawa*—comb, hair ornament.
COMPLETED: July 1957.
ILLUSTRATED: *Collectors' Netsuke*, Figure 345.

30 Sukeroku

Sukeroku, who gives his name to this play, is an *otokodate*, a popular hero and champion of the common people—handsome, resourceful, and audacious. He is opposed by Ikyū, a detested samurai, for the affections of Agemaki, a leading courtesan of the licensed quarter. Ikyū's wealth and power are no match for Sukeroku's manly charm and bravado.

Sukeroku's mother remonstrates with him over his constant brawling. She threatens to visit his father's grave to commit suicide, whereupon Sukeroku is forced to confess the motive for his continuous brawling in the licensed quarter, that he quarrels with samurai in order to goad them into drawing their swords. He is searching for one special sword which will identify the murderer of his father. His mother is appeased, in the knowledge that her family honor will be upheld. At last Sukeroku goads Ikyū into drawing, recognizes the sword, and cuts him down as the murderer of his father.

I carved Sukeroku as he dances holding an umbrella. He wears a purple headband, a color reserved for daimyō, to show his bravado and he carries a flute on his back to indicate that he is romantic and an aesthete as well as being fearless.

SIGNED: Masatoshi, in red *nikawa* in an oval reserve.
MATERIAL: ivory.
BASIC COLOR: *yashadama*; *sumi*—hair, make-up, umbrella, kimono, *obi*; purple acetic acid—headband.
COMPLETED: December 1952.
ILLUSTRATED: *Arts of Asia*, July/August 1973.

31 Man about Town
Tsūjin

This figure is a minor character in *Sukeroku* (Plate 30). He is a *tsūjin*, a man about town, a dandy and conceited womanizer. His speech is affected but funny, and his manners vain and ridiculous. He furnishes contrast and comic relief.

SIGNED: Masatoshi.
MATERIAL: ivory.
BASIC COLOR: *yashadama*; *sumi*—hair, make-up, coat pattern, kimono, fan design; gold *nikawa*—coat fastening.
COMPLETED: March 1971.

32 Sumizome

The Love Story at the Snow-covered Barrier, like *The Arrowroot Leaf* (Plate 21), is a *shosagoto*, a drama enacted in dance. Sumizome, a courtesan, is the paramour of Yasusada, a loyal supporter of the emperor. Yasusada thwarts a plot to overthrow the emperor hatched by Sekibei, the head of the Barrier Guard. In revenge, Sekibei kills him.

Sumizome learns of the murder. She uses her magical powers to transform herself into the spirit of the "Black Cherry Tree," which stands at the barrier and blooms even though it is winter. Sekibei seizes an axe and attempts to cut down the tree, but his axe is rendered powerless. Sumizome fights him with a branch of the cherry tree and vanquishes him, whereupon she vanishes back into the tree.

I carved Sumizome wielding a branch of the "Black Cherry Tree" and using it as a weapon.

SIGNED: Masatoshi *tō*.
MATERIAL: ivory.
BASIC COLOR: *yashadama*; *sumi*—hair, make-up, kimono patterns; red *nikawa*—lips.

COMPLETED: August 1957.
ILLUSTRATED: *Collectors' Netsuke*, Figure 340.

33 Piling Branches
Nishikigi

I find Noh cold and austere and lacking the drama and excitement of Kabuki. I have made only two pieces from Noh, this one and the mask of Kagekiyo (Plate 146). Noh makes me very uncomfortable and gives me a headache.

Nishikigi (Piling Branches) is a Noh play based on revenge (*shūnenmono*). The name of the play comes from an ancient, regional custom in which a young man asks a girl to marry him by piling twigs for firewood outside her home. If she takes the firewood into her home, he is accepted. If she refuses the firewood for a period of three years, his proposal is rejected. The story is of a rejected and heartbroken suitor who commits suicide. His spirit returns to earth to condemn the girl and her family for rejecting him.

I carved the principal actor of the play, the spirit of the rejected suitor. I applied *yashadama* to his mask to distinguish it from the actor's face.

SIGNED: Masatoshi *tō*.
INSCRIPTION: *Nishikigi nochijite* (principal actor of the second scene).
MATERIAL: ivory.
COLOR: natural; black lacquer—hair; *yashadama*—mask; green acetic acid—kimono; purple acetic acid—trousers.
COMPLETED: March 1956.
ILLUSTRATED: *Arts of Asia*, July/August 1973.

34 Adachigahara

Adachigahara is the name of a desolate wilderness in which a solitary hut stands. It is occupied by Iwate, a fiendish old vampire. She lives by robbing lost travelers after first having bitten their throats until they expire. A young couple asks Iwate for permission to rest. The wife is pregnant and exhausted. The crone finds an excuse to send the husband away, intending to murder the young woman in order to tear out the embryo for use in her philters. She is unmoved, even when she discovers that the woman is her own daughter.

I carved the scene of the daughter begging Iwate to spare the life of her unborn child.

SIGNED: Masatoshi *tō*.
MATERIAL: ivory.
BASIC COLOR: *yashadama*; *sumi*—hair, make-up, kimono patterns, knife; red *nikawa*—lips.
COMPLETED: December 1954.
ILLUSTRATED: *Arts of Asia*, July/August 1973.

35 Oiwa

Oiwa is the wife of Iemon, who is in love with his neighbor's daughter, Oume. When Oiwa takes sick, Iemon treats her cruelly and, instead of administering her medicine, gives her poison which causes her hair to fall out and turns her into a hideous caricature. In despair she kills herself. As Kohei, a faithful old servant, is the only witness to his guilt, Iemon kills him too and ties the bodies of the pair to opposite sides of a plank, which he pushes into the river. He marries Oume, but when he removes her head covering after the marriage ceremony he sees the face of Oiwa. Panic-stricken he flees in terror and comes to the river. Out of the depth of the river the ghost of Oiwa rises, still bound to the plank, and holds out her arms to him beseechingly. Iemon pushes it away, but it turns over, and there is the ghost of Kohei begging medicine for his mistress. Iemon goes mad with terror and drowns in the river.

This is the famous play *Yotsuya kaidan*, which is based on an actual incident that occurred in the seventeenth century. There is a shrine in Yotsuya dedicated to the appeasement of the ghost of Oiwa. A Kabuki actor, given the part of Oiwa, invariably precedes his performance with a prayer visit to her shrine to placate her ghost.

I carved the ghost of Oiwa as it is portrayed on stage.

SIGNED: Masatoshi, in an oval reserve.
MATERIAL: ivory.
EYES: black tortoise shell.
BASIC COLOR: *yashadama*; *sumi*—hair, make-up.
COMPLETED: August 1965.

36 Yaegaki

The heroine of *Honchō nijushikō* (The Twenty-Four Examples of Filial Piety) is Yaegaki. Assassins are pursuing her lover Katsuyori, though he is unaware of the danger he is in. There is no way she can warn him. In desperation she prays at the Suwa Shrine, where the sacred helmet, the heirloom of Katsuyori's family, is enshrined. She holds the helmet over the water of Lake Suwa and miraculously sees it reflected as a white fox, which beckons her to follow it. The animal is the messenger of the god of the Suwa Shrine. She follows the white fox safely across the paper-thin ice that covers the lake and intercepts Katsuyori in time to save him.

I represented Yaegaki as she dances with the sacred helmet. The position and movement of her left hand is called *kitsune-de* (the fox's paw).

SIGNED: Masatoshi *tō*.
MATERIAL: ivory.
BASIC COLOR: *yashadama*; *sumi*—hair, kimono patterns, make-up; red *nikawa*—lips.
COMPLETED: April 1958.

37 Tamausagi

Tamausagi (Moon Rabbit) is a dance performed on the Kabuki stage. It is a gay, sprightly dance, full of the spirit of fairy tales. It represents the rabbit on the moon pounding rice cakes and then leaving the moon to play pranks elsewhere. The singing that accompanies the dance is in the *kiyomoto* style (see Plate 21).

The dancer wears a head band (*hachimaki*) tied to resemble the long ears of a rabbit. He stoops as he dances to suggest the hopping movement of the rabbit. The design on the actor's jacket is dewy grass, the rabbit's domain.

I carved the actor pounding rice cakes at the start of the dance.

SIGNED: Jikishiin Masatoshi *tō*.
INSCRIPTION: *Tsuki yuki hana nagori no bundai* (Repository of remembrances of moon, snow, and flowers—the title of the lyrics) *kiyomoto tama-usagi*.
MATERIAL: ivory.
COLOR: incense smoke; *sumi*—hair, make-up, coat patterns.
COMPLETED: October 1974.

38 Narukami Shōnin

Narukami Shōnin, after whom the play is named, is a great priest who is offended by the emperor and employs his powers of magic to capture the Rain Dragon and bring a drought upon the land. Princess Taema volunteers to seduce him in order to release the Rain Dragon. She gains admission to his retreat and professes her love for him in more and more erotic terms until the priest is transported with passion. Suddenly Taema complains of a pain. Narukami says that he is well versed in medicine. He examines her more and more intimately and describes her physical charms in a curious mixture of vulgar, earthy expressions and metaphysical, religious terms. Finally he grows wild with carnal desire, causing him to lose his priestly power, whereupon the Rain Dragon escapes and rain falls on the land.

I represented Narukami as he begins his examination of Princess Taema.

SIGNED: Masatoshi *tō*.
MATERIAL: ivory.
BASIC COLOR: *yashadama*; *sumi*—hair, make-up, kimono patterns, tassel on prayer beads; gold *nikawa*—hair decoration.
COMPLETED: May 1953.

3. Birds

39 Fudō Myō-ō

Fudō—like *Sukeroku* (Plate 30) and *Narukami* (Plate 38)—is one of the *jūhachiban* (eighteen plays) reserved for the Kabuki actor family of Ichikawa Danjūrō. It is rarely performed and I have never seen it. The idea for my carving came from a painting I once saw of the principal actor as he appears on the stage. The actor wears the brilliant make-up (*kumadori*) of Kabuki. It is this facial paint that distinguishes Fudō Myō-ō on stage from representations of him as a god.

SIGNED: Masatoshi, in an oval reserve.
MATERIAL: ivory.
BASIC COLOR: *yashadama*; *sumi*—hair, make-up, patterns on shoulder sash and apron; gold *nikawa* —sword handle, arm bands.
COMPLETED: August 1956.

40 Java Sparrow
Bunchō

I simplified the design of the Java sparrow by eliminating details but without going so far as to make the species no longer recognizable.

In the chapter on materials, I described hippopotamus tooth as flat towards the bark or rind but very finely ridged at the center. An examination of the Java sparrow shows the right side of the bird to be flat and the left side to be finely ridged, indicating how the bird lay in the tooth.

I carved the larger of the *himotoshi*, the knot hole, in a triangular shape to enhance the suggestion of tail feathers.

SIGNED: Masatoshi *tō*.
MATERIAL: hippopotamus tooth.
EYES: black coral.
COLOR: *yashadama*.
COMPLETED: March 1976.

41 Abstract Bird
Chūshō-dori

I had no particular species in mind when I designed this bird. Instead, I aimed at a high degree of simplification and abstraction, while striving for an appealing, avian shape in a size suitable for use with an *inrō*. I selected teak for the subject—one of teak's advantages in this case being that its numerous pores, a little enlarged, suggest the feathers of a bird (see page 39). The symmetrical bulges on the sides represent wings, and the slight elevation at the rear, tail feathers.

I inlaid my signature on a label of red hornbill because of the difficulty of carving characters clearly on a porous surface, especially in the case of a small netsuke (see page 66).

SIGNED: Masatoshi.
MATERIAL: teak.
EYES: carved; pupils—black tortoise shell.
COLOR: natural.
COMPLETED: December 1962.

42 Color-toned Bird
Oshare-dori

The body of this bird resembles that of a duck, but not so the bill. Here again, as with the Abstract Bird (Plate 41), I was more concerned with creating an attractive netsuke than with carving an identifiable species.

The ivory I used had a strongly marked grain. The contrast between the darker shade near the rind and the lighter shade near the core was also very marked. I incorporated this contrast by cutting the ivory so that the underside of the bird was carved from nearer the rind. The darkness was increased by the greater tendency of areas near the rind to absorb color from the incense smoking (see page 36). An additional contrast was created by an "oil spot" (oil spots are patches of ivory bark or husk) and a natural light band across the dark underside that resisted coloring. The smoking emphasized a faint surface crack on the underside.

When I carve human figures, I usually avoid the rind because of its darker shade; but in the case of animals, whether of land, sea, or air, I can often use the darkness for contrast.

SIGNED: Jikishiin Masatoshi *tō*.
MATERIAL: ivory.
EYES: black tortoise shell.
COLOR: incense smoke.
COMPLETED: June 1967.

43 Black Woodpecker
Kumagera

The wings of the woodpecker are considerably darker than the rest of the body. I secured this effect by cutting the block from the narrow tip of the tusk, placing both wings at the outer circumference under the rind with the head and body at the center. As I explained in the description for Plate 42, the rind area is usually darker and more porous, and absorbs more color from the incense. The woodpecker polished with a pleasing two-tone effect.

I balanced the bird on a center near the *himotoshi* so that it rocks gently without tumbling.

SIGNED: Masatoshi.
MATERIAL: ivory.
EYES: carved; pupils—black coral.
COLOR: incense smoke.
COMPLETED: August 1973.

44a, 44b White-Eye and Bush Warbler
Mejiro to uguisu

The two birds I have carved here are the white-eye (*mejiro*) and the bush warbler (*uguisu*). As they are similar in appearance, I thought that pairing them head to tail on a branch would make a good model. Of all Japanese birds the bush warbler figures the most prominently in poems and songs.

I included the branch in the composition for two reasons: firstly, it furnishes a place of attachment for the cords, avoiding the necessity for holes; and secondly, the birds' talons envelop the round branch, providing a slightly flattened base on which the netsuke stands firmly upright.

SIGNED: Masatoshi *tō*.
MATERIAL: boxwood.
EYES OF WHITE-EYE: ivory and black coral.
EYES OF BUSH WARBLER: black coral.
COLOR: potassium permanganate.
COMPLETED: November 1965.

45 Domestic Duck
Ahiru

As a craftsman, I try to make my carvings beautiful rather than scientifically correct. A netsuke of a bird succeeds for me to the degree that it is attractive and well made, not to the extent that it replicates the living creature.

I selected a whale-tooth for its contrasting coloration between rind and core. A dentine flake developed under the bill, as did a few faint natural cracks, which were accented by resin deposits from the incense smoking. In whale-tooth it is impossible to anticipate the presence of yellowish flecks of dentine (see page 36).

This is the first illustrated figure that exemplifies my technique for inlaying eyes that follow the viewer (see page 46). Eyes that follow are composed of transparent tortoise shell and lampblack. Hereafter, the use of the phrase "eyes follow" in the descriptions will indicate this feature.

SIGNED: Masatoshi *tō*.
MATERIAL: whale-tooth.
EYES: transparent tortoise shell and lampblack.
EYES FOLLOW.
COLOR: incense smoke.
COMPLETED: August 1965.

46 Wild Duck
Kamo

I carved this wild duck from a central section of whale-tooth that was flawless. I made the size slightly smaller than I would have preferred in order to avoid extending into the rind. As I utilize more and more of the outer circumference of the whale-tooth, the risk of poor material increases.

I signed with only the first character of my *gō* so as not to crowd the available space.

The eyes follow, but not as clearly as I would like, owing to their small size. Besides, I may have carved the surface of the tortoise shell too flat.

SIGNED: Masa *tō*.
MATERIAL: whale-tooth.
EYES FOLLOW.
COLOR: incense smoke.
COMPLETED: January 1965.

47 Mandarin Duck
Oshidori

Many of my designs are the product of my imagination. There are no models for them. In the case of a common subject, however, such as a mandarin duck, I have no doubt seen thousands of representations in paintings, prints, and sculptures, in zoos and museums, on the wing and in the water. But rather than imitate any one of them, I have synthesized all my impressions to express my own feeling in my portrayal of the subject.

SIGNED: Masatoshi.
MATERIAL: ivory.
EYES FOLLOW.
COLOR: incense smoke.
COMPLETED: July 1967.

48 Kaigyokusai Crane
Kaigyokusai tsuru

Mr. Bushell suggested that I copy with complete fidelity a crane carved by Kaigyokusai. I agreed to undertake the task of attempting to duplicate this master's incomparable technique as an exercise in craftsmanship.

I began by selecting a superb piece of ivory (see page 35). I cut a block from the inner core of the tusk to assure uniform color and texture. I copied Kaigyokusai meticulously: I engraved the feathers with precise parallel lines carved to a uniform depth; I registered the weight of the crane's bill on its breast, the bulge of the pouch caused by the twist of its head, the delicate markings on the underside, the ridges on the legs and claws, and the subtle separation of leg from body to provide for the *himotoshi*; and I inlaid the eyes in transparent tortoise shell, drilling the center to accommodate a second inlay of the pupil in black tortoise shell. This was Kaigyokusai's method. I polished the natural ivory without color or stain, just as Kaigyokusai had done. I added the character for "*sha*" to my name to show that I had copied the model (see page 60).

SIGNED: Masatoshi *sha*.
MATERIAL: ivory.
EYES: transparent and black tortoise shell.
COLOR: natural.
COMPLETED: September 1974.

49 Heron
Sagi

I am in awe of the pure beauty and grace of Mitsuhiro's designs, his simple artistry, and immaculate finish. I tried to carve this heron in his style. This effort was something quite different from the Kaigyokusai Crane (Plate 48), where I was consciously copying one of Kaigyokusai's carvings. The model for the heron was my own; for if Mitsuhiro ever carved the subject, I never saw it. What I was attempting to do was to carve it as Mitsuhiro might have. I wanted to emulate his style, as if I were an actor playing a role as he imagines it performed by another actor. In copying the Kaigyokusai Crane I was only a craftsman—I repressed any inclination towards self-expression. In imitating Mitsuhiro's style my role was that of artist as well as craftsman.

I seldom stain ivory with gamboge. But I used it in this case because I felt that the orangy yellow tinge would best approximate the glazelike texture of the stain, so characteristic of Mitsuhiro's work.

SIGNED: Masatoshi, with *kakihan*.
MATERIAL: ivory.
EYES: black coral.
COLOR: gamboge.
COMPLETED: June 1974.
ILLUSTRATED: *Netsuke Familiar and Unfamiliar*, Figure 379.
Catalogue, Raymond Bushell Collection, Tokyo.

50 Goose
Gan

The goose is gathering momentum to rise from the water in flight. In nature the goose's head and neck would be extended in the direction of flight, but in order to achieve a good netsuke shape I represented the goose looking backward.

I carved the netsuke entirely from the inner part of the whale-tooth. There is a tiny depression, not visible in the illustration, on the bird's back between the wings and a small whitish area on the right side of the neck. These two faint but natural blemishes mark the passage of the nerve channel of the tooth. The channel is filled with tooth material by some fortunate process of nature and is, therefore, what *netsuke-shi* describe as a "sleeping channel," a common phenomenon in whale-tooth but rare in elephant tusk (see page 35).

I did not mark my signature with *sumi*, as I normally do, in order to avoid marring the natural color and luster of the material.

SIGNED: Masatoshi *tō*.
MATERIAL: whale-tooth.
EYES: black tortoise shell.
COLOR: natural.
COMPLETED: April 1975.

51 Wild Goose
Karigane

This is one of the very few examples in my work of the type of netsuke known as *manjū* for their resemblance to *manjū* buns (see Plate 61 and Diagram D

on page 64). The design is based on the family crest (*mon*) known as the wild goose pattern (*karigane-moyō*). I adapted the pattern into a *manjū* suitable for use with a cloth or leather pouch.

I arranged the stylized wings to meet in a simple floral design, then undercut them to reduce the weight of an otherwise solid piece. I notched a few bruises and specks and colored the piece deeply to suggest the condition frequently seen in old *manjū*. A few faint surface cracks on the underside were accentuated by the incense coloring.

SIGNED: Tokisada *koku*.
MATERIAL: ivory.
EYES: black tortoise shell.
COLOR: incense smoke.
COMPLETED: November 1962.

52 Whippoorwill
Yotaka

I thought that the whippoorwill would be interesting to carve because of the characteristic thick patches of feathers at its throat. What could be more amusing than a bird with whiskers? I carved the whiskers in raised relief. This bird is more frequently mentioned in conversation than actually sighted because "*yotaka*" (literally, "night hawk") is a popular expression for a streetwalker.

As I was carving the bird, four dentine specks suddenly appeared when I had almost finished shaving it (see page 36). Had the blemishes appeared on the bird's head, I might have been forced to discard it, but, fortunately, two of the flecks appeared evenly on each wing and were not unattractive.

Sometimes the flakes come loose leaving unsightly pits. When this happens the piece must be discarded.

I signed my *gō* in red as an attractive contrast to the creamy white material.

SIGNED: Masatoshi *tō*.
MATERIAL: whale-tooth.
EYES FOLLOW.
COLOR: natural.
COMPLETED: August 1972.

53 Swelling Sparrow
Fukura-suzume

The "Swelling Sparrow" is the plump, little sparrow of the fairy tale. I represented the sparrow in the stylized form in which children see it in their picture books. I chose stag-antler for its suitability for caricature and its markings that suggest feathers.

There is one small area visible in the illustration that was porous and developed a cavity as I carved. This sometimes occurs even when the antler appears solid. I remedied the situation by making a mixture of pulverized antler and *nikawa* and filling the cavity with this mixture.

I signed the work "Toki" instead of "Tokisada" because I felt that the single character centered in the square between the two *himotoshi* and the two legs was more attractive.

SIGNED: Toki.
MATERIAL: stag-antler.
EYES: black coral.
COLOR: natural.
COMPLETED: October 1962.

54 Sparrows and Bamboo
Take ni suzume

The tooth was given to me, and I am not even sure of the animal it comes from, but it may be the tooth of a bear. My design is original, though based on the popular association of sparrows and bamboo. It was influenced by family crests and traditional patterns. There is no other significance or symbolism.

I signed my *gō* in an etched reserve in the design of a bamboo node and leaves.

SIGNED: Masatoshi.
MATERIAL: animal tooth.
EYES: carved; pupils—red tortoise shell.
COLOR: incense smoke.
COMPLETED: October 1974.

55 Swallows
Tsubame

I used to see swallows (*tsubame*) frequently in my area. Once I heard nestlings complaining raucously and traced the sound to its source, where I saw the baby birds urging their mother to find them some juicy worms for breakfast. Their mouths gaped as wide as their heads, but the mother sat serenely in

the nest in no hurry to feed them. This is the scene I carved. In recent years swallows have almost disappeared from my neighborhood, as new constructions have replaced trees with concrete.

SIGNED: Masatoshi *tō*.
MATERIAL: boxwood.
EYES: black tortoise shell.
COLOR: potassium permanganate.
COMPLETED: January 1965.

56 Eagle
Washi

I portrayed the eagle in that instant of tension when he has spotted his prey and is about to spring into flight. One of my problems was to treat the head so that it lost nothing in ferocity, despite the need to place the curved beak in contact with the edge of the branch in order to prevent it acting as a snare or catch. Carving the inaccessible left side of the head and inlaying the left eye was a mere matter of technique.

SIGNED: Masatoshi *tō*.
MATERIAL: ivory.
EYES FOLLOW.
COLOR: incense smoke.
COMPLETED: May 1965.

57 Eagle
Washi

I stylized the model with the goal of making the bird attractive whether it is viewed from above or below or in profile. I also tried to obtain a two-tone effect with the wing edges lighter than the back and stomach by using the two more absorbent parts of the tusk, the rind and the core, for the eagle's back and stomach respectively.

The eagle balances on its legs and *himotoshi*, with both head and tail above the ground.

SIGNED: Masatoshi *tō*.
MATERIAL: ivory.
EYES: black tortoise shell.
COLOR: incense smoke.
COMPLETED: June 1968.

58 Cormorant and Young
U no oyako

I browsed through the natural history section of a bookshop searching for some inspiration for a cormorant netsuke. The contrast provided by the idea of this voracious fisher bird tenderly feeding its young appealed to me. The problem was to compose the elements of the model—the cormorant, the young, and the fish—into a proper netsuke.

The cormorant's coloration is black and bluish black. A fine, deep black piece of ebony was a natural choice for the subject. The quality of the block I used was excellent. The feather markings were easy to carve and the surfaces polished beautifully.

SIGNED: Tokisada, in a smooth oval reserve.
MATERIAL: ebony.
EYES: carved.
COLOR: natural.
COMPLETED: November 1960.
ILLUSTRATED: *Collectors' Netsuke*, Figure 349. Catalogue, Raymond Bushell Collection, Tokyo.

59 Cormorant
U

Mr. Bushell urged me to repeat the cormorant in Plate 58, this time as a solitary bird. I did so reluctantly, eliminating the young bird and reducing the size of the sweetfish (*ayu*) until it became merely a detail. For variety I changed the arrangement of the feathers. I used the same fine ebony as I had used in the previous piece.

I prefer my first effort. I do not feel that the elements of the young bird and the fish burdened the design. The composition was rounded, and the space between the young bird's foot and the mother's body provided for the *himotoshi*. In the case of the solitary cormorant, I had to carve *himotoshi* in the body.

The eyes of both models are carved. As they protrude and are polished smooth, they give the impression of being inlaid.

SIGNED: Jikishiin Masatoshi *tō*.
MATERIAL: ebony.
EYES: carved.
COLOR: natural.
COMPLETED: January 1972.

60 Japanese Crane
Tanchō-zuru

The Japanese crane (*tanchō-zuru*) is prominent in legend and religious art. Except for its legs, it is pure white with a red crest like the holy mark on Buddha's forehead. These beautiful birds are still to be found in a few parts of northern Japan.

I curved the crane's neck to emphasize its grace and length. I simplified the bird and marked the tail feathers in regimental array as a contrast to the smoothness of the body. I represented the distinguishing red crest on the bird's crown with the red part of hornbill ivory polished to a high luster.

SIGNED: Masatoshi *tō*.
MATERIAL: ivory.
CREST: red hornbill.
EYES FOLLOW.
COLOR: *yashadama*.
COMPLETED: July 1974.

61 Crane
Tsuru

I was trained to carve figures in-the-round. My father never taught me how to carve netsuke of the *manjū* or *ryūsa* type, and that is why I have carved so few of them (see Diagram D on page 64). When I do, it is usually because I have some material on hand that is particularly suitable for this type.

My design is of a crane in flight across a full moon, represented by the circular disc. I undercut the crane in order to create some illusion of distance between bird and moon. Since the crane and tortoise are both symbols of longevity and often associated, I represented the tortoise by carving the *himotoshi* as one segment in a turtle-shell pattern (*kikkō*).

I marked a number of dents and blemishes on the ivory to represent the hard wear usually suffered by old *manjū* netsuke.

SIGNED: Tokisada *tō*.
MATERIAL: ivory.
EYES: black tortoise shell.
COLOR: incense smoke.
COMPLETED: September 1962.

64 Plover
Chidori

I derived the design for this stylized plover from the same traditional kimono pattern as the plover shown in Plate 63. The result, however, is very different because of the uniquely unusual quality of the material I used. It is a single, solid block of *umoregi* (semipetrified wood). The sharp, straight demarcation line between brownish black and seal gray makes it hard to believe, however, that the material is solid and the color natural. The outer circumference of the material is the light part, the inner core the darker part. *Umoregi* varies vastly in hardness, weight, grain, and color. This exceptional specimen was harder and heavier than ebony.

As I worked, two hairline cracks developed in the seal gray section of the *umoregi*. I made a mixture of pulverized *umoregi* and *nikawa* and used it to heal the cracks.

SIGNED: Tokisada *tō*.
INSCRIPTION: *umoregi*.
MATERIAL: *umoregi*.
EYES: ivory and black coral.
BEAK: *kōki*.
LEGS: coral.
CRESCENT: boxwood.
COLOR: natural.
COMPLETED: December 1963.

62 Plover
Chidori

I took this design from an old netsuke and tried to improve on it. The bird at either end is the plover. Plovers are often represented in pairs or in formation as they skim the ocean, rising and falling with the waves. The ridges between the birds may represent the crests and troughs of waves. I have also heard that they represent sheafs of a popular paper that was watermarked with this design.

The netsuke balances upright and rocks on its base.

SIGNED: Masatoshi *sha*.
MATERIAL: ivory.
EYES: coral.
COLOR: incense smoke.
COMPLETED: February 1960.

63 Plover
Chidori

I stylized the plover into a design that we often see on kimono. The plover walks with a peculiar, tottering waddle and has given its name to the word we use for the drunkard's unsteady gait, "*chidori-ashi*" or "plover legs." I designed the stumpy legs and tail of the bird so that it stands leaning either to right or to left but not straight up.

I engraved the reverse with a stylized blue seawave pattern (*seikaiha*), using a curl of spray to form the *himotoshi*. I intended these design elements to symbolize the association of bird and wave. The inlaid modified crescent is a design element from the original kimono pattern.

SIGNED: Masatoshi, in a smooth oval reserve.
MATERIAL: ivory.
EYES: black coral.
BEAK: red coral.
CRESCENT: silver metal.
COLOR: incense smoke.
COMPLETED: June 1955.

65 Fulmar
Furuma-kamome

I have never seen a fulmar in the flesh, but I was fascinated by pictures of this ungainly seabird with its strange beak and decided to carve it.

While carving the fulmar, a crack appeared at the breast, but as it was natural and almost imperceptible, I ignored it. But the penetrating and coloring effect of the incense smoking accentuated and exaggerated the flaw. The heat from the incense may be responsible for enlarging a crack or even for causing new ones. Sometimes a crack develops after I have already finished staining a netsuke with incense. One of the dangers in coloring with incense is to hold the netsuke too near the incense in order to hasten the process or increase coloration. This is likely to cause cracks (see page 52).

My practice in representing feathers is to engrave the outline of each one individually, starting from the center and moving outward (see page 42). After outlining the feathers, I return to carve the quills and barbs.

SIGNED: Masatoshi.
MATERIAL: whale-tooth.
EYES FOLLOW.
COLOR: incense smoke.
COMPLETED: December 1966.

66 Cock and Hen
Ondori to mendori

I took the model for this composition from an illustration of a Kaigyokusai netsuke. It is not a copy, however, in the sense that Plate 48 is a copy. Vain though it may seem, my goal here was not to duplicate but to improve. Duplication involves only technical skills, while the attempt to excel calls for all a carver's talents as an artist and originator. One improvement I can claim is in the inlays of the eyes, which follow the viewer. The material that I carved this netsuke from is tōkata.

SIGNED: Masatoshi koku.
MATERIAL: ivory.
EYES FOLLOW.
COLOR: natural.
COMPLETED: June 1979.
ILLUSTRATED: Catalogue, Raymond Bushell Collection, Tokyo.

67 Flight
Shō

I wanted to experiment with a design in modernistic style and chose as my model a swan in flight. I selected a block of ivory that had a very faint grain, almost like pure white marble. The head and neck form a straight line with the tail. I curved the wings to the body in a downward flap to form hollow cylinders. I do not feel that the design is too radical but rather that it falls somewhere between the traditional and the avant-garde.

SIGNED: Masatoshi tō.
MATERIAL: ivory.
EYES FOLLOW.
COLOR: incense smoke.
COMPLETED: September 1978.

4. Insects

68a, 68b "Helmeted Bug"
Kabutomushi

The kabutomushi, which resembles the June bug, is a beetle (kōchū) with an arched metallic back. I applied silver nitrate over the dorsal portion of the insect to represent the reflective surface of metal, and then exposed the silver nitrate to the smoke of burning incense to mellow its metallic harshness.

I see many inrō with designs of insects and moths, subjects that are uncommon in netsuke. I therefore make most of my insects in a smaller size, suitable for use with inrō.

SIGNED: Masatoshi tō.
MATERIAL: ivory.
EYES: black tortoise shell.
COLOR: silver nitrate and incense smoke.
COMPLETED: February 1973.

69 Tsutsugamushi

I saw the horrifying tsutsugamushi in a drawing in the Obake no zukan (Illustrated Book of Apparitions) and decided to carve it. Later I learned that it was not an imaginary creature but a living, disease-carrying parasite and later still that the disease it transmits is known as "tsutsugamushi disease" in English.

The disease used to be rife in Niigata Prefecture, on the northwest coast of Japan. In the old days a common farewell to travelers was "Tsutsuga naku," meaning "Stay safe from the tsutsuga tick."

While the material I used is clearly the tooth of a whale, I am not sure which sort of whale. It is narrow and pointed and therefore different in shape from the tooth of the sperm whale. It may have been the tooth of the killer whale—or, alternatively, of the tiger shark.

I flattened the area around the himotoshi slightly so that the tooth sits securely on a base, with the insect upright.

SIGNED: Masatoshi.

MATERIAL: whale-tooth.
EYES: black coral.
COLOR: natural; *sumi*—markings.
COMPLETED: March 1979.

70a, 70b Sashi Cicada
Sashi semi

I elongated the ordinary shape of a cicada to make a *sashi* netsuke, the type worn thrust into the *obi* (see Diagram E on page 64). The wing tips are slender but they are not fragile, as hippopotamus tooth is stronger than ivory. I could not decide on any satisfactory distortion to act as a catch on the bottom edge of the *obi*, without spoiling the sleek effect of the design. In the end I everted the wing tips into a slight outward curve that tends to secure the netsuke to the *obi*. As a guide to carving the veining on the wings I drew the network in pencil directly on the tooth.

SIGNED: Jikishiin Masatoshi.
MATERIAL: hippopotamus tooth.
EYES: carved.
COLOR: incense smoke.
COMPLETED: October 1975.
ILLUSTRATED: Catalogue, Raymond Bushell Collection, Tokyo.
SCALE: three-fifths life size.

71a, 71b Eccentric Cicada
Kawari-zemi

I named the cicada "eccentric" as my excuse for exploiting artistic license and oddity. Most of the netsuke versions of this common art motif are realistic.

SIGNED: Masatoshi *tō*.
MATERIAL: hippopotamus tooth.
EYES: transparent tortoise shell.
INLAID EMBELLISHMENTS: hornbill ivory, abalone shell, black tortoise shell.
COLOR: incense smoke; gold *nikawa*—collar.
COMPLETED: March 1976.

72a, 72b House-fly
Hae

It must have been summer. It came to me in a flash that the biting, buzzing, bothering house-fly, a common enough nuisance, is rare in netsuke. I swatted one to study at my leisure as a model for a netsuke.

SIGNED: Masatoshi *tō*.
MATERIAL: whale-tooth.
EYES: *sumi*.
COLOR: incense smoke; *sumi*—markings.
COMPLETED: February 1970.

73a, 73b Moth
Ga

One problem with moths is to represent them as light and airy insects without making them fragile and brittle at the same time. The wing patterns consist of circular inlays of tortoise shell combined with pricking and scoring of the ivory to increase absorption of *sumi*. The idea for the model came from a picture book on insects which I had bought for my daughter.

SIGNED: Masatoshi *tō*.
MATERIAL: ivory.
INLAYS: tortoise shell.
EYES: transparent tortoise shell.
COLOR: incense smoke; *sumi*—wing markings; gold *nikawa*—antennae, thorax.
COMPLETED: September 1960.
ILLUSTRATED: *Arts of Asia*, July/August 1973.

74a, 74b Firefly Moth
Hotaru-ga

I modeled the firefly moth on an illustration in a popular scientific magazine. I had to modify the drawing extensively to eliminate hooks and extensions. I have depicted the insect at rest with its wings folded.

I found a variety of mother-of-pearl known by the picturesque name *shirochō-gai* (white butterfly pearl shell) particularly suitable for representing the insect's bulbous eyes.

SIGNED: Masatoshi *tō*.
MATERIAL: hippopotamus tooth.
EYES: white butterfly pearl shell.
COLOR: incense smoke.
COMPLETED: November 1967.
ILLUSTRATED: *Collectors' Netsuke*, Figure 353. Catalogue, Raymond Bushell Collection, Tokyo.

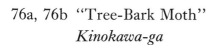

75a, 75b "Under-Leaf Moth"
Shitaba-ga

I represented the moth with wings folded as it "lies" on the underside of a leaf, its favorite haunt. I scored the surface so it would absorb the *sumi* and form a realistic wing pattern.

SIGNED: Masatoshi *tō*.
MATERIAL: ivory.
EYES: transparent tortoise shell.
COLOR: incense smoke; *sumi*—markings.
COMPLETED: January 1973.

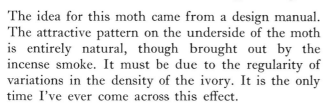

76a, 76b "Tree-Bark Moth"
Kinokawa-ga

The idea for this moth came from a design manual. The attractive pattern on the underside of the moth is entirely natural, though brought out by the incense smoke. It must be due to the regularity of variations in the density of the ivory. It is the only time I've ever come across this effect.

SIGNED: Masatoshi *tō*.
MATERIAL: ivory.
EYES: carved.
COLOR: incense smoke.
COMPLETED: December 1979.

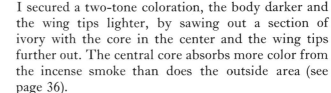

77a, 77b "Dead-Leaf Moth"
Kareha-ga

I secured a two-tone coloration, the body darker and the wing tips lighter, by sawing out a section of ivory with the core in the center and the wing tips further out. The central core absorbs more color from the incense smoke than does the outside area (see page 36).

SIGNED: Masatoshi *tō*.
MATERIAL: ivory.
EYES: carved.
COLOR: incense smoke.
COMPLETED: January 1980.

5. Botanical Subjects

78 Blade of Grass
Kusa no ha

I once saw a picture of a carving representing nothing more than a simple blade of grass. It was an *okimono* attributed to Kaigyokusai. I decided to carve it in my own way. I designed it as a *sashi* netsuke (see Plate 70 and Diagram E on page 64), doubling the blade of grass back on itself and adding beads of dew and a firefly. I selected a section of pure white ivory from the core of a fine-grained tusk.

SIGNED: Masatoshi, with *kakihan*.
MATERIAL: ivory.
COLOR: natural.
COMPLETED: August 1975.
ILLUSTRATED: Catalogue, Raymond Bushell Collection, Tokyo.
SCALE: two-thirds life size.

79 Fungus and Turtle
Reishi to kame

The subject symbolizes long life—the fungus is the Ten-Thousand-Year Mushroom (*Mannendake*), and the Sacred Turtle (*Kame*) lives for ten thousand years. In combination the fungus and turtle constitute a powerful prayer for a long life.

I designed the subject as a *sashi* netsuke, the turtle acting as a safety catch on the lower edge of the *obi* (see Diagram E on page 64). The form is like that of a *nyo-i*, or priest's scepter. I balanced the netsuke so that it stands securely on its narrow base and sprinkled the surface sparsely with gold powder for its contrast with the black and for its suggestion of magical properties.

The material is similar to ebony but not as fine. I cannot identify it with certainty, but it is probably Indonesian ironwood.

SIGNED: Masatoshi *tō*.
MATERIAL: Indonesian ironwood.
EYES: carved.
COLOR: natural; fine gold powder.
COMPLETED: November 1976.
SCALE: two-thirds life size.

80a, 80b Weird Mushrooms
Henna kinoko

My material appeared to be a choice block of amber, and I was elated. I had just begun to carve a large animal when an apparently minor crack developed into a group of major fissures. The only solid piece of the amber boulder left was a shallow triangular shape—a trick of fate. I salvaged the carving by transforming it into a group of mushrooms (*kinoko*) and vented my own mockery by carving them to resemble weird human faces. If mushroom tops look like faces, we should not be surprised, as mushrooms are endowed with magical properties.

Defects in amber cannot be discerned by a visual examination. Carving is the only sure test of solidity. Amber often tends to granulate as it is shaved.

SIGNED: Masatoshi *tō*.
INSCRIPTION: *kohaku* (amber).
MATERIAL: amber.
COLOR: natural.
COMPLETED: July 1977.

6. Supernatural Animals

81 Water Sprite and Cucumber
Kappa to kyūri

Everyone knows that the cucumber is the *kappa*'s favorite food. To eat one, he will postpone whatever mischief he is up to. I carved this *kappa* from a solid block of stag-antler. When he was imprisoned in the antler, he lay at the base of the main stem with his back against the stag's skull—this part is usually solid material, free of the spongy marrow found further up the tine. I made sure there was no doubt that the *kappa*'s gender is male.

SIGNED: Masatoshi *tō*.
MATERIAL: stag-antler.
EYES: black tortoise shell.
COLOR: incense smoke.
COMPLETED: April 1975.

82 Long-haired Water Sprite
Chōhatsu kappa

This *kappa* is tasting the head of a turtle before engulfing it for his dinner. This is my second version of the same subject. I had made my earlier version many years before and I felt I could improve on it. The earlier version is illustrated in *Masterpieces of Netsuke Art* (Figure 993).

I exaggerated the *kappa*'s long, smooth hair as a contrast to his scaliness. I carved the eyes of the *kappa* and of the turtle but sharply differentiated the sockets, pupils, and lids to give the impression of inlays. The ebony was night black and of superb quality.

SIGNED: Masatoshi.
MATERIAL: ebony.
EYES: carved.
COLOR: natural.
COMPLETED: March 1977.

83 Water Sprite's Cranial Vegetable Bowl
Kappa no yasai kōbe donburi

The depression at the top of the *kappa*'s head contains a magic liquid. If it dries, he dies. The burlesque of a *kappa* using this vital depression as a vegetable bowl amused me. I carved the *kappa* as he reaches for his lunch and gave him a form-fitting shell instead of a carapace and a pebble-grain hide instead of scales.

SIGNED: Masatoshi *tō*.
MATERIAL: boxwood.
EYES: carved; pupils—black coral.
COLOR: potassium permanganate.
COMPLETED: December 1978.

84 Feasting Water Sprite
Kappa no gochisō

A *kappa* enjoys a feast of his three favorite foods: cucumber, *sake*, and *shirigodama*, the ball-shaped hip joint popularly understood to be an imaginary bone in the anus. He sits on cucumbers, holds an open *sake* bottle, and bites into a *shirigodama*.

When I was a child, my father taught me the words of a song: "When you entertain *kappa*, you must serve *sake*, cucumbers, and *shirigodama*." We often warn children when they go out to play to be careful not to lose their *shirigodama*.

SIGNED: Masatoshi *tō*.
MATERIAL: boxwood.
EYES: black tortoise shell.
COLOR: potassium permanganate.
COMPLETED: August 1968.

85 Water Sprite
Kappa

A *kappa* sits comfortably with one of his webbed flippers resting on a clam. I marked all of his hide with a pine-bark pattern, and, in order to avoid interrupting the pattern, I signed my name inside the knot hole.

SIGNED: Masatoshi.
MATERIAL: boxwood.
EYES: black coral.
COLOR: natural except for faint *yashadama*.
COMPLETED: October 1967.
ILLUSTRATED: *Arts of Asia*, July/August 1973.

86 Water Tiger
Suiko

The *suiko*, literally "water tiger," is a relative of the *kappa*. In countenance and deportment he is more solemn than *kappa*. His back is composed of overlapping fish scales instead of a carapace. I represented this *suiko* in a contemplative mood as he sips his *sake*. I designed the *suiko* based on drawings in the *Minzokugaku zenshū*.

SIGNED: Masatoshi *tō*.
INSCRIPTION: *suiko*.
MATERIAL: boxwood.
EYES: carved.
COLOR: potassium permanganate.
COMPLETED: March 1978.

87 *Nue*

The story is well known of Ii no Hayata's fearless service for the emperor. He killed a *nue*, a beast as large as a horse with the head of a monkey, the body and claws of a tiger, and a poisonous snake for a tail.

SIGNED: Masatoshi.
MATERIAL: ivory.
EYES: transparent tortoise shell; pupils—black tortoise shell.
COLOR: incense smoke; *sumi*—hide, scales, markings.
COMPLETED: July 1960.

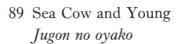

88 Dragon Bat
Ryū-kōmori

The design is entirely imaginary. I carved the dragon

bat with the horns of a dragon, the trunk of a tapir (*baku*), the wings of a bat, and the tail of a serpent. I composed the elements into a compact shape representing a flying *kaibutsu* (supernatural animal). The piece balances on its belly with both wings off the ground. I made a few nicks and colored the piece to enhance its antique appearance.

SIGNED: Tokisada *tō*.
MATERIAL: ivory.
EYES: black tortoise shell.
COLOR: incense smoke.
COMPLETED: September 1959.

89 Sea Cow and Young
Jugon no oyako

Somewhere I saw an illustrated article about the sea cow, or dugong. The article said it was an aquatic mammal that fed on marine vegetation and kept rivers in Malaysia from clogging. What impelled me to carve it was the information that the sea cow is believed to be the factual basis for the legend of the mermaid. My design is original, though based on the sea cow.

I flattened the tail of the parent so that the piece stands without support. The slight flattening did not disturb the overall nodular pattern of the sea cow's hide.

SIGNED: Masatoshi *tō*.
MATERIAL: boxwood.
EYES: black coral.
COLOR: potassium permanganate.
COMPLETED: December 1964.
ILLUSTRATED: *Collectors' Netsuke*, Figure 344.
Catalogue, Raymond Bushell Collection, Tokyo.

90 Weird Animal Eating Snake
Hebi o kuu kaibutsu

This weird specimen is in a quandary. It has the tip of the snake's tail between its teeth, but its arms are too short to push the snake further in for a second bite. If it opens its jaws the snake will escape. Apparently heedless of the problem, the snake inspects his captor's huge orifice. The idea for the model came from the *Ehon hyakki yagyō* (Illustrated Book of Nighttime Apparitions).

SIGNED: Masatoshi *tō*.
MATERIAL: stag-antler.
EYES: black tortoise shell.
COLOR: incense smoke.
COMPLETED: May 1971.

91 Rain Dragon
Amaryū

I tried to visualize an interesting subject in a misshapen segment of stag-antler. I thought that the Rain Dragon might "escape" from the material, provided I twisted his head and shortened his muzzle. I hoped there would be whimsy in the distortion, as there is in many of Kokusai's carvings.

The dragon is a *sashi*, and so his body is slightly convex to match the curve in the human body (see Diagram E on page 64). The forked tip of his tail is turned outward to catch on the lower edge of the *obi*. His beard forms the *himotoshi*, so that when he is in place, his head is peering out over the *obi* as he smiles at the rainfall.

This *sashi* is designed so that it can also be used as a brush rest (*fudetate*). The dragon sits firmly on his side, supported by his short legs, tail, and neck.

SIGNED: Masatoshi *tō*.
MATERIAL: stag-antler.
EYES: black coral.
COLOR: incense smoke.
COMPLETED: September 1976.
SCALE: life size.

92 Mythical Lion
Shishi

The *shishi* (mythical lion) is so familar that it seems strange to classify him as a supernatural animal. We know him in a thousand varieties and variations. My model is formidable in size, but I avoided bulkiness by substantially undercutting his beard, mane, and tail and by separating his legs.

SIGNED: Masatoshi *tō*.
MATERIAL: ivory.
EYES: black coral.
COLOR: *yashadama* and faint *sumi* wash.
COMPLETED: December 1975.

93 Lion Incense Burner
Kōro-jishi

My model was a Bizen ware incense burner in the shape of a *shishi* (mythical lion). The pottery piece was thick and heavy and may have unconsciously influenced my design. Were I to carve it again, I believe I would reduce the size a little or I would redesign the shape to make it a little less bulky.

I chose rhinoceros horn for my material. Rhinoceros horn is coarsest at the root, particularly around the rind. Surprisingly, it is this rough area that polishes most lustrously, though it requires polishing, more polishing, and repolishing to bring out the natural beauty of the material. I am glad that I resisted the temptation to engrave relief designs.

SIGNED: Masatoshi *tō*.
INSCRIPTION: *saikaku* (rhinoceros horn).
MATERIAL: rhinoceros horn.
COLOR: natural.
COMPLETED: May 1977.

94 Monster with Goat's Head
Yōtō kaijū

It amused me to imagine a goat standing upright with front legs ending in hands instead of hoofs and shaking with laughter.

The legs of standing figures, whether human or animal, are a weak point when separated one from the other and are often damaged. I brought the tail round and into contact with the hind hoofs to give the legs additional strength.

SIGNED: Masatoshi *tō*.
INSCRIPTION: *saikaku* (rhinoceros horn).
MATERIAL: rhinoceros horn.
EYES: carved.

COLOR: natural.
COMPLETED: August 1976.
ILLUSTRATED: Catalogue, Raymond Bushell Collection, Tokyo.
The Kotto, No. 3.
SCALE: life size.

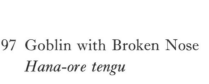

97 Goblin with Broken Nose
Hana-ore tengu

The strap of the *tengu*'s wooden clog (*geta*) broke, throwing him to the ground. The fall snapped his long nose, of which—like all *tengu*—he is inordinately proud. The joke is that the *tengu* broke both his "*hana*" at the same time: his nose (*hana*) and his clog strap (*hana-o*). The *tengu* wears a *tokin*, the peculiar hat of the mountain priest.

SIGNED: Masatoshi *tō*.
MATERIAL: ivory.
EYES: black coral.
COLOR: incense smoke; *sumi*—hair, markings.
COMPLETED: November 1968.

95 Fire-breathing Monster
Hi o haku kaibutsu

I marveled at the simplicity and power of an ancient Chinese jade carving of a monster. The elements of the sculpture were in perfect harmony. Very little modification was needed to adapt the design for a netsuke. I decided on rhinoceros horn as the most suitable material for representing a Chinese jade carving.

SIGNED: Masatoshi *tō*.
INSCRIPTION: *saikaku* (rhinoceros horn).
MATERIAL: rhinoceros horn.
EYES: carved.
COLOR: natural.
COMPLETED: July 1976.

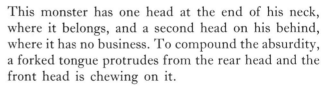

98 Double-headed Monster
Sōtō no kaibutsu

This monster has one head at the end of his neck, where it belongs, and a second head on his behind, where it has no business. To compound the absurdity, a forked tongue protrudes from the rear head and the front head is chewing on it.

SIGNED: Masatoshi *tō*.
MATERIAL: ivory.
EYES: black tortoise shell.
COLOR: incense smoke.
COMPLETED: April 1963.

96 Ming Bronze Animal
Minchō seidō dōbutsu

I was fascinated by a Chinese Ming Dynasty bronze of an imaginary animal. In order to preserve the attraction of the original, I modified the shape and redesigned a few of the features to the extent that was essential for a netsuke.

The next problem was to imitate the bronze color of the original. After much preliminary experimentation, I roughened the surface of the ivory and gave the piece a thorough bath in acetic acid to increase absorption and penetration of color. I used a hot, thick solution of *yashadama*, and this imparted a brownish color. I followed it with an application of thick *sumi*, which turned the brown to a satisfactory imitation of a metallic bronze texture.

SIGNED: Masatoshi *tō*, in a smooth reserve.
MATERIAL: ivory.
COLOR: *yashadama* and *sumi*.
COMPLETED: December 1977.

99 *Kirin*

A Japanese proverb has it that even a *kirin* runs like a hack when it ages. This *kirin*, however, is in its prime. It has the long, slender legs and supple body that assure great speed.

Aided by ebony of superb quality, I felt that the *kirin* itself was supervising my work and commanding perfect performance. Each individual scale, each twirl of hair, and each tongue of flame registered precisely. My model was an old netsuke, which I tried to improve on with better surface detail.

SIGNED: Masatoshi *tō*.
MATERIAL: ebony.
COLOR: natural.
COMPLETED: March 1977.
SCALE: life size.

100 Hippo-Frog
Kaba-gaeru

A picture I saw showed a creature with a head and tail resembling those of a hippopotamus attached to the body and legs of a frog. Both hippos and frogs spend a lot of time in the river. If they mated, I imagine that they would produce offspring like the creature in this plate. It amused me to think of a froggy hippopotamus trying to leap onto a branch.

SIGNED: Masatoshi *tō*.
MATERIAL: ivory.
EYES: black coral.
COLOR: incense smoke.
COMPLETED: August 1977.

101 *Kudan*

I vaguely recall that the model for this carving was an old netsuke, and I also remember reading somewhere or other that the *kudan* looks like a bearded goat with six horns and nine eyes.

SIGNED: Masatoshi *tō*.
MATERIAL: ivory.
EYES: black tortoise shell.
COLOR: incense smoke; *sumi*—hide, head markings
COMPLETED: August 1966.

102 *Kudan*

The *kudan* is not as familiar to me as are other imaginary animals like the *shishi* and the *kirin*. The guide for this model was an old netsuke.

SIGNED: Masatoshi *sha*.
MATERIAL: ivory.
EYES: black tortoise shell.
COLOR: incense smoke; *sumi*—hair, beard.
COMPLETED: May 1972.

103 Mythological Dolphin
Shachihoko

The *shachihoko* is a monster fish like an elaborate dolphin. It is familiar as the corner decoration of castle roofs, the great gilded ones at Nagoya Castle being the most famous. As the *shachihoko* is always represented standing on its chin with its tail curled high overhead, "*shachihoko-dachi*" has come to mean "standing on one's head."

SIGNED: Masatoshi *tō*.
MATERIAL: boxwood.
EYES: black coral.
COLOR: potassium permanganate.
COMPLETED: March 1966.

104a, 104b Double-ended Monster
Sōmen kaibutsu

The paintings and drawings of Kawanabe Gyōsai are a great source of ideas for preposterous creatures of all kinds. As far as I can remember, it was one of his flights of fancy that was the inspiration for this double-ended monster. One end, like a one-eyed worm, gorges on leaves, while the other end, with its humanoid head, stretches its mouth wide as though complaining of an empty gullet.

SIGNED: Masatoshi *tō*.
MATERIAL: boxwood.
EYES: black coral.
COLOR: potassium permanganate.
COMPLETED: August 1963.

7. Turtles and Crabs

105 Snapping Turtle, Parent and Child
Suppon no oyako

I observed the snapping turtle at Ueno Zoo in Tokyo. It is so fierce and formidable that it has no need of a shell into which to withdraw for safety like other turtles. A proverb has it that when the snapping turtle bites it won't let go, even when Kaminari, the god of thunder, releases a bolt. I wanted to show the contrast between the snapping turtle's predatory nature and the tender dialogue with its baby.

I carved each nodule of the carapace and each node of the leathery neck of the parent individually.

SIGNED: Masatoshi, in a smooth reserve.
MATERIAL: ivory.
EYES: black coral.
COLOR: incense smoke; dust—for mellowing.
COMPLETED: July 1973.

106 Turtle and Snapping Turtle
Kame to suppon

There are only two segments of the turtle's back shell that nature joins to corresponding segments of the belly shell. The joinings, or fusings, called *chūōban* in Japanese, occur at either side between the front and rear flippers. These are the only parts of a turtle's shell which are of sufficient bulk for carving in the round, and it was this part of the shell—fused, as it is, by nature not man—that I used as my material here. The netsuke illustrated in Plates 107, 180, and 181 are carved from natural tortoise shell, but their great thickness results from manually fusing layers using heat and pressure.

The contrast between turtle and snapping turtle is interesting. The larger of the two, the turtle, is protected by a thick, hard shell, into which it can retract all its appendages including its head. The snapping turtle has a soft shell which barely covers

its body and leaves its appendages exposed. The turtle is slow and gentle, the snapping turtle swift and voracious.

SIGNED: Masatoshi.
MATERIAL: transparent tortoise shell.
EYES: carved.
COLOR: natural.
COMPLETED: August 1969.

107 Snapping Turtle
Suppon

Soup made from the blood and meat of the snapping turtle is regarded as a source of male energy and virility and fetches a high price at special restaurants.

The dealer who sold me this material had to fuse ten or twelve layers of tortoise shell in order to obtain the thickness I needed. He joined the layers perfectly with no fusion lines visible. Although the material is classed as black tortoise shell, some areas are greenish and the head and neck are streaked with translucent yellow.

SIGNED: Jikishiin Masatoshi *tō*.
MATERIAL: black tortoise shell.
EYES: carved.
COLOR: natural.
COMPLETED: October 1969.

108a, 108b "Goose-flesh Crab"
Samehada-gani

I carved this crab in a suitable size for use with an *inrō*. The nodules are all carved individually. I applied silver nitrate to parts of the back shell to make it look more realistic. I followed this with incense smoke to give an overall coloring and to mellow the metallic character of the silver nitrate.

SIGNED: Masatoshi *tō*.
MATERIAL: ivory.
EYES: silver nitrate.
COLOR: silver nitrate and incense smoke.
COMPLETED: June 1961.

8. Gods and Sages

109 Taishin Ō Fujin

The design is from a *kakemono* (hanging scroll). Taishin Ō Fujin, a figure from Chinese mythology, rides a dragon through the clouds and plays on her harp music of such extraordinary sweetness that the birds stop in their flight to listen.

The carving is too elaborate and complicated for the piece to be practical as a netsuke, though I managed to ensure that the numerous elements did not become points and hooks. Twenty-five years ago I took a young carver's pride in displaying technical virtuosity. Even now I feel a qualified admiration for my laborious, detailed carving and undercutting. It takes experience to realize that a demonstration of talent does not necessarily make a good netsuke.

SIGNED: Masatoshi, in an oval reserve.
MATERIAL: ivory.
EYES OF DRAGON: gold *nikawa*; pupils—black tortoise shell.
COLOR: *yashadama*; *sumi*—hair, eyes, eyebrows, markings; red *nikawa*—lips; gold *nikawa*—hair ornaments.
COMPLETED: November 1957.

110 Kannon Mounted on a Dragon
Ryūzu Kannon

My inspiration was a painting by Harada Naojirō, a famous Western-style painter of the Meiji Era.

Although there is a general similarity in the subject matter, my feeling toward Kannon, a revered Japanese deity, is quite different from what I feel about Taishin Ō Fujin (Plate 109), a mythological Chinese figure. I have such reverence for Kannon that I feel a certain uneasiness over representing her. When I had completed Ryūzu Kannon, I placed her in the palm of my hand and bowed my head to her

as an affirmation of my respect and of my hope for her understanding. This fear of committing sacrilege accounts for the rarity of netsuke representing Kannon and Buddha, but it never disturbed painters, since their representations of Kannon are hung in the *tokonoma* (alcove) or serve as altarpieces.

The crown worn by Kannon is a figure of Amida Buddha.

SIGNED: Masatoshi, in a smooth oval reserve.
MATERIAL: ivory.
EYES OF DRAGON: black tortoise shell.
COLOR: *yashadama*; *sumi*—hair, eyes, eyebrows; gold *nikawa*—crown, necklace, earrings.
COMPLETED: November 1953.

111 Temple Guardian God
Niō

Whenever I visit the Kaminari Gate in Asakusa, Tokyo, I concentrate my attention on the head and expression of the Niō, the two gods whose traditional role is that of guardian of the temple gates. I tried to give my Niō the same frightening fierceness without compromising his dignity. My basic design however came from an old wood netsuke. I carved his tobacco pouch in heroic proportions to accord with the gigantic size of his straw sandals (*waraji*).

SIGNED: Masatoshi *tō*.
MATERIAL: ivory.
EYES: black tortoise shell.
COLOR: *yashadama*; *sumi*—hair, patterns; gold *nikawa*—tobacco pouch.
COMPLETED: January 1975.
ILLUSTRATED: *Clipper* (Pan American Airlines), February 1976.

112 The Dragon God of the Seas
Ryūjin

Ryūjin controls the seas and tides. They ebb and flow at his command. Taking the idea from an old wood netsuke, I combined man and dragon in a single body. Ryūjin's hands and feet are dragon's claws and his chest dragon's scales. The dragon's tail curls at his knees. He wears a belt decorated with a demon's head.

SIGNED: Masatoshi *sha*.
INSCRIPTION: *ko netsuke yori* (from an old netsuke).
MATERIAL: ivory.
EYES OF RYŪJIN: *sumi*.
EYES OF DEMON'S HEAD: black tortoise shell.
COLOR: incense smoke; *sumi*—dragon scales; gold *nikawa*—demon's head.
COMPLETED: August 1972.
ILLUSTRATED: *Arts of Asia*, July/August 1973.
　　　　　The Imperial (cover), Autumn 1978.
　　　　　Catalogue, Raymond Bushell Collection, Tokyo.
SCALE: seven-eighths life size.

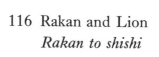

113 Banko

According to Chinese metaphysics, Banko is the god who represents infinity, eternity, and creation. He was born of the original egg and he is the creator of heaven and earth. His eyes are the sun and the moon. I represented Banko in the form of a celestial, human-headed dragon as he emerges from the primordial egg that rests on the earth and supports the heavens.

SIGNED: Masatoshi, with *kakihan*.
INSCRIPTION: *Banko*.
MATERIAL: ivory.
EYES: *sumi*.
COLOR: incense smoke.
COMPLETED: April 1971.
ILLUSTRATED: *Arts of Asia*, July/August 1973.

114 The Evil Deity of Heaven
Amanojaku

Although Amanojaku is a legitimate inmate of the Buddhist pantheon, he is regarded as a devil. He is

a heretic. He perverts and debases true doctrine, and his name has come to represent "perverseness" in everyday, colloquial Japanese. The great sculptors of the Kamakura Period (1118–1333) often represented Amanojaku squatting on hands and knees and supporting on his back the warrior guardians of Buddhism. My design is based on the folk tale *Urikohime monogatari* (The Romance of Princess Uriko), in which Amanojaku intimidates the princess and steals her ball.

SIGNED: Masatoshi, in a smooth reserve.
MATERIAL: ivory.
EYES: *sumi*.
COLOR: *yashadama*; *sumi*—hair, tiger stripes; gold *nikawa*—ball, loincloth.
COMPLETED: April 1979.
SCALE: seven-eighths life size.

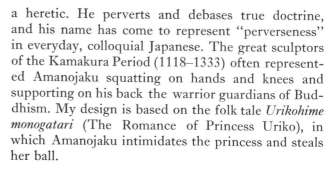

115 Handaka Sonja

Handaka Sonja is one of the *rakan*, the sixteen principal disciples of Buddha. His companion, the dragon, issues from his begging bowl (*teppatsu*). Handaka wears an angry expression because he has an angry disposition, not because the dragon contests his possession of the jewel of Buddha (*hōshu no tama*).

The piece balances easily on one foot despite being slightly top-heavy.

SIGNED: Masatoshi *tō*.
INSCRIPTION: *Handaka*.
MATERIAL: boxwood.
EYES: carved.
COLOR: potassium permanganate.
COMPLETED: July 1978.
SCALE: seven-eighths life size.

116 Rakan and Lion
Rakan to shishi

Buddhist literature is not clear in identifying which

is the *rakan* who is associated with the *shishi* (mythical lion) nor in explaining why he holds the *shishi* by two paws upside down. To know his character might have helped me to portray the strangeness of the relationship.

I chose *kōki* for the carving, a strange material for a strange subject. *Kōki* is a kind of red sandalwood. It is beet red when first cut, but on exposure it gradually darkens to a reddish black. It is coarse grained, and often the carving quality of the same block varies considerably, a fact that can lead to distressing developments, especially if I have almost finished working on a piece.

SIGNED: Masatoshi *tō*.
MATERIAL: *kōki*.
EYES: carved.
COLOR: natural.
COMPLETED: April 1974.
SCALE: seven-eighths life size.

117 Kinko Sennin

Kinko Sennin (*sennin* are Taoist hermits and sages who remain youthful into great, old age) preached the sacredness of all life and particularly the protection of fish. He is often portrayed mounted on a gigantic carp, which carries him to the Submarine Kingdom. I treated the subject humorously. One of Kinko's scrolls slips from his grasp, and both he and the carp are thrown into confusion as they scramble to recover it from the waves.

SIGNED: Masatoshi *tō*.
MATERIAL: ivory.
EYES OF CARP: black coral.
COLOR: *yashadama*; *sumi*—hair, eyes, patterns, scales, markings; gold *nikawa*—Buddhist scepter.
COMPLETED: January 1954.
ILLUSTRATED: *Arts of Asia*, July/August 1973.

118 Hichōbō Sennin

Hichōbō befriended an eccentric dealer in philters who slept in a pot suspended from a lintel over his shop. The old drug dealer taught him occult magic and finally he became a *sennin*. His distinguishing

feature is a Japanese crane (*tanchō*), which flies him about the heavens. The crane has a red crest and carries a gold treasure ball (*hōshu*) in his beak.

Hichōbō Sennin is illustrated in Hasegawa Tōun's *Ehon hōkan*. As in a number of my early pieces, I carved and undercut excessively, increasing the fragility of the netsuke.

SIGNED: Masatoshi, on a raised oval reserve.
MATERIAL: ivory.
EYES OF CRANE: black tortoise shell.
COLOR: *yashadama*; *sumi*—hair, beard, eyes, tail feathers, patterns, markings; scarlet *nikawa*—lips, crane's crest, tongue; gold *nikawa*—treasure ball.
COMPLETED: January 1955.

119 Seiōbo Sennin

Seiōbo is the only woman among the many *sennin* of Chinese origin. Her emblem is the magic peach. She is usually represented carrying a branch, basket, or bowl of the fruit. Her peaches confer longevity on those fortunate enough to be her guests.

As a netsuke, this is more functional than the *sennin* in Plates 117 and 118. It is less fragile, better protected, and more compact.

SIGNED: Masatoshi, in red in an oval reserve.
MATERIAL: ivory.
COLOR: *yashadama*; *sumi*—eyes, eyebrows, hair, kimono patterns, markings; red *nikawa*—lips, fan; gold *nikawa*—crown, hair ornaments.
COMPLETED: November 1952.
ILLUSTRATED: *Arts of Asia*, July/August 1973.

120 Tōbōsaku Sennin

Like Seiōbo, Tōbōsaku carries a peach as a symbol of his own longevity. According to legend, Tōbōsaku stole three peaches from Seiōbo, thereby acquiring a life span of three thousand years.

Tōbōsaku wears on his right hip a complete *inrō*, *ojime* (slide bead), and netsuke with gold cords. Despite undercutting, this is a reasonably functional netsuke.

SIGNED: Masatoshi.
MATERIAL: ivory.
COLOR: *yashadama*; *sumi*—hair, eyebrows, whiskers, eyes, kimono patterns; gold *nikawa*—Buddhist scepter, *inrō* cords.
COMPLETED: February 1953.

121 Tekkai Sennin

The accounts say that Tekkai Sennin was crippled by leprosy. He walked with the support of a cane, around which he wrapped his withered leg. Tekkai had the unique capacity of being able to exhale his spiritual essence. In painting he is usually represented with a faint replica of himself in the distance. For practical reasons, I designed his "spiritual essence" as a solid figure which he holds in his hand.

I experimented with a stain that imparted a strange violet shade to the ivory. At the time, it did not please me at all, and so I never tried it again. Now that the mellowing effect of a quarter of a century has transformed the color to a rare and attractive lavender tinge, I would like to use the stain again, but I've forgotten my formula and method.

SIGNED: Masatoshi.
MATERIAL: ivory.
EYES: carved.
COLOR: faint lavender.
COMPLETED: September 1955.

122 Ikkaku Sennin

Ikkaku (One-Horn) Sennin was the result of a liaison between a sturdy mountain priest and a beautiful deer. He inherited his single horn from his mother's side and earned his status as a *sennin* through his celibacy and acts of asceticism. One fateful day he met Sendara, a beauty suffering from exhaustion, and offered to carry her. Her womanly warmth aroused his carnal desire, causing him to lose his occult powers.

Sendara steadies herself by gripping Ikkaku's horn. The patterns on her garments are cloud, chrysanthemum, and wave. She wears a swan-shaped decoration in her hair.

SIGNED: Masatoshi.
MATERIAL: ivory.
COLOR: *yashadama*; *sumi*—hair, eyebrows, chin stubble, kimono patterns; gold *nikawa*—hair ornaments.
COMPLETED: April 1970.

123 Tōran Sennin

There are very few *sennin* of Japanese origin, and of the few only one, Tōran, is a woman. She is illustrated in the *Minzokugaku zenshū*. She stands on clouds, spying on mountain strongholds where *tengu* (goblins) and *yamabushi* (mountain priests) gather and women are prohibited. She holds the fingers of her left hand in a position symbolizing magic and spells. Even mountains are no barrier to her movements.

SIGNED: Masatoshi, in an oval reserve.
INSCRIPTION: *Tōran Sennin*.
MATERIAL: hippopotamus tooth.
COLOR: *yashadama*; *sumi*—hair, eyebrows, eyes, skirt.
COMPLETED: January 1974.

9. Customs, Festivals, Ceremonies

124 Floating Lanterns
Tōrō nagashi

Obon is the annual holiday when our deceased relatives return to earth to visit us. In the old days at the end of the festivities, families placed paper candle-lit lanterns on rafts to accompany their relatives on their return to the other world. Thousands of floating lanterns made an eerie nocturnal spectacle, as they floated downriver or out to sea.

I carved a floating lantern in the shape of a pigeon. The antique effect imparted by a few nicks and coloring with incense smoke was accentuated by natural cracks.

SIGNED: Tokisada *koku*.
MATERIAL: ivory.
EYES: black coral.
COLOR: incense smoke; *sumi*—lantern folds.
COMPLETED: September 1962.

125 Happiness In, Evil Out
Fuku uchi, ki gai

The elements, symbols, and allusions that are recognized in the old lunar New Year are numerous and are regularly combined in a multitude of designs. I carved Otafuku, who represents happiness, *inside* the bean box and a demon (*oni*), representing evil, *outside*. Otafuku roasts beans with which to pelt the demon, while he tries to distract her by enticing her with the offer of a mushroom, the male symbol, of which she is inordinately fond.

The marks on the bean box are "*isshō*" (1.8 liters) and "*tei*" (verified). I formed the *himotoshi* by separating the demon's ankle from the box.

SIGNED: Masatoshi.
MATERIAL: ivory.

COLOR: *yashadama*; *sumi*—hair, eyes, eyebrows, patterns, leopard spots; red *nikawa*—lips; gold *nikawa*—demon's loincloth; potassium permanganate—oven, mushroom top, demon's hair.
COMPLETED: August 1958.

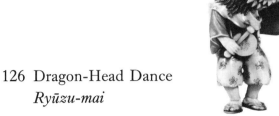

126 Dragon-Head Dance
Ryūzu-mai

In times of depression, Edo townsmen found it difficult to earn a living. As one step above outright begging, some went from door to door dancing, chanting, or beating drums. They were not professional performers, and the entertainment they offered was crude—just enough to eke out an existence by relying on the generosity of neighbors. I carved an itinerant entertainer performing a dance with a dragon headdress and a drum. I got the idea from the cover of a program for a variety show (*yose*) at Ueno in Tokyo.

SIGNED: Masatoshi *tō*.
MATERIAL: ivory.
EYES: carved.
COLOR: *yashadama*; *sumi*—patterns, markings.
COMPLETED: March 1975.

127 Miniature Lion Dance
Miniachua shishimai

The lion dance is performed at New Year to scare away evil spirits. I carved the lower jaw of the *shishi* (mythical lion) separately but from the same block of ivory as the figure. I fixed the movable jaw in place with an ivory pin, the head of which is disguised as the center of a *shishi* hair (*keman*) pattern. The jaw drops to reveal the face of the boy dancer. The ears of the *shishi* are separate and are made of water buffalo horn (*suigyū no tsuno*.) I discuss some of the considerations involved in miniature netsuke on page 68.

SIGNED: Masatoshi *saku.*
MATERIAL: ivory; *shishi*'s ears—water buffalo
horn.
EYES: carved.
COLOR: *yashadama*; *sumi*—eyes, nostrils, patterns.
COMPLETED: July 1952.

128 Indian Dance
Tenjiku no mai

This dance is one of mixed elements. The performer
wears a costume with voluminous Chinese-style
sleeves, a skirt, and a headdress in the shape of a
goat's head. I carved stylized sun and cloud patterns
on the dancer's costume.

SIGNED: Masatoshi.
MATERIAL: ivory.
EYES: carved.
COLOR: incense smoke.
COMPLETED: August 1967.

10. People

129 Ueda Akinari

Ueda Akinari (1734–1809) was an Edo Period critic
and novelist. Mizoguchi Kenji turned Akinari's most
famous story, *Ugetsu monogatari*, into a motion
picture which won international acclaim.

Akinari's facial structure was startling. I carved
him from a painting made during his lifetime and
engraved his name on the back of his coat to identify
him.

SIGNED: Masatoshi.
MATERIAL: ivory.
EYES: carved.
COLOR: *yashadama*; *sumi*—eyes, eyebrows, brush
tip.
COMPLETED: September 1976.
SCALE: nine-tenths life size.

130 Gensō and Yōkihi

Gensō, the Tang Dynasty emperor, teaches his chief
concubine, Yōkihi, to play the flute. The emperor's
dissipation with her, his neglect, and her extravagance
impoverished his subjects and resulted in a rebellion.
I once saw a print by Yoshitoshi of the two lovers
seated on a couch, but I designed them standing to
make a better netsuke.

SIGNED: Masatoshi *tō.*
MATERIAL: boxwood.
EYES: carved.
COLOR: natural; gold *nikawa*—hair ornament,
character "*gen*" on crown.
COMPLETED: April 1976.

131 Townsman and Earthquake Fish
Chōnin to namazu

A townsman is jarred out of his senses when a huge earthquake fish comes to life with a wriggle that sets the earth trembling.

SIGNED: Masatoshi tō.
MATERIAL: ivory.
FISH'S EYES FOLLOW.
COLOR: incense smoke; silver nitrate and sumi—fish's back; sumi—eyes, towel pattern, fins.
COMPLETED: September 1974.

132 Woman Diver
Amu

My experience with the tusk of wild boar (inoshishi no ha) is limited. It has a hard enamel rind about one millimeter or more in thickness which should be removed before carving—a job that is difficult to do cleanly. Beneath the rind the material is uniform and carves easily.

I was once asked to repair a boar tusk netsuke by smoothing the surface, which had become pitted and scarred. But I found it impossible to do the work because the carver had not removed the enamel rind but had used it his design.

I imagined an ama (woman diver) holding an abalone as she enjoys a siesta.

SIGNED: Masatoshi.
MATERIAL: boar tusk.
COLOR: yashadama; sumi—hair, eyebrows, eyes, abalone.
COMPLETED: June 1966.

133 Amateur Sumō
Shirōto-zumō

When I was a boy, I used to go to Shitaya Shrine in my neighborhood to watch amateur wrestlers (sumō-tori) practicing. A burly sumōtori named Ikedagawa won by the technique known as tsuridashi (lift out), but as he carried his opponent out of the ring, he fell on top of me. I still feel the wrench on my knees. That is the bout I carved.

SIGNED: Masatoshi tō.
MATERIAL: boxwood.
EYES: carved.
COLOR: natural.
COMPLETED: March 1976.
ILLUSTRATED: Catalogue, Raymond Bushell Collection, Tokyo.
Sumo World, January 1980.

134 Old Man Crazy about Painting
Gakyō rōjin

In a daily newspaper, I once saw a self-portrait (jigazō) drawn by Hokusai at the age of eighty. He signed it "gakyō rōjin" (old man crazy about painting). I decided to turn drawing into carving, to netsuketize the subject. Hokusai deserves the praise of all netsuke-shi. His prolific production of drawings is a rich source of models and ideas for us.

SIGNED: Masatoshi tō.
INSCRIPTION: gakyō rōjin.
MATERIAL: boxwood.
EYES: carved.
COLOR: natural except for a faint yashadama wash.
COMPLETED: March 1976.

135 Dutchman on Horseback
Orandajin jōba

I admired the way the anonymous carver of an old netsuke composed a subject with such difficult design problems into a safe, compact, and balanced model and decided to see what I could do with my version of the design.

SIGNED: Masatoshi *sha*.
MATERIAL: ivory.
EYES: carved.
COLOR: incense smoke.
COMPLETED: December 1958.

136 Making Faces
Akanbei

Before there was cinema, television, radio, and pinball games like *pachinko*, ordinary people relied on themselves for fun and amusement. I portrayed a common laborer entertaining his friends by contorting himself into an absurd position, pulling his eyes down and twisting his mouth. He balances on his rump.

SIGNED: Masatoshi.
MATERIAL: ivory.
EYES: carved.
COLOR: incense smoke; *sumi*—hair, eyes, eyebrows, loincloth.
COMPLETED: August 1966.

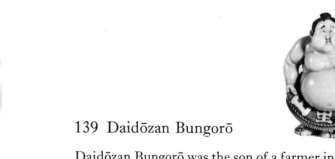

137 Albuquerque
Arubukeruke

I once saw in the magazine *Kinsei sanbyakunen shi* (Three Hundred Years of Modern History) a picture of a bust of Albuquerque, the Portuguese navigator who established the colony of Goa in India. I decided to carve a standing figure, composing my model from the bust and from representations of Portuguese in old screens.

SIGNED: Masatoshi *tō*.
MATERIAL: ivory.
EYES: carved.
COLOR: incense smoke; *sumi*—hair, eyes, eyebrows, hat.
COMPLETED: June 1972.

ILLUSTRATED: *Arts of Asia*, July/August 1973.
SCALE: seven-eighths life size.

138 Rapid Advancement
Unagi-nobori

The eel swims with a sinuous upward motion as though it were trying to break the surface and enter a higher realm. "*Unagi-nobori*" (literally, "eel climb") denotes speedy success. I carved an ordinary laborer clutching a giant eel and hoping it will carry him straight up to his dream of prosperity.

SIGNED: Masatoshi.
MATERIAL: ivory.
EYES OF MAN: carved.
EYES OF EEL: black tortoise shell.
COLOR: incense smoke; *sumi*—hair, eyes, eyebrows, eel's skin.
COMPLETED: October 1965.
ILLUSTRATED: *Collectors' Netsuke*, Figure 339.

139 Daidōzan Bungorō

Daidōzan Bungorō was the son of a farmer in northern Japan, where many *sumō* giants originate. At the age of eight, Daidōzan packed 205 pounds in his 4-foot 4-inch frame. He was known everywhere as the oversized boy wonder of *sumō* and he became the youngest wrestler to participate in the parade of champions.

I joined his feet for additional security with a *sumō* referee's fan (*gunbai*). I engraved his name, Daidōzan, on his ceremonial apron (*kesshō-mawashi*).

SIGNED: Jikishiin Masatoshi *tō*.
MATERIAL: ivory.
EYES: carved.
COLOR: *yashadama*; *sumi*—hair, apron; silver nitrate—belt.
COMPLETED: April 1975.
ILLUSTRATED: *Sumo World*, January 1980.

140 Amakusa Shirō

Amakusa Shirō was a seventeen-year-old samurai, a Christian, who led the revolt of the farmers at Shimabara. He was killed in the fall of Hara Castle in 1638, and his head was exposed at Nagasaki.

I carved this young leader the way I imagined him. He wears a cross and a cloak, emblems of foreign religion and foreign influence. He holds an iron fan (*tessen*) in his hand, the insignia of his command. The pattern on his cloak is that of leaves that fall within the year, symbolizing the brevity of his life.

SIGNED: Masatoshi.
MATERIAL: hippopotamus tooth.
EYES: carved.
COLOR: *yashadama*; *sumi*—hair, eyes, eyebrows, bracelets, patterns; silver nitrate—fan.
COMPLETED: June 1973.

142 Kōbō Daishi

I once saw a standing figure—it was not a netsuke as it lacked *himotoshi*—about two centimeters in height carved by Morita Sōko. I marveled at his skill in conveying so much in so small an area and decided to try to emulate his accomplishment.

I represented Kōbō Daishi, the famous propagator of Buddhism in Japan, as a child, when he had already displayed his brilliance in calligraphy. He holds special paper for writing poems (*kaishi*) in one hand and a writing brush in the other. His hair style is typical of that of children of the Heian Period (794–1185).

UNSIGNED.
MATERIAL: boxwood.
EYES: carved.
COLOR: natural except for a faint *yashadama* wash.
COMPLETED: August 1952.
ILLUSTRATED: *Netsuke Familiar and Unfamiliar*, Figure 432.

141 Snow-Country Child
Yukiguni no ko

This little girl is from Akita Prefecture in the "snow country" of northern Japan. She wears padded trousers (*monpe*) and a padded kimono jacket (*wataire no chanchanko*). She shrinks her neck and withdraws her hands into her sleeves to stave off the cold.

When the snows are deepest in Akita, the children have a festival. They gather in *kamakura*, huts built of snow, where braziers keep them warm and rice cakes keep them fed. The warm *kamakura* is a happy respite for the children during the cold and monotonously long winter.

SIGNED: Masatoshi.
MATERIAL: ivory.
EYES: black tortoise shell.
COLOR: incense smoke; *sumi*—hair, eyes, eyebrows.
COMPLETED: March 1961.

143 A Blind Man Fears Not the Snake
Mekura hebi ni ojizu

I wanted a subject for the Year of the Snake and decided to represent this familiar proverb. In the old days handicapped people were despised and ridiculed. Artists often represented them with ugly tumors and wens in addition to their principal defects. People regarded their afflictions in this life as punishment for evil committed in their previous lives. Moreover, masseurs were especially contemptible because they were also moneylenders and usurers.

I carved the figure of a *zatō*, the lowest of the four grades of masseurs. He is unaware that he has trod on a snake, which strikes at the cord of his *hakama* (skirt).

When I attended primary school, all my classmates wore *hakama* except for one upstart who wore Western clothes. Today the reverse is the case.

SIGNED: Masatoshi *tō*.
MATERIAL: ivory.
EYES OF SNAKE: black tortoise shell.
BASIC COLOR: *yashadama*; *sumi*—eyebrows, scales, patterns.
COMPLETED: March 1977.

144 Long-legged Beauty
Ashinaga no bijin

My long-legged beauty is a Japanese—she is not a primitive *ashinaga*. Her slender, elongated legs combined with her massive breasts appealed to my sense of whimsy.

I carved the netsuke as a *sashi* (see Diagram E on page 64). The feet act as a safety catch on the lower edge of the *obi* and the crook of her elbow as the *himotoshi*. I colored her skirt in a two-tone effect.

SIGNED: Masatoshi *tō*.
MATERIAL: hippopotamus tooth.
EYES: carved.
COLOR: incense smoke; *sumi*—hair, eyes, eyebrows.
COMPLETED: September 1973.
SCALE: two-thirds life size.

145 Takarai Kikaku

Takarai Kikaku was one of the ten great students of Bashō, the master of *haiku* (seventeen-syllable poems). I carved Kikaku in the act of composing a poem which is at the same time a prayer for the end of a ruinous drought. His poem, indeed, is credited with having brought the rainfall which ended the drought. The characters on the paper are "Yūdachi" (Evening Rain), the title of his poem. He protects his poem card with a rain hood (*sōsho zukin*).

SIGNED: Masatoshi.
MATERIAL: ivory.
EYES: carved.
COLOR: *yashadama*; *sumi*—eyes, eyebrows, cap, brush tip, coat.
COMPLETED: October 1974.

11. Masks and Heads

146 Kagekiyo

Kagekiyo was a leader of the defeated Taira clan. Rather than witness the triumph of his enemy, he blinded himself and went into self-imposed exile. He is the hero of a Noh play.

The mask of Kagekiyo is considered one of the most difficult to carve. It must show blindness and despondency without compromising the resolute pride and unbroken will of an old warrior.

I added the word for copy, "*sha*," to my signature to indicate that my model was an ancient Noh mask.

SIGNED: Masatoshi *sha*.
INSCRIPTION: *Kagekiyo*.
MATERIAL: ivory.
COLOR: incense smoke.
COMPLETED: December 1955.

147 Batō

Batō is a Bugaku mask. "*Ba*" means "to pull out," and "*tō*" means "head," so that the figurative sense of Batō is tearing out the hair in fury. The dancer, a barbarian, expresses his consuming hatred for the tiger that ate his father. He moves vigorously as he throws his hemp hair about and rakes it with claw-like hands. I pitted the pate to show that much of the hair has already been pulled out.

The original of the mask is a national treasure kept at the famous Itsukushima Shrine near Hiroshima.

SIGNED: Shunzan *tō*.
INSCRIPTION: *Batō*.
MATERIAL: ivory.
EYES: carved.
COLOR: red lacquer—face; black lacquer—hair, eyebrows.

COMPLETED: November 1956.
ILLUSTRATED: *Arts of Asia*, July/August 1973.

148 Gyōdō Jūniten

This mask is of one of the *jūniten*, the Twelve Gods of Heaven. It is a Gyōdō mask, a religious mask worn by priests when they take part in solemn processions around a temple or shrine. Unlike the emotional masks of the theater, Gyōdō masks must convey spiritual serenity and the life of contemplation and withdrawal. The Gyōdō mask is large; it envelops the entire head, not just the face as in Noh.

SIGNED: Masatoshi *tō*.
INSCRIPTION: *jūniten*.
MATERIAL: ivory.
EYES: carved.
COLOR: *yashadama*; *sumi*—eyes; gold *nikawa*—crown; red lacquer—lips; silver nitrate—hair, eyebrows, beard.
COMPLETED: November 1975.

149 Five Great Kings of Light
Go dai myō-ō

I used the streak of red in the hornbill ivory to convey the dramatic effect produced by a narrow ray of afternoon sunlight blazing down on the face of a dimly lit Buddhist figure, one of the Go Dai Myō-ō, the Five Great Kings of Light.

SIGNED: Masatoshi *tō*.
INSCRIPTION: *gojitsu nyūmei* (signed later).
MATERIAL: hornbill ivory.
COLOR: natural.
COMPLETED: June 1972.
ILLUSTRATED: *The Inrō Handbook*, Figure 97.

150 Arabesque Mask
Karakusa men

The mask is entirely the product of my imagination, though the design is rooted in arabesques.

> SIGNED: Masatoshi *tō*.
> MATERIAL: ivory.
> COLOR: *yashadama*; *sumi*—markings.
> COMPLETED: January 1975.

151 Rakan Mask
Rakan no men

This is not a theatrical mask such as might be seen in Noh, Kabuki, or Gigaku but the face of a *rakan* in mask form.

> SIGNED: Masatoshi *tō*.
> MATERIAL: ivory.
> COLOR: incense smoke.
> COMPLETED: October 1978.

152 "Heike Crab" Mask
Heike-gani men

The Heike (Taira) clan was finally beaten by the Genji (Minamoto) at Dannoura in the Inland Sea, and many of them drowned. We call the crabs of the area "*heike-gani*" (Heike crabs), because of the uncanny resemblance of the peculiar markings on the crabs' shells to the faces of helmeted samurai.

I tried to combine elements of a crab and a warrior's face in the mask.

> SIGNED: Masatoshi *tō*.
> MATERIAL: boxwood.
> EYES: black coral.
> COLOR: natural.
> COMPLETED: August 1975.

153 Demon Mask
Oni no men

Hornbill ivory is a rare material, but it is even rarer to find a piece sufficiently large for a carving in-the-round. The small size of this block just about dictated the choice of a mask for my subject.

I inlaid the eyes separately for better effect, though I used the same piece of hornbill.

> SIGNED: Masatoshi *tō*.
> INSCRIPTION: *hōten nite* (from hornbill).
> MATERIAL: hornbill.
> EYES: hornbill.
> COLOR: natural.
> COMPLETED: September 1968.

154 Noh Style Mask
Nō men

I call this mask a "Noh style" mask because, when I carved it, I did not have in mind a particular mask with prescribed elements and characteristics.

The hornbill polished to brilliant shades of red and yellow. It was a shame that the material was not large enough for a carving in-the-round.

> SIGNED: Masatoshi *tō*.
> INSCRIPTION: *gojitsu nyūmei* (signed later).
> MATERIAL: hornbill ivory.
> EYES: carved.
> COLOR: natural.
> COMPLETED: April 1972.

155 Amber Mask
Kohaku men

My model was an ancient Chinese mask in translucent, pale green jade. I decided on yellow amber as the best material to match the quality and reflect the rarity of the original. In the few years since I carved it, I am pleased to find that the color and texture have improved. To my amazement, natural color markings suggesting a dragon developed on the back of the mask. I discuss amber as a material for carving in the description of Plate 80.

SIGNED: Masatoshi *sha*.
MATERIAL: amber.
EYES: carved.
COLOR: natural.
COMPLETED: September 1974.

156 Head of Snake
Hebi no kubi

I thought the head of a fanciful snake would make an unusual netsuke. I am now thinking of carving another version in ivory.

SIGNED: Jikishiin Masatoshi, with *kakihan*.
MATERIAL: boxwood.
EYES: follow.
COLOR: natural except for a faint *yashadama* wash.
COMPLETED: June 1969.

157 Hawk's Head
Taka no atama

I acquired a pair of tiger fangs (*tora no ha*) many years ago and carved one of them into a hawk's head. I had spent a long time studying the tooth and wondering what to make of it, when in a flash I saw the beak of a bird in the enamel and the head in the root. Nature had given it the proper shape and color contrast. I had little carving to do to give the bird its crest and eyes. I felt as if I had freed the hawk from the fang, in which it had been confined.

I studied the second fang searching for another inspiration, but this time there was no flash and no insight. Finally I gave up and carved it into a twin, the mirror image of the first. It flies in the opposite direction. If the two were brought together, they would be in confrontation—just as hawks should be.

SIGNED: Masa *tō*.
MATERIAL: tiger fangs.
EYES: black coral.
COLOR: incense smoke.
COMPLETED: February 1972.
SCALE: seven-eighths life size.

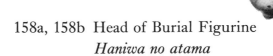

158a, 158b Head of Burial Figurine
Haniwa no atama

I have never seen *haniwa* (clay burial figurines) depicted in old netsuke. They have an elusive but distinctive charm, so it's hard to know why *netsuke-shi* did not take to them. It may be because Hokusai and other draftsmen didn't think to include them in their design manuals.

The head I copied is from a famous *haniwa* reproduced in many catalogues with critical essays by scholars. The critics do not agree on whether the head belongs to a man or to a woman, whether it is laughing or crying, and whether the object atop the head is a helmet or a coiffure. I carved the head as a "warrior with helmet," but it is also described as a woman with a sort of symmetrical hair style called *taiseishiki*. The confusion in no way diminishes the attractiveness of the subject.

I nicked the head here and there to imitate the condition of the *haniwa*.

The material was given to me. It was about sixteen centimeters long and just over three centimeters in diameter, a solid, straight cylindrical shape. I am quite unable to identify it. All I know is that I have never used or seen it before, and I can say positively that it is not ivory, whale-tooth, hippopotamus, walrus, narwhal, boar's tusk, or boar's tooth. It mystifies me.

SIGNED: Masatoshi *sha*.
MATERIAL: unidentified.
EYES: carved.
COLOR: incense smoke; *sumi*—markings.
COMPLETED: February 1975.

159a, 159b Woman with Ponytail
Keppatsu onna

The original clay head was found in the grave of Emperor Ōjin. I admired it for its basically cubic shape, its spare simplicity, and unpretentious sophistication.

The surface texture of the original is smooth. I thought that a pitted surface would make a more interesting netsuke.

SIGNED: Masatoshi *tō*.
MATERIAL: ivory.
EYES: carved.
COLOR: incense smoke and dust.
COMPLETED: October 1966.

160 Man with Eyebrows
Mayu no aru otoko

Eyebrows are an unusual feature in *haniwa* and account for the special designation of the clay original.

The impression which I tried to convey by reproducing the turned-up mouth and the crescent-shaped eyes of the original is that of a man laughing uproariously. Some authorities, however, say the man is crying. As this indicates, our understanding of the meaning of *haniwa* is highly conjectural. I made a few nicks to imitate the condition of the original.

SIGNED: Masatoshi *tō*.
INSCRIPTIONS: *Jōshū shutsudo* (excavated in Jō Province, i.e., Gunma Prefecture); *Mayu no aru otoko* (man with eyebrows).
MATERIAL: whale-tooth.
EYES: carved.
COLOR: incense smoke; *sumi*—eyebrows.
COMPLETED: July 1976.

161a, 161b Sharaku Big Head
Sharaku no ōkubi

I copied the head of the villain Washizuka Kandayū as portrayed on stage by the great Ichikawa Danjūrō from a print by Sharaku. To imitate Sharaku's strong lines marking the eyes and nose, I used the residue of the resin deposited from incense smoke mellowed with house dust (see page 53).

SIGNED: Jikishiin Masatoshi, with *kakihan*.
INSCRIPTIONS: *Sharaku no ōkubi* (Sharaku big head); *Gose Danjūrō* (Fifth-Generation Danjūrō).
MATERIAL: ivory.
EYES: black coral.
COLOR: incense smoke; silver nitrate—hair, eyebrows, lips; *sumi*—inscription.
COMPLETED: October 1968.
ILLUSTRATED: *Arts of Asia*, July/August 1973.

162 Monster of Mount Tenmoku
Tenmoku-zan no kaibutsu

There is a legend that a monster lived on Mount Tenmoku. A live snake grew out of his head, and his teeth were tiger tusks. The legend says nothing about the rest of his body, so I decided to carve only his head.

SIGNED: Masatoshi *tō*.
MATERIAL: ivory.
EYES: black coral.
COLOR: incense smoke; *sumi*—markings.
COMPLETED: July 1978.

163 Head of "Woman Daruma"
Onna daruma

I represented the head only of Onna Daruma. I treated the *umoregi* (semipetrified wood) in which I set her face as an allusion to Daruma: an abundance of flowing hair suggesting Daruma's cloak, a rounded base imitating his shape as a roly-poly toy, and, from the rear, Daruma's traditional papier-mâché form for good luck at New Year.

SIGNED: Jikishiin Masatoshi *tō*.
MATERIALS: *umoregi* and ivory.
EYES: black coral.
COLOR OF IVORY: incense smoke; *sumi*—eyebrows, nostrils, mouth.
COLOR OF *umoregi*: natural.
COMPLETED: September 1969.

164 Conflicting Eyes
Me-kurabe

The idea for this subject came from a children's picture book of ghosts. The monster's head is equipped with seven uncoordinated eyeballs that stare in conflicting directions. Two of the four eyes visible in the illustration are black coral. The others are transparent tortoise shell differentiated in color by underlying applications of red and gold lacquer—all except for the seventh eye, which is uncolored.

SIGNED: Masatoshi *tō*.
INSCRIPTION: *me-kurabe* (conflicting eyes).
MATERIAL: rhinoceros horn.
EYES: black coral and transparent tortoise shell, colored with red or gold lacquer.
COLOR: natural.
COMPLETED: November 1978.

12. Fish

165 Carp
Koi

I altered the natural anatomy of the carp here, especially the tail fins, in the interests of a safe, sturdy design. I exaggerated the teeth and tongue and rearranged the head to make it more amusing. But it is still recognizably a carp.

SIGNED: Masatoshi *tō*.
MATERIAL: ivory.
EYES: black tortoise shell.
COLOR: incense smoke; *sumi*—scales, fins.
COMPLETED: August 1961.

166 Seahorse
Tatsu no otoshigo

I once saw a live seahorse at the aquarium in Inage City near Tokyo. Its name, *tatsu no otoshigo*, means "pouched child of the dragon." I designed it to exaggerate its dragonet aspects and I needle-pricked the entire skin for realism. As I cut the material from the central core of the tusk, it absorbed color evenly from the incense smoke.

SIGNED: Masatoshi *tō*, in a smooth reserve.
MATERIAL: ivory.
EYES: black coral.
COLOR: incense smoke.
COMPLETED: January 1968.
ILLUSTRATED: *Arts of Asia*, July/August 1973.

167 Seahorse Skeleton
Tatsu no otoshigo no gaikotsu

The subject is the same as that of the netsuke shown in Plate 166, but the treatment is entirely different.

I modeled the previous seahorse on the live animal, while I modeled this one on the skeleton—the empty eye sockets leave no doubt about this. It is the skeleton that is sold in the Chinese medicine shops. The *yashadama* coloring is thick and uniform.

SIGNED: Masatoshi *tō*.
MATERIAL: ivory.
COLOR: *yashadama*.
COMPLETED: November 1977.

168 Imaginary Fish
Sōzō uo

I envisioned this imaginary, finless fish in the tip of an antler with heavy nodules. For amusement's sake, I gave it a large, flat tongue and enough teeth for a sperm whale.

SIGNED: Masatoshi.
MATERIAL: stag-antler.
EYES: black coral.
COLOR: incense smoke.
COMPLETED: October 1969.
SCALE: life size.

169 Carp
Koi

I curled the carp's tail and fins against its body to give it sufficient protection for a netsuke. The loop formed by the joining of breast fin and tail is the *himotoshi*.

SIGNED: Masatoshi.
MATERIAL: ivory.
EYES: black coral.
COLOR: incense smoke; *sumi*—markings.
COMPLETED: March 1959.

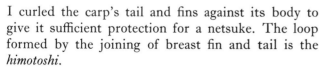

170 Carp with Young
Koi no oyako

The carp swims against the current and is a symbol of strength and courage. Here, the mother carp cuddles her baby in the shelter of her dorsal and tail fins. The design is my own.

SIGNED: Masatoshi.
MATERIAL: boxwood.
EYES: black coral.
COLOR: potassium permanganate.
COMPLETED: May 1963.
ILLUSTRATED: *Wonderful World of Netsuke*, Figure 56.

171 Carp with Mate
Koi no fūfu

The carp is admired for its conjugal devotion as well as for its courage. I made one a little larger than the other to indicate which is husband and which wife. They frolic together affectionately. In paintings, carp couples are usually represented swimming head to head, or, when destined for the kitchen, hanging head to head. But to make a compact netsuke, I designed the pair head to tail. I needle-pricked the heads to simulate the carp's leathery hide.

SIGNED: Tokisada.
MATERIAL: boxwood.
EYES: black coral.
COLOR: natural except for faint *yashadama* wash.
COMPLETED: March 1961.

172 Whale
Kujira

A drawing I once saw of a whale awakened me to the strange fact that *netsuke-shi* make frequent use of whales' teeth but rarely represent the animal itself in a netsuke, and so I decided to try my hand at carving one. I reproduced the color of the whale's back with silver nitrate mellowed by incense smoke.

SIGNED: Tokisada *tō*.
MATERIAL: ivory.
EYES: carved.
COLOR: silver nitrate and incense smoke.
COMPLETED: January 1962.

173 Freshwater Carp
Funa

At the time I felt like a change and so I finished the piece by applying *negoro* lacquer, even though the basic material is boxwood. I applied the lacquer in the standard *negoro* technique: an application of black lacquer followed by a coat of red, which I polished unevenly to produce the blotched red-black effect. I embellished it with a sprinkling of gold powder.

SIGNED: Tokisada, in an oval reserve.
MATERIAL: boxwood.
EYES: lacquer.
COLOR: *negoro* lacquer and gold powder.
COMPLETED: May 1962.
ILLUSTRATED: *Arts of Asia*, July/August 1973.

174 Flathead
Kochi

The live flathead served as my model. The flathead has a rough scaly skin, is broader than it is long, and is sinuous. As my carving is smooth, long, and angular, it is clearly not true to life. The fins of the two flathead overlap to form the *himotoshi*.

Oil spots (patches of skin or bark in the ivory) and cracks on the underside are natural.

SIGNED: Masatoshi *tō*.
MATERIAL: ivory.
EYES: black tortoise shell.
COLOR: incense smoke; *sumi*—markings.
COMPLETED: March 1963.

175 Goldfish
Kingyo

In spring the cry of the peddler of goldfish is as common as that of the baked sweet potato seller in winter. Many varieties of goldfish are exotic in shape and delicate in fin. They require extensive modification to make good netsuke. I brought the rear fins together for the *himotoshi*. The goldfish "stands" securely on its fins with head and tail above the ground.

SIGNED: Masatoshi.
MATERIAL: ivory.
EYES: black tortoise shell.
COLOR: incense smoke; *sumi*—markings.
COMPLETED: May 1965.

176 Prehistoric Fish
Kodai uo

A fossil I once saw illustrated was described as a prehistoric armored fish. I happened to have a section of whale-tooth on hand that was suitable for this prehistoric fish for the very reason that it was unsuitable for any other: it was covered with unsightly dentine flecks. These blemishes would blight the appearance of other subjects, but they enhanced the armor-plated unreality of this grotesque monster.

SIGNED: Tokisada.
MATERIAL: whale-tooth.
EYES: black coral.
COMPLETED: February 1962.
ILLUSTRATED: *Arts of Asia*, July/August 1973.

177 Flute-playing Sea Bream
Fuefuki-dai

One of the many varieties of sea bream (*tai*) is the *fuefuki-dai*, the "flute-playing sea bream." It gets its fanciful name from the position of its lips, pursed as though blowing out its breath. I carved it with a fox because, at the time, I thought there was a resemblance between the face of the fox and that of the fish. Now that I look at it again, I can't help thinking my notion was ridiculous!

I made the fox small to fit into a good netsuke shape and its fur smooth for contrast with the scaly skin of the fish. The separation of the fox's belly from the fish provides for the *himotoshi*.

SIGNED: Masatoshi.
MATERIAL: boxwood.
EYES OF FISH: black coral.
EYES OF FOX: carved.
COLOR: potassium permanganate.
COMPLETED: November 1965.

178 Octopus
Tako

I was amused by the idea of an octopus annoyed by a sea louse (*funamushi*) crawling on its head—like the priest disturbed in his meditations by a buzzing fly.

I inlaid the eyes in ivory and black coral and exaggerated their bulbous appearance. They look toward the sea louse and register annoyance at its intrusion.

SIGNED: Tokisada *tō*.
MATERIAL: boxwood.
EYES: ivory and black coral.
COLOR: potassium permanganate.
COMPLETED: August 1962.

181 Earthquake Fish
Namazu

The tortoise shell material for this version of the earthquake fish was much easier to obtain than the material for the netsuke illustrated in Plate 180. It was smaller and it was black, except for a mottled brown and yellow area on and around the tail. It was still necessary, however, to fuse manually several layers of tortoise shell in order to get the thickness I needed. Not that the problem was any different for carvers of the Edo Period who wished to make a carving in-the-round in tortoise shell.

SIGNED: Masatoshi *tō*.
MATERIAL: black tortoise shell.
COLOR: natural.
COMPLETED: September 1969.

179 Goby
Haze

I used to fish for goby in the Nakagawa, a river not far from my home. The real goby would look more like my model if it had a smooth skin, spread its fins out like fans, and appeared ready to make a speech. I exaggerated and distorted for amusement. The goby stands firmly on its fins.

SIGNED: Tokisada *koku*.
MATERIAL: ivory.
EYES: black coral.
COLOR: incense smoke; *sumi*—markings on fins.
COMPLETED: July 1962.

182 Sea Bream in Chrysanthemum Bowl
Kikubachi no tai

This sea bream lies in a chrysanthemum bowl (*kikubachi*) with sixteen stylized petals. I wouldn't have dared carve a chrysanthemum design of sixteen petals before the war. A chrysanthemum design of fourteen or eighteen petals was permissible, but sixteen was the imperial crest and was reserved for the imperial family.

I colored the bowl evenly with *yashadama*. A uniform shade was essential to convey the impression of a porcelain glaze.

SIGNED: Masatoshi *tō*.
MATERIAL: ivory.
EYE FOLLOWS.
COLOR: *yashadama*; *sumi*—scale markings.
COMPLETED: January 1966.

180 Earthquake Fish
Namazu

My main problem in producing this model was with the material. I needed a block of transparent tortoise shell, ten to twelve layers thick. The order taxed to the limit the resources and capabilities of the tortoise shell dealer. Reluctantly, he accepted the order because of his long friendship with me and my father. He faced a financial loss if his efforts failed.

What he had to do was fuse the layers with applications of heat and pressure. He fused twelve layers, and he managed to do it very neatly, except for a faint center line where heat and pressure were weaker. I thought it would polish out but a vestige remains. I paid him ¥35,000 (about $175). Transparent tortoise shell, which varies in both transparency and shade from shell to shell, is three or four times the cost of black tortoise shell. I have never seen a block of transparent tortoise shell of this thickness (see page 39).

SIGNED: Jikishiin Masatoshi *tō*.
MATERIAL: transparent tortoise shell.
COLOR: natural.
COMPLETED: May 1966.
ILLUSTRATED: *Collectors' Netsuke*, Figure 352.
SCALE: life size.

183 Five Eels
Go man

At the fish market a tangle of live eels writhing and coiling like snakes is a common sight. I composed a group of five eels into a compact netsuke, although the individual eels are separated. The tail of one of the eels provides place for the *himotoshi*.

SIGNED: Tokisada *tō*.
MATERIAL: ivory.
EYES: black tortoise shell.
COLOR: incense smoke; *sumi*—markings.
COMPLETED: January 1962.

184 Catfish and Gourd
Hyōtan namazu

A friend got me the material from a dealer, who said it was walrus tusk (*seiuchi no ha*). I myself cannot be absolutely certain, since the part I was given was only the top of the tusk. I would need a lower section, showing coloration, grain, and nerve channel, for positive identification. Although I cannot confirm identity of the material as walrus, I can, to some extent, confirm it negatively: it is not elephant, whale-tooth, hippopotamus, or narwhal, and it is too large for the tusk of a boar or the tooth of a tiger or bear. It accords with walrus in density and feel.

SIGNED: Masatoshi *tō*.
MATERIAL: walrus tusk.
EYES FOLLOW.
COLOR: incense smoke; *sumi*—fish markings.
COMPLETED: November 1964.
ILLUSTRATED: *Collectors' Netsuke*, Figure 347.

185 Catfish and Gourd
Hyōtan namazu

Catfish and gourd designs are countless. They represent futility—a wasted or ridiculous effort like trying to capture a catfish in a gourd. This treatment and that of catfish and gourd shown in Plate 184 are my own additions to the count. I regard this version as the more amusing and skillful but the previous one as its superior in simplicity and balance.

SIGNED: Masatoshi *tō*.
MATERIAL: ivory.
EYES FOLLOW.

COLOR: *yashadama*; *sumi*—armor plate, nostrils.
COMPLETED: May 1976.

186 "Ugly Fish" of Mushima
Mushima jorō

Mushima Jorō is illustrated in the *Minzokugaku zenshū*. The legend tells of the sacrifice of a girl from Mushima, an island in the Inland Sea, to pacify the seas when they were angry and nets were hauled in empty. In revenge for her cruel fate, she prayed to be transformed into an ugly fish, and her spiteful wish was granted. The "ugly fish" is found in the waters around Mushima.

SIGNED: Masatoshi *tō*.
INSCRIPTION: *Mushima jorō*.
MATERIAL: hippopotamus tooth.
EYES FOLLOW.
COLOR: incense smoke.
COMPLETED: May 1971.
SCALE: seven-eighths life size.

187 Blowfish
Fugu

I designed the blowfish as a pair and arranged them facing opposite one another and tail to belly for a protected model. They are frightened and bloated to the point of bursting.

I raised pimples, or nodules, to convey the leathery quality of the skin of the fish using the *ukibori* technique (see page 47). The pimples are smaller on the bellies of the fish and larger on their backs. I find few opportunities to utilize *ukibori*, and I prefer relief carving when there is a choice—for example, in inscribing my signature. A carved signature is more durable than one in *ukibori*. I discuss my one attempt at using the *ukibori* technique in ivory in the description of Plate 354.

SIGNED: Masatoshi *tō*.
MATERIAL: boxwood.
EYES: black coral.
COLOR: potassium permanganate; silver nitrate—back of one of the fish.
COMPLETED: March 1959.

188 Chinese Octagonal Bowl with Fish
Hakkaku shinabachi no kouo

I once saw an ingenious netsuke of a bowl of fish. It acted as a challenge, goading me into trying to produce something better. I carved a Ming bowl with a red glaze which I imitated in red lacquer. I carved thirty-four separate and distinct whitebait (*shirasu*) plus a crayfish (*zarigani*) and a sprig of bamboo leaves. Each little fish has inlaid eyes of tortoise shell. As black tortoise shell looks brown and lacks intensity in small specks, I put *sumi* at the bottom of each eye socket.

SIGNED: Shunzan, in an oval reserve.
MATERIAL: ivory.
EYES: black tortoise shell.
COLOR: *yashadama*; *sumi*—bamboo leaves; red lacquer—bowl, crayfish.
COMPLETED: February 1956.

189 Chinese Round Bowl with Fish
Shina marubachi ni kouo

I had two reasons for trying a second version of the subject. Firstly, the red lacquer on the base of the earlier bowl curled due to improper drying. And secondly, Mr. Bushell criticized the addition of the crayfish as an unnecessary embellishment, an excess decoration.

The treatments and techniques are identical in both versions. The second version has one more whitebait than the first.

SIGNED: Masatoshi, in an oval reserve.
MATERIAL: ivory.
EYES: black tortoise shell.
COLOR: *yashadama*; *sumi*—bamboo leaves; red lacquer—bowl.
COMPLETED: January 1957.
ILLUSTRATED: *Arts of Asia*, July/August 1973. Catalogue, Raymond Bushell Collection, Tokyo.

13. Lizards, Snakes, Bats, Owls

190 Gecko and Fly
Yamori to hae

I imagined a farm in the heat of summer. A fly alights on a straw sandal and a gecko silently glides toward it.

SIGNED: Masatoshi *tō*.
MATERIAL: ivory.
EYES FOLLOW.
COLOR: incense smoke; dust.
COMPLETED: February 1970.

191 Gecko with Young
Yamori no oyako

Mr. Bushell likes this netsuke, but I feel it is a little flat. The animal looks more like a crocodile than a gecko. If I were to carve it again, I would bring the legs closer together and heighten the lizard's stance.

The nodules on the lizard's back are carved in relief; they are not raised by *ukibori*.

SIGNED: Tokisada.
MATERIAL: boxwood.
EYES: black coral.
COLOR: natural except for faint *yashadama*.
COMPLETED: December 1961.
ILLUSTRATED: *Collectors' Netsuke*, Figure 348.
SCALE: life size.

192 Lizard and Fingered Citron
Tokage to bushukan

The lizard hunts for insects on a *bushukan* (fingered citron). I really don't know whether the *bushukan* is a likely fruit on which to find insects, but I am an admirer of Tomioka Tessai (1836–1924), who frequently included the *bushukan* in his paintings. So I thought I would include one in a carving.

SIGNED: Masatoshi *tō*.
MATERIAL: ivory.
EYES: black tortoise shell.
COLOR: natural except for faint *yashadama*.
COMPLETED: November 1955.

193 Lizard and Fingered Citron
Tokage to bushukan

I can't remember why I tried a second version of this subject, especially since the two are identical. In all probability I wanted to try the effect of deep color. I prefer the natural ivory of the first.

SIGNED: Masatoshi *tō*.
MATERIAL: ivory.
EYES: black tortoise shell.
COLOR: silver nitrate and incense smoke.
COMPLETED: October 1960.

194 Lizard and Fly
Tokage to hae

Before my house was enlarged, I had a small garden that was home for many lizards. The first time I ever tried to catch a lizard, I grabbed hold of its tail but was amazed to see the creature scurry away leaving its tail in my hand. But I needn't have worried—the lizard grows a replacement. I find these miniature dinosaurs fascinating.

I carved the lizard as it lies concealed in a rotted pumpkin waiting to ambush a fly.

SIGNED: Masatoshi.
MATERIAL: ivory.
EYES: *sumi*.
COLOR: incense smoke; *sumi*—scales, markings.
COMPLETED: January 1961.

195 Lizard and Ant
Tokage to ari

Stag-antler is a good material with which to represent a cucumber—the arena in this design for the lizard's pursuit of the ant. The texture and markings of stag-antler and cucumber bear certain similarities. I did not, however, make use of the natural nodules (*ibo*) of the antler, but carved each wart of the cucumber individually.

SIGNED: Masatoshi *tō*.
MATERIAL: stag-antler.
EYES: *sumi*.
COLOR: incense smoke.
COMPLETED: April 1977.
SCALE: nine-tenths life size.

196 Salamander
Sanshō-uo

I did a lot of experimenting with carving and materials in order to represent realistically the metallic quality of the salamander's hide. I carved each nodule or tubercle individually, and I colored and spotted with silver nitrate in various concentrations until I attained the effect I wanted.

SIGNED: Jikishiin Masatoshi *tō*.
MATERIAL: whale-tooth.
EYES: black tortoise shell.
COLOR: incense smoke and silver nitrate.
COMPLETED: January 1970.
ILLUSTRATED: *Arts of Asia*, July/August 1973.

197 The Sparrows' Dwelling
Suzume no oyado

At Nikkō, bird lovers cut windows in gourds and hang them in their gardens so that sparrows can nest in them. A local train station is even named Suzume no Miya (Sparrows' Shrine). Out of sympathy for the bird-loving spirit of the area, I carved a lizard feeding worms to hungry nestlings.

SIGNED: Jikishiin Masatoshi *tō*.
MATERIAL: hippopotamus tooth.
EYES: *sumi*.
COLOR: incense smoke; *sumi*—cords.
COMPLETED: July 1968.

198 Gecko on a Branch
Ki no ue no yamori

The gecko is motionless but vigilant as he stalks an insect. The segments around his mouth are natural markings; they are not teeth. His eyes follow, but the movement lacks clarity due to some opaqueness in the transparent tortoise shell. The gecko colored deeply, as I roughened his hide considerably before applying incense smoke.

SIGNED: Masatoshi.
MATERIAL: ivory.
EYES FOLLOW.
COLOR: incense smoke; dust.
COMPLETED: May 1967.

199 Two Snakes
Nihiki no hebi

Although the mouth of one snake is open and that of the other closed, I did not conceive of them as a complementary pair representing the duality of nature—like the Niō standing guard at temple gates—but rather as two males moving in deadly opposition.

I carved the coils distinctly and separately but close enough to maintain compactness.

SIGNED: Masatoshi *tō*.
MATERIAL: ivory.
EYES FOLLOW.
COLOR: incense smoke; dust.
COMPLETED: September 1964.

200 Bat
Kōmori

Bats are weird and fascinating, and I have designed many models. For this one I used Chinese rosewood, which is closely related to red sandalwood in carving characteristics and texture (see page 39). In comparison with boxwood or ebony, it is coarse grained and soft and is therefore suitable for larger forms but not for details. The unusual coloration of rosewood enhanced the attractiveness of this model.

I inlaid the bat's eyes in black tortoise shell placed low in its head to accord with the bat's natural anatomy.

SIGNED: Masatoshi *tō*.
MATERIAL: rosewood.
EYES: black tortoise shell.
COLOR: natural.
COMPLETED: July 1963.
ILLUSTRATED: *Collectors' Netsuke*, Figure 350.
Horizon, Autumn 1965.

201 Sleeping Bat
Nemuri kōmori

The bat sleeps hanging head down—strange behavior is quite normal for this abnormal creature. To portray the bat, I used lignum vitae (*yusōboku*), a wood every bit as peculiar as the bat itself. The wood's natural streaks of light brown and yellowish brown seemed appropriate for a bat in moonlight. Lignum vitae is very dense and heavy. It remains oily and moist to the touch, no matter how carefully it is seasoned and dried. The dust is sticky and adhesive. It constantly clogs the teeth of saws and files and quickly coats sandpaper. Tools require frequent cleaning and sharpening, and sandpaper replenishing. Progress is slowed. The material is responsive but it is unsuitable for embellishments. (See Plate 298 for another example of lignum vitae.)

SIGNED: Tokisada *tō*.
MATERIAL: lignum vitae.
EYES: carved.
COLOR: natural.
COMPLETED: April 1965.

202 "Chrysanthemum-head Bat"
Kikugashira-kōmori

The "chrysanthemum-head bat" is so grotesque that I found the most effective way to portray it was to remain completely true to nature. It was named for its nostrils and nose, which flare and flower like the chrysanthemum. It has, besides, a protuberance like a horn above its nose and a stubby tail. Its ears are segmented like the legs of a centipede. A grinning maw and sharp teeth complete the nightmare.

I balanced the piece so it stands upright without compromising the design.

SIGNED: Masatoshi, in a smooth reserve.
MATERIAL: ebony.
EYES: carved.
COLOR: natural.
COMPLETED: July 1973.

203 Bat and Two Young
Kōmori to nihiki no kodomo

I carved this bat family from my imagination. I have no idea whether a mother bat actually cuddles her babies in this manner, and I don't know what the species of bat may be or how it accords with nature. I am content in my unscientific ignorance. The model satisfies me if it is a good netsuke. And this is my main concern, that the design be right for a netsuke, not that it be scrupulously loyal to nature.

SIGNED: Masatoshi *tō*.
MATERIAL: boxwood.
EYES: black tortoise shell.
COLOR: natural except for faint *yashadama*.
COMPLETED: January 1968.

204 Bat with Young
Kōmori no oyako

I tried to convey the same feeling of love and trust between mother bat and baby that is experienced by a human mother and child.

SIGNED: Masatoshi, in a smooth reserve.
MATERIAL: boxwood.
EYES: black tortoise shell.
COLOR: potassium permanganate.
COMPLETED: August 1968.
ILLUSTRATED: *Arts of Asia*, July/August 1973.

205a, 205b Flying Bat
Hiyō kōmori

The bat flies swiftly in irregular, darting motions, and the light is usually dim so that it is difficult to observe the position of head and legs and the extension of wings. A realistic rendering, however, might not have made a good netsuke. My design is principally a product of my imagination.

I balanced the bat so that it rests securely on its belly, with head and wings above the ground as though flying.

SIGNED: Masatoshi *tō*.
MATERIAL: ebony.
EYES: carved.
COLOR: natural.
COMPLETED: January 1976.

206 Dual Bats
Kōmori nihiki

I paired these bats to represent the duality of nature, like the Niō, who guard temples, and the *shishi* that stand guard at shrines. One bat has a slightly larger head, an open mouth, and eyes inlaid in black tortoise shell. He is the male. The other has a smaller head, a closed mouth, and carved eyes. She is the female.

SIGNED: Masatoshi.
MATERIAL: black persimmon.
EYES OF MALE: black tortoise shell.
EYES OF FEMALE: carved.
COLOR: natural.
COMPLETED: January 1961.

207 Bat with Young
Kōmori no oyako

This species of bat has a fierce head with predatory

jaws and teeth. The mother shields her young within the protective barricade of her wings.

SIGNED: Masatoshi.
MATERIAL: ebony.
EYES: carved.
COLOR: natural.
COMPLETED: September 1979.

208 Owl
Fukurō

My inspiration was a comical, old netsuke I once saw. I designed my owl as a caricature and tried to give it the character of a cartoon. I selected red sandalwood with a heavy porous grain as best suited for this treatment.

SIGNED: Masatoshi *tō*.
MATERIAL: red sandalwood.
EYES: carved.
COLOR: natural.
COMPLETED: December 1967.

209 Manjū Owl
Fukurō manjū

This carving can be classified as a *manjū* even though I made it more spherical in shape and less flat than the usual *manjū* (see Plates 51 and 61 and Diagram D on page 64). The effect is more that of a carving in-the-round and less that of a relief carving. As a further modification of the conventional *manjū* form, I modeled the talons so that the owl stands upright on them. The round shape symbolizes the full moon.

SIGNED: Masatoshi.
MATERIAL: boxwood.
EYES: carved.
COLOR: potassium permanganate.
COMPLETED: July 1961.

210 Owl
Fukurō

A dealer from whom I sometimes buy material found in his storeroom an extraordinarily large stag-antler that had been cut and forgotten more than a generation ago. The material carved like wood and was exceptionally large and solid with a natural two-tone gray coloration. I doubt that it is from our native deer. I cut a block so that the wing sides of the owl would be smooth and light gray, the front and back pitted and dark gray.

SIGNED: Masatoshi *tō*.
MATERIAL: stag-antler.
EYES FOLLOW.
COLOR: natural.
COMPLETED: May 1979.
ILLUSTRATED: Catalogue, Raymond Bushell Collection, Tokyo.

211 Owl
Fukurō

I carved this owl in response to a suggestion from Mr. Bushell that I duplicate an owl in stag-antler attributed to Kokusai.

SIGNED: Masatoshi.
MATERIAL: stag-antler.
EYES: black coral.
COLOR: *yashadama*.
COMPLETED: June 1980.

14. Objects

212 Smudge Pot
Kayari

The original is a popular pottery pig for burning incense to repel insects. The pottery was produced at the Imado kiln on the banks of the Sumida River in Tokyo. The rotund shape of the pig accommodated coiled incense of a standard size. The pottery pig is suggestive of summer, insects, and incense.

The poem inscribed on the pig is a *haiku*: "Although smoky, we sleep comfortably." It was composed by Kaga no Chiyō, a woman poet.

SIGNED: Masatoshi *koku*.
MATERIAL: water buffalo horn; ivory—handle.
COLOR: natural.
COMPLETED: June 1955.

213 Vase with Duck Handles
Ahiru no totte tsuki kabin

I saw this vase in a magazine on ancient Egyptian art. In spite of my design modifications, the subject remains a vase. The feeling that the piece imparts is more that of a foreign vase than a Japanese one and more an *okimono* than a netsuke.

SIGNED: Shunzan *tō*.
MATERIAL: ivory.
EYES: black tortoise shell.
COLOR: incense smoke.
COMPLETED: October 1956.

214 Ming Vase
Min no kabin

The original is a Ming Dynasty porcelain vase. The design is secure and functional, but like the vase in Plate 213 it is an ornamental vase and the lingering

impression it gives is that of an *okimono*. I formed the *himotoshi* by separating the dragon's tail from the body of the vase.

SIGNED: Masatoshi *tō*.
MATERIAL: ivory.
EYES: carved.
COLOR: incense smoke.
COMPLETED: April 1955.

215 Burial Figurine of Woman
Haniwa no onna

Stag-antler is a good material for simulating the crude clay of *haniwa* (burial figurines). It has the advantage over teak, the material I used for the two following versions, of permitting the representation of details like the buttons on the woman's robe.

Haniwa figures that accompanied our remote royalty to their graves are common exhibits in museums.

SIGNED: Jikishiin Masatoshi, with *kakihan*.
MATERIAL: stag-antler.
EYES: carved.
COLOR: incense smoke.
COMPLETED: April 1969.

216 Burial Figurine with Comb in Hair
Kushi o sashita onna

I selected teak as a good medium for simulating the rough red clay of *haniwa*. Teak is coarse and porous. It is satisfactory for carving large features but not for small details. In this respect its carving characteristics are similar to red sandalwood and rosewood (page 39 and Plates 200 and 208).

The projection of breasts beneath her dress is marked and indicates the potter's interest in the beauty of women.

SIGNED: Tokisada *tō*.
MATERIAL: teak.
EYES: carved.
COLOR: natural.
COMPLETED: February 1962.

217 Burial Figurine of Warrior
Haniwa no yūshi

The more I studied *haniwa* as models for my netsuke, the more I appreciated their subtle sophistication and the difficulty of conveying the simple charm of the originals.

SIGNED: Tokisada *tō*.
MATERIAL: teak.
EYES: carved.
COLOR: natural.
COMPLETED: February 1962.
SCALE: seven-eighths life size.

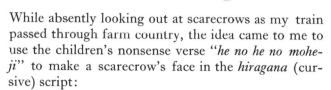

219 Scarecrow
Kakashi

While absently looking out at scarecrows as my train passed through farm country, the idea came to me to use the children's nonsense verse "*he no he no mohe-ji*" to make a scarecrow's face in the *hiragana* (cursive) script:

he he	eyebrows
no no	eyes
mo	nose
he	mouth
ji	face

I clothed the scarecrow in a rough coat, a hood towel (*hōkaburi*), and a woven hat.

SIGNED: Tokisada *tō*.
MATERIAL: ivory and teak.
EYES: carved.
COLOR: ivory—incense smoke.
      teak—potassium permanganate.
COMPLETED: May 1962.
ILLUSTRATED: *Collectors' Netsuke*, Figure 342.
SCALE: life size.

218 Naked Burial Figurine
Hadaka no onna

Of the thousands of *haniwa* that have been excavated all were clothed except for this one. It is the only known example of the representation of a woman's private parts on a *haniwa*.

The material is a rare white ivory almost free of grain. It looks like pure marble. I used no stain whatsoever. Rather than spoil her flawless back with holes I used her elbow for the *himotoshi*, and for proper balance, I turned her head in the direction away from her bent elbow.

SIGNED: Masatoshi *tō*.
INSCRIPTIONS: *Yashū shutsudo* (excavated in Ya Province, i.e., Tochigi Prefecture); *hoto no shoken* (first time women's private parts exposed).
MATERIAL: ivory.
EYES: carved.
COLOR: natural.
COMPLETED: November 1979.

220 Melting Deer
Shika nomerikomi

The original was carved in stag-antler. The idea of carving a stag subject out of stag material is a compelling one. I decided however on ivory—a more tractable medium for representing the subtle melt of the stag's neck and legs into the handle of the seal.

SIGNED: Masatoshi *sha*.
MATERIAL: ivory.
EYES: carved.
COLOR: incense smoke.
COMPLETED: November 1958.

15. Subjects from Ukiyo-e

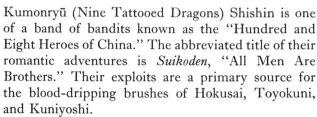

221 Carpenter
Daiku

A popular theme of *ukiyo-e* artists was the various artisans at their occupations: carpenter, swordsmith, lacquerer, weaver, the makers of hats, paper, cords, umbrellas, fans, mats, and a hundred other things.

The carpenter squints at the cutting edge of his plane to make sure it is level. He wears a short jacket, the *shirikire-hanten* (hip-cut coat), now known as *happi-kōto* (happy coat). He uses the towel on his shoulder for wiping perspiration.

If I were to repeat the subject today, I would try to make it more compact.

SIGNED: Masatoshi, in red in an oval reserve.
MATERIAL: ivory.
COLOR: *yashadama*; *sumi*—hair, eyebrows, eyes, shirt, towel pattern, tobacco pouch, hammer head.
COMPLETED: April 1952.

223 Kumonryū Shishin

Kumonryū (Nine Tattooed Dragons) Shishin is one of a band of bandits known as the "Hundred and Eight Heroes of China." The abbreviated title of their romantic adventures is *Suikoden*, "All Men Are Brothers." Their exploits are a primary source for the blood-dripping brushes of Hokusai, Toyokuni, and Kuniyoshi.

Kumonryū is identified by his tattoo of nine dragons. I carved him grimacing with satisfaction as he scratches his itch with a priest's scepter that he appropriated from a temple.

SIGNED: Masatoshi, in red in an oval reserve.
MATERIAL: ivory.
COLOR: *yashadama*; *sumi*—hair, eyebrows, eyes, tattoo, trouser pattern; gold *nikawa*—scepter.
COMPLETED: April 1953.
ILLUSTRATED: *Arts of Asia*, July/August 1973.

222 Sharaku Print
Sharaku ukiyo-e

Sharaku's representation of the actor Ichikawa Komazō III in the part of Sagami no Jirō is a stunning masterpiece. I used the print for my model, modifying and contracting costume and pose as required for a netsuke. Contemporary reports say that the actor's nose was misshapen, but I carved it long and large. The character on the actor's sleeve is the "*ji*" of Jirō.

SIGNED: Masatoshi.
MATERIAL: ivory.
COLOR: *yashadama*; *sumi*—hair, eyebrows, eyes, armguards, legging, kimono stripes.
COMPLETED: March 1972.

224 Boyasha Sonjirō

Two of the bandits among the "Hundred and Eight Heroes of China" are women, one of whom is Boyasha Sonjirō (see description of Plate 223). Among her Amazonian exploits is the decapitation of an antagonist who enraged her with his lustful and contemptuous attitude. Even in death, however, he continues to exhibit an expression of lewd derision.

SIGNED: Masatoshi, in a smooth reserve.
MATERIAL: ivory.
COLOR: *yashadama*; *sumi*—hair, eyes, eyebrows, beard, kimono patterns; red *nikawa*—lips; gold *nikawa*—hair ornament.
COMPLETED: October 1954.
ILLUSTRATED: *Arts of Asia*, July/August 1973.

225 Protruding Navel
Debeso

The subject is imaginary but my treatment is in genre style. The man is a workman drunk with *sake*. His wife's navel is oversized and protruding (*debeso*) and he determines to tear out the eyesore. He strains every muscle, while she screams with anguish.

SIGNED: Masatoshi.
MATERIAL: ivory.
COLOR: *yashadama*; *sumi*—hair, eyebrows, eyes, short coat.
COMPLETED: January 1971.
ILLUSTRATED: *Arts of Asia*, July/August 1973.

226 Picture of a Beautiful Woman
Bijin-ga

Beautiful women (*bijin*), especially geisha, were a popular theme of *ukiyo-e* artists. I carved a beautiful geisha enjoying the cool after her bath.

The design on her kimono is an all-over fan pattern (*ōmen-moyō*), and the design on her fan the autumn moon and chrysanthemums. In one of the fan-shaped outlines, I carved a group of radishes and signed my name in *sumi* as though I were the artist who painted the picture.

SIGNED: Masatoshi *tō*.
MATERIAL: ivory.
COLOR: *yashadama*; *sumi*—hair, eyebrows, eyes, kimono patterns.
COMPLETED: June 1953.
ILLUSTRATED: *Collectors' Netsuke*, Figure 343.

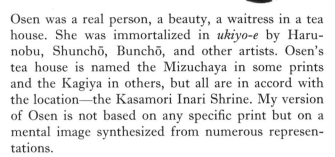

227 Osen

Osen was a real person, a beauty, a waitress in a tea house. She was immortalized in *ukiyo-e* by Haru-nobu, Shunchō, Bunchō, and other artists. Osen's tea house is named the Mizuchaya in some prints and the Kagiya in others, but all are in accord with the location—the Kasamori Inari Shrine. My version of Osen is not based on any specific print but on a mental image synthesized from numerous representations.

SIGNED: Masatoshi *tō*.
MATERIAL: ivory.
COLOR: *yashadama*; *sumi*—hair, eyebrows, eyes, kimono pattern, clogs; red *nikawa*—lips; gold *nikawa*—serving cloth.
COMPLETED: December 1953.

228 The Bath
Yuami

The mother prepares to enter the bath with her child. Her hair is meticulously arranged in the style of a married woman, a style known as *marumage*. She is the wife of a rich merchant. Her skin is as soft and white as a rice cake. The mother is beautiful and intelligent, but the child has the appearance of an ugly simpleton (*nōtarin*). I wanted to convey the idea that the boy resembles his father in ugliness and stupidity.

A woman's hair stylishly arranged and decorated was her crown. As soap was unknown in the Edo Period, women bathed in water which had been used for washing rice and which generated enough lather for shampooing. Only wealthy women could afford the luxury of fastidiously maintaining their coiffures.

I arranged the *himotoshi* around the mother's arm. It is not the ideal place, but I did not want to puncture her long graceful back.

SIGNED: Masatoshi *tō*.
MATERIAL: ivory.
COLOR: *yashadama*; *sumi*—hair, eyebrows, eyes, towel pattern; red *nikawa*—lips; gold *nikawa*—hair ornament.
COMPLETED: March 1977.
SCALE: seven-eighths life size.

229 Mother and Child
Haha to ko

My design here represents an ordinary scene between a mother and her child. The mother washes her feet in a metal tub (*kanadarai*), while the boy offers her a cake but hides the one he prefers behind his back. He wears a bib (*haragake*) designed to keep his stomach warm—the stomach was considered the most vulnerable of a child's organs. His hair is in the typical style for boys of the Edo Period. The character on the bib is "*kin*" standing for Kintarō, the name of a fairy tale hero.

SIGNED: Masatoshi *tō*.
MATERIAL: ivory.
COLOR: *yashadama*; *sumi*—hair, eyebrows, eyes, bib; red *nikawa*—lips.
COMPLETED: September 1953.

230 Hair Combing
Kami-suki

The woman combs her hair after finishing her bath and plays with her cat. The woman I had in mind is neither geisha nor housewife. She is—as I picture her—unmarried and independent, a teacher of music or calligraphy. She keeps a cat as a pet to avoid loneliness. The pattern on her kimono is bamboo, pine, and plum (*shōchikubai*).

SIGNED: Masatoshi, in red in an oval reserve.
MATERIAL: ivory.
COLOR: *yashadama*; *sumi*—hair, eyebrows, eyes, kimono pattern; red *nikawa*—lips.
COMPLETED: February 1952.

16. Legends and Myths

231 Sea God Race
Kaijin-zoku

There is an old legend that a race of sea gods was born from salt water. They spent their lives in the ocean, always laughing and happy. I carved one in the way I imagine a sea god might appear. He holds in his hands a lotus, the emblem of Buddha. I chose two-tone greenish rhinoceros horn (*saikaku*) as the most suitable material for representing a creature made from the sea.

SIGNED: Masatoshi *tō*.
INSCRIPTIONS: *kaijin-zoku*; *saikaku*.
MATERIAL: rhinoceros horn.
EYES: carved.
COLOR: natural.
COMPLETED: August 1978.

232 Headstone of Masakado
Masakado no kubizuka

Masakado of the Taira clan revolted against the emperor in A.D. 935. Hidesato, a deadly archer, engaged Masakado in battle. To thwart his enemy, Masakado dressed up several of his retainers to resemble himself. Hidesato was forced to shoot three of the doubles before downing the true Masakado and identifying his head. As though to continue the deception after death, there are numerous sites which are supposed to mark the place where Masakado's head is buried. There is even one in Ōtemachi in the center of Tokyo.

I carved the character "*masa*" standing for Masakado on the headstone.

SIGNED: Masatoshi *tō*.

MATERIAL: ivory.
EYES: black tortoise shell.
COLOR: *yashadama*; *sumi*—hair, eyebrows, mustache, markings; red *nikawa*—head wound.
COMPLETED: November 1974.

233 Peeping Tom
Shōkera

When I was a child a Peeping Tom was arrested for obscenity. He was called "Debagame" because of his protruding teeth, and his abnormal behavior was described in the newspapers in lurid terms.

The *shōkera* is a legendary Peeping Tom. Old houses have skylights, through which the *shōkera* watched when women bathed. *Shōkera* are illustrated in many books about apparitions and ghosts.

SIGNED: Masatoshi, in a raised oval reserve.
MATERIAL: ebony.
EYES: carved.
COLOR: natural.
COMPLETED: January 1979.

234 "Temple-pecker"
Tera-tsutsuki

The *tera-tsutsuki* is a legendary bird equipped with a huge bill, which it uses to peck away at the pillars and beams of old temples causing them to collapse. Should anyone try to capture the *tera-tsutsuki*, it will fly to the would-be captor's home and rip it to pieces.

SIGNED: Masatoshi.
MATERIAL: ivory.
EYES: black coral.
COLOR: gamboge; *sumi*—hair, eyebrows, feathers.
COMPLETED: December 1978.

235 Old Woman of Flames
Ubagabi

In the old days, old women were often carried away to the mountains by their families and left to die.

The custom was known as "*uba-sute-yama*," old women abandoned in the mountains. The heartlessness was justified by the need to conserve food for the young, while the aged—usually, but not always—stoically accepted the custom when their time came. Occasionally an old woman would protest her abandonment and fly into a hysterical rage. Women who reacted like this were called "*ubagabi*," old women of flames. I carved the spirit of an *ubagabi* flying through the clouds, enveloped in flames, and shrieking in anger.

SIGNED: Masatoshi *tō*.
INSCRIPTION: *ubagabi*.
MATERIAL: ivory.
EYES: black coral.
COLOR: incense smoke.
COMPLETED: January 1979.

236 Issun Bōshi

Issun Bōshi (One-Inch Priest) is the Japanese Tom Thumb. He set out for Kyoto to seek his fortune using a wooden soup bowl as a boat, a chopstick for his oar, and a needle as a sword. The magic hammer incised on the bowl represents his transformation into a handsome samurai.

In this case the material determined the subject. I had a remnant from some ivory of excellent quality that was too small for a regular-sized netsuke. Issun Bōshi was the result.

SIGNED: Masatoshi *tō*.
MATERIAL: ivory.
EYES: carved.
COLOR: *yashadama*; *sumi*—hair, eyebrows, eyes; red *nikawa*—lips.
COMPLETED: February 1955.
ILLUSTRATED: *Netsuke Familiar and Unfamiliar*, Figure 428.
Catalogue, Raymond Bushell Collection, Tokyo.

237 Kashima Myōjin

The earthquake fish lives in the mud at the bottom of rivers. When it flexes its long feelers, the earth trembles, and when it swings its powerful tail, the earth quakes.

There is a boulder set in the earth near the Kashima Shrine in Ibaraki Prefecture. The legend is that it weighs down an earthquake fish, preventing it from wriggling its tail, and that it is Kashima Myōjin who protects the neighborhood from disastrous quakes by keeping the stone in place. I engraved the character for *"kaname,"* as the stone is known as "Kaname Ishi" (Pivot Stone).

SIGNED: Masatoshi *tō.*
INSCRIPTION: *Kashima Myōjin.*
MATERIAL: ivory.
EYES OF GOD: carved.
EYES OF FISH: black coral.
COLOR: incense smoke; *sumi*—hair, eyebrows, markings.
COMPLETED: February 1973.

238 "Tongue-cut Sparrow"
Shitakiri suzume

The fable of *Shitakiri suzume* (Tongue-cut Sparrow) is one of our five great nursery tales. There are many versions and incidents in the story. I carved the sparrow as he carries the greedy old woman to his home in the forest. I copied the design of a netsuke by Hidemasa, though I used ivory in preference to wood, altered details, and inlaid eyes that follow.

SIGNED: Masatoshi *sha.*
INSCRIPTION: *Hidemasa netsuke yori* (from a Hidemasa netsuke).
MATERIAL: ivory.
EYES FOLLOW.
COLOR: incense smoke; *sumi*—hair, feathers, kimono.
COMPLETED: August 1972.

239 Fox Wife
Kitsune no nyōbō

The creature that is a gentle housewife by day and a wild fox by night is a popular figure in Japanese folklore. I intended my carving to be a travesty of the normal treatment of the subject, which emphasizes the tenderness of the fox wife and the innocence of the infant. The mother is a mean, cruel vixen and the infant, with enlarged head and adult features, more like a grotesque dwarf than a babe in arms. A friend said that it looks like Fukusuke, a dwarf with a swollen head who was famous as a storyteller. If so, the resemblance is unintentional.

The pattern on the fox's kimono is the blue sea wave (*seikaiha*); that on her head covering, the pine, bamboo, and plum (*shōchikubai*); and on the infant's kimono, the hemp leaf (*asa no ha*).

SIGNED: Masatoshi *tō.*
MATERIAL: ivory.
EYES: carved.
COLOR: incense smoke; *sumi*—fox's face, kimono, towel patterns.
COMPLETED: October 1963.

240 Mermaid and Young
Ningyo to kodomo

The mermaid nurses her baby. The infant suckles one breast as he fondles the other. The fondling is instinctive. We say that the baby is afraid that the other breast will be stolen.

SIGNED: Masatoshi.
MATERIAL: ivory.
EYES: carved.
COLOR: incense smoke; *sumi*—hair, eyes, fins.
COMPLETED: April 1963.
ILLUSTRATED: *Introduction to Netsuke,* Plate 30.

241 Mermaid and Flathead
Ningyo to kochi

The mermaid frolics with her pet, a flathead.

SIGNED: Masatoshi *tō.*
MATERIAL: ivory.
EYES: carved.
COLOR: incense smoke; *sumi*—hair, eyebrows, eyes, scales, markings.
COMPLETED: July 1968.

242 Merman
Sekiju

Creatures half human half fish are generally mermaids. But where there are mermaids, there must be mermen. One species of merman, called a *sekiju*, is illustrated in the *Sankaikyō*. I carved the arms of the unfortunate merman too short to scratch the itch on his face. He twists his mouth in discomfort and frustration.

SIGNED: Masatoshi *tō*.
INSCRIPTION: *sekiju*.
MATERIAL: ivory.
EYES: black coral.
COLOR: incense smoke; *sumi*—eyebrows, hair, scales.
COMPLETED: May 1977.

243 Merman
Ningyo

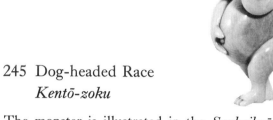

The *Minzokugaku zenshū* quotes from a biography of Prince Shōtoku found in the *Nihongi* ("Chronicles of Japan"): "A merman appeared in the Third Month of the twenty-seventh year of Suiko [A.D. 619] in the Gamo River in Omi [Shiga Prefecture]. The prince's followers presented it for his inspection." A drawing, which gave me the idea for my design, accompanies the account quoted in the *Minzokugaku zenshū*.

SIGNED: Masatoshi *tō*.
INSCRIPTION: *Ōmi Gamogawa ningyo*.
MATERIAL: ivory.
EYES: black tortoise shell.
COLOR: *yashadama*; *sumi*—hair, eyebrows.
COMPLETED: July 1975.
ILLUSTRATED: Catalogue, Raymond Bushell Collection, Tokyo.

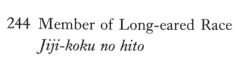

244 Member of Long-eared Race
Jiji-koku no hito

Like the long-legged (*ashinaga*) and long-armed (*tenaga*) races, the long-eared people originated in China. They had to carry their ears when they walked and they used them as mufflers and pillows. The folklore books say nothing about the acuteness of their hearing. I wonder whether our ancestors believed in the existence of these weird tribes? Maybe these old picture books were like the cartoon strips of today.

SIGNED: Masatoshi *tō*.
MATERIAL: boxwood.
EYES: carved.
COLOR: natural except for faint gamboge.
COMPLETED: March 1978.

245 Dog-headed Race
Kentō-zoku

The monster is illustrated in the *Sankaikyō*, where he is described as a member of the dog-headed race. I carved the figure in a previous version that included a baby dog-head. I consider the earlier version the better one. Simplifying a design does not necessarily improve it.

SIGNED: Masatoshi.
MATERIAL: ivory.
EYES: black tortoise shell.
COLOR: incense smoke.
COMPLETED: March 1975.

246 *Waira*

The *waira* is a ferocious beast found in rural areas. It lurks in distant neighborhoods and on remote roads and preys on unruly children. Each of its paws has a single nail like a dagger. I found only one reference to the *waira* in books on folklore, and that was in a book called *Japanese Grotesqueries*.

SIGNED: Masatoshi *tō*.
INSCRIPTION: *waira*.
MATERIAL: boxwood.
EYES: black coral.
COLOR: potassium permanganate.
COMPLETED: April 1978.

247 Kikujidō

Kikujidō (Chrysanthemum Boy) was an attendant on the emperor of China, until one day he unintentionally touched with his foot the cushion on which the emperor was resting; for this "crime" he was sentenced to exile. Kikujidō spent his days writing aphorisms on chrysanthemum leaves, which he then sent floating downriver. These leaves conferred magical benefits on those who found them. I wonder whether the legend accounts for the belief of some people that chrysanthemum leaves have medicinal value. We eat them cooked in various ways.

I carved Kikujidō sitting on a giant chrysanthemum as he writes on a leaf.

SIGNED: Masatoshi *tō*.
MATERIAL: ivory.
EYES: carved.
COLOR: *yashadama*; *sumi*—hair, eyebrows, eyes, brush tip, kimono pattern; red *nikawa*—lips; gold *nikawa*—*inrō* and netsuke.
COMPLETED: March 1957.

248 Net Ripper
Amikiri

In the Edo Period, during the summer heat, people usually slept under mosquito nets. Tears in the netting that occurred mysteriously during the night were blamed on the *amikiri*. The *amikiri* was a flying creature with clipping claws and a tearing beak. It flew about at night shredding mosquito netting.

I designed the *amikiri* grasping a treasure ball (*hōshu*), a device to prevent the claws from becoming hooks or brittle appendages.

SIGNED: Masatoshi *tō*.
MATERIAL: boxwood.
EYES: black coral.
COLOR: *sumi* wash; gold *nikawa*—circle on treasure ball.
COMPLETED: May 1971.

249 Net Ripper
Amikiri

I was not satisfied with the way the *amikiri* illustrated in Plate 248 polished, nor with the effect of a *sumi*

wash on its color. I decided to carve it again using ivory instead of boxwood. Usually it is my first of two efforts that I prefer, but in this case it is the second.

SIGNED: Masatoshi *tō*.
MATERIAL: ivory.
EYES: black coral.
COLOR: gamboge; gold *nikawa*—ring on treasure ball.
COMPLETED: April 1978.

250 Songokū

The adventures of Songokū, the monkey, and Sanzō Hōshi, the priest, as recounted in the famous book *Saiyūki* ("Monkey") read like fairy tales, but they are often allegorical or satirical in nature. Songokū was boastful of his feats and accomplishments. He wrote a poem on an enormous column: "O Heaven, the great one is here to amuse himself for a while." He learns that the column he wrote on is a finger of Buddha and that his travels of thousands of miles have not covered Buddha's hand. He is chastened to realize that he cannot escape the power of Buddha.

SIGNED: Masatoshi *tō*.
INSCRIPTION: *Seiten taisei koko ni itarite ichiyūsu* (O Heaven, the great one is here to amuse himself for a while).
MATERIAL: ivory.
EYES: carved.
COLOR: *yashadama*; *sumi*—hair, stockings, markings; black lacquer—inscription.
COMPLETED: February 1966.
ILLUSTRATED: *Collectors' Netsuke*, Figure 351.
Orientations, October 1970.

251a, 251b Spider and Kojorō
Kojorō-gumo

The story is told of Dazai Shobu Tsunefusa, a daimyō who ransomed a courtesan called Hakata Kojorō. She was on her way to join him in his castle when a huge "earth spider" (*tsuchigumo*) attacked and ate her whole.

I represented the spider with all that remains of Hakata Kojorō: her beautiful face, hair, and head.

SIGNED: Masatoshi *tō*.
MATERIAL: ebony.
EYES: carved.
COLOR: natural.
COMPLETED: June 1971.

252 Shirafuji Genta and Water Sprite
Shirafuji Genta to kappa

Shirafuji Genta, a samurai of enormous strength, is credited with the capture of a *kappa*, the only instance recorded. I represented Genta holding the *kappa* by the scruff of his neck while the *kappa* begs him frantically to spare his life. The large character on the back of Genta's kimono is the *"gen"* of Genta.

SIGNED: Masatoshi *tō*.
MATERIAL: ivory.
EYES: carved.
COLOR: *yashadama*; *sumi*—hair, eyebrows, pupils, *kappa* markings, *obi*, kimono pattern; silver nitrate —sword scabbard.
COMPLETED: May 1974.

253 The Long-Sleeve Fire
Furisode kaji

The Furisode (Long-Sleeve) Fire of 1657 destroyed the city of Edo (modern Tokyo) and burned to death more than 100,000 people. A legend grew to explain the fire. A girl of sixteen went with her mother to worship at the Honmyōji temple. The girl fell madly in love with a young priest and persuaded her mother to make her a kimono of the same pattern as his. When the priest rejected her love, she died of heartbreak. Thereafter, every girl who wore the ill-fated kimono died tragically within the year. Finally the

chief abbot of the temple declared the kimono cursed and ordered it to be burned. The *furisode* (long sleeves) were set aflame but were not consumed. A strange wind carried them here and there, starting fires that merged into the immense conflagration known as the Furisode Fire.

I combined the elements of the legend in my design: the head of the priest, the long-sleeve kimono carried on the wind, and the unquenchable flames.

SIGNED: Masatoshi.
MATERIAL: ivory.
COLOR: *yashadama*; *sumi*—eyebrows, pupils, *obi* patterns.
COMPLETED: March 1955.

17. Animals

254 Rabbit
Usagi

The idea for this unusual rabbit came from an old ivory incense box (*kōgō*). I say "idea" because, by the time I have modified the design for a netsuke and treated it in my own way, all that remains of the model from which I copied is the idea. Many of my ideas come from old paintings and sculptures.

SIGNED: Masatoshi *tō*.
EYES FOLLOW.
MATERIAL: ivory.
COLOR: incense smoke.
COMPLETED: December 1977.
ILLUSTRATED: Catalogue, Raymond Bushell Collection, Tokyo.

255 Fighting Rabbits
Usagi no kassen

The idea of rabbits fighting and biting one another like dogs or cats appealed to me for its absurdity. I composed the model so that one rabbit is gnawing his antagonist's ear while the other bites his paw. The *himotoshi* are formed by the separation of paw and body.

SIGNED: Masatoshi *tō*.
MATERIAL: ivory.
EYES FOLLOW.
COLOR: incense smoke.
COMPLETED: September 1964.

256 Stone Monkey
Ishi-zaru

The idea for this netsuke came from a catalogue devoted to stone sculpture. The design was as compact as imagination could conceive, and almost no modification was necessary in order to transform it into a netsuke. My problem was one of technique: how to preserve the original's monolithic character, and its quality of stone. I obtained the effect of stone (*ishime*) by stippling and flecking the surface (see page 46).

In order to avoid marring the uniformity of the texture, I carved my signature inside the larger of the *himotoshi*.

SIGNED: Masatoshi.
MATERIAL: ivory.
EYES: carved.
COLOR: natural except for faint *yashadama*.
COMPLETED: September 1959.

257 Monkey
Saru

The monkey is intently peeling a "nothing" vegetable, a shallot (*rakkyō*). It is all peel with not a morsel of substance on the inside. He is beginning to worry but has not yet come to his ultimate disappointment.

I used boxwood of immaculate texture and quality from Mikura Island (see page 38).

SIGNED: Masatoshi.
MATERIAL: boxwood.
EYES: black tortoise shell.
COLOR: natural.
COMPLETED: June 1975.

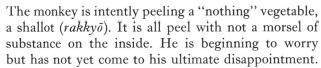

258 Monkey, Young, and Daruma Toy
Saru no oyako to daruma no omocha

I carved the larger monkey's eyes so that they appear to threaten the young one with a whack if he comes any closer to the daruma toy. I chose a monkey subject to commemorate the Senior Gold Year of the Monkey (as it is described according to the traditional sexagenary cycle), Shōwa 55 (1980).

SIGNED: Masatoshi *tō*.
MATERIAL: boxwood.
EYES: black coral.
COLOR: natural except for faint *yashadama*.
COMPLETED: January 1980.

259 Horse
Uma

I took this design for a horse from a picture of an old netsuke. The model was unusual, and I decided to carve it. Even if I had wanted to duplicate the model exactly, it would have been impossible to do so, as the pictures did not show the size, back, bottom, or the *himotoshi*, while color and texture were barely hinted at. An exact copy can be made from the actual netsuke but not from a picture.

SIGNED: Masatoshi *sha*.
MATERIAL: ivory.
EYES: black coral.
COLOR: incense smoke; *sumi*—mane, tail, head markings.
COMPLETED: September 1975.

260 Grazing Horse
Kusa o kuu uma

The horse has found a patch of particularly juicy grass. He smiles broadly as he grazes and sweeps his tail accommodatingly across his legs, thereby furnishing a place for the *himotoshi*.

SIGNED: Masatoshi *tō*.
MATERIAL: ivory.
EYES FOLLOW.
COLOR: incense smoke; *sumi*—markings.
COMPLETED: September 1961.

261 Horse on Three Legs
Sanbon ashi de tatsu uma

I copied this horse from a picture of an old netsuke, although I modified the treatment freely to accord with my own feelings about the subject. In order to simulate age, I ground down the mane and tail and I polished out hair lines in areas where normal use would have shown wear. I used incense smoke—the best coloring for an antique appearance.

SIGNED: Masatoshi *sha*.
MATERIAL: ivory.
EYES: black tortoise shell.
COLOR: incense smoke; *sumi*—coat, mane, tail.
COMPLETED: August 1961.

262 Fat Horse
Futotta uma

The inspiration for this horse came from an old lacquer incense box. The model is the perfect netsuke composition. The horse's long neck, mane, legs, and tail are laid flat against his body, completely neutralizing their hazards as appendages. The design is a remarkable achievement in compression and compactness.

SIGNED: Tokisada.
MATERIAL: boxwood.
EYES: carved.
COLOR: *yashadama*.
COMPLETED: June 1961.

263 Horse and Mare
Osu uma to mesu uma

An old netsuke of a horse and mare nuzzling each other bore the stigma of an enforced triangular form dictated by the "pie-slice" shape of the ivory block. Many otherwise fine old netsuke were spoiled by the carver's need to account for the weight of the precious ivory he received from the dealer. I copied the old model but in a natural, rounded shape. I simulated an antique coloration by applying a great deal of incense smoke and a thick coat of *sumi*. Cracks in the tails of both horse and mare are natural flaws in the material.

SIGNED: Masatoshi *sha*.
MATERIAL: ivory.
EYES: carved.
COLOR: incense smoke; *sumi*—horse's coat, manes, tails, markings.
COMPLETED: November 1961.

264 Horse from Gourd
Hyōtan kara koma

I carved this piece to illustrate the proverb *Hyōtan kara koma* (a horse issues from a gourd), meaning that there's no telling what may happen. There is also the story of Chokarō, the *sennin* who stabled his horse in a gourd, but it was not my inspiration for this netsuke.

Stag-antler is a challenge to a carver's imagination and ingenuity. I used the coin-shaped segment of the stem that is attached directly to the skull as a base for the horse and gourd. This part is usually solid bone, permitting greater latitude in choice of subjects. Those parts of an antler where the tines join are also sometimes sufficiently solid for carving in-the-round, but the tines themselves, at least for part of their length, are generally filled with soft marrow and spongy material that severely limits choice and treatment of subject.

Netsuke made of antler are more resistant to wear than those of ivory.

SIGNED: Masatoshi *tō*.
MATERIAL: stag-antler.
EYES: carved.
COLOR: incense smoke; *sumi*—mane, eyes, tail, underside.
COMPLETED: December 1965.

265 Tiger and Cub
Tora no chichi to ko

The tiger cub plays with his father. I carved the eyes of both animals spherical and full, clearly marking the pupils. The effect is to simulate the inlay of some black material like *umimatsu*. I raised the whiskers with individual hairs carved in relief. The technique I used to raise the whiskers involved shaving away the surrounding material and not *ukibori*.

SIGNED: Masatoshi.
MATERIAL: ebony.
EYES: carved.
COLOR: natural.
COMPLETED: August 1973.

266 Tigress and Cub
Oyako-dora

I wanted to try to get distinctive tiger stripes in natural colors, and so I experimented by using silver nitrate for the stripes with incense smoke to mellow the metallic texture. I was not satisfied with the initial result; the stripes were too harsh. But I have noted further mellowing since the original application, and I expect the mellowing will continue, especially if the piece is handled. I raised the whiskers by relief carving.

SIGNED: Masatoshi.
MATERIAL: ivory.
EYES: black coral.
COLOR: *yashadama*; silver nitrate and incense smoke—stripes.
COMPLETED: September 1975.

267 Tiger
Tora

I imagined this tiger as a silly animal making a great effort to appear intimidating and dangerous. I enjoy treating netsuke humorously. My inclination is to emphasize the aspects of my subjects that are comical, amusing, absurd, or even ludicrous.

I cut the block of material for this piece from the part of the rhinoceros horn that is at the outer circumference near the base. This part is lighter in color and rougher in texture, but it is also the part that polishes most brilliantly. In cutting out a block from this area, there is some breakup and spreading into coarse, individual strands of hair which must be chiseled away. The tiger's paws were just inside the rind at the base where the horn joins the skull. By chance, there happened to be natural bands of color near the *himotoshi* which suggested tiger stripes. I regretted that the whole section was not naturally tiger-striped.

SIGNED: Masatoshi.
MATERIAL: rhinoceros horn.
EYES: black coral.
COLOR: natural.
COMPLETED: April 1966.

268 Wild Boar and Young
Inoshishi no oyako

The design and treatment are my own. I formed the *himotoshi* by creating a gap between the mother's hind leg and body. I ground some of the hair lines to give a pleasing effect of natural wear and to avoid a monotonous coloration of the hide. The eyes of both parent and child follow, but as boars' eyes are small the feature is not particularly obvious.

SIGNED: Masatoshi *tō*.
MATERIAL: ivory.
EYES FOLLOW.
COLOR: incense smoke; *sumi*—hair lines.
COMPLETED: September 1964.

269 Wild Boar and Snake
Inoshishi to hebi

The idea for this subject came from a poor, thumbnail-sized picture of an old netsuke. Although I signed the netsuke as a copy, there is little similarity between my treatment and the original. The boar and snake are a favored combination as they occupy opposite positions in the zodiacal circle.

I inlaid the eyes of the snake with black coral but carved the boar's eyes, as they were too small to be improved by inlays.

SIGNED: Masatoshi *sha*.
MATERIAL: ebony.
EYES OF SNAKE: black coral.
EYES OF BOAR: carved.
COLOR: natural.
COMPLETED: February 1974.

270 Dog
Inu

The idea for this carving came from an old Chinese jade. I marveled at the craftsmanship involved. Starting with a pancake-shaped stone that seemed to offer no possibility other than that of a flat pendant, the artist had had the imagination to envision a dog shaped in the round. He gave form to his vision by grinding away excess material until he had released his dog.

I selected a section of rhinoceros horn showing two distinct areas, one a yellowish tan and the other a brownish black. The coloration and translucency of the horn were just right for simulating jade.

SIGNED: Masatoshi *tō*.
INSCRIPTION: *saikaku* (rhinoceros horn).
MATERIAL: rhinoceros horn.
EYES: carved.
COLOR: natural.
COMPLETED: December 1977.

271 Fox
Kitsune

The fox has two pieces of his favorite food, fried bean curd (*abura-age*), in his jaws. Worshipers place bean curd on the pedestals of stone foxes at Inari shrines. (The fox is the messenger of Inari, the god of rice.) I carved the animal's whiskers individually in raised relief. A space between his right leg and haunch serves for the *himotoshi*.

SIGNED: Masatoshi.
MATERIAL: boxwood.
EYES: black coral.
COLOR: potassium permanganate.
COMPLETED: March 1979.

272 Chinese Goat
Chūgoku yagi

I found my model in a book of Chinese seals. I believe the animal is a kind of Chinese goat. I carved it squatting on a narrow, circular base, as it was drawn in the book. I thought about eliminating the base, but I did not want to risk spoiling its Chinese flavor.

SIGNED: Masatoshi *sha*.
INSCRIPTION: *saikaku nite* (from rhinoceros horn).
MATERIAL: rhinoceros horn.
EYES: carved.
COLOR: natural.
COMPLETED: February 1966.

273 Goat and Monkey
Yagi to saru

This goat belongs to the same camel-necked Chinese species as the goat illustrated in Plate 272. I gave the monkey the amusing task of grooming the goat's beard.

To suggest old age, I colored the piece densely with incense smoke. This particular block of ivory was porous and readily absorbed color, darkening deeply.

SIGNED: Masatoshi *sha*.
MATERIAL: ivory.
EYES: carved.
COLOR: incense smoke.
COMPLETED: August 1961.

274 Badger
Tanuki

The badger, or raccoon dog, one of the most common animals in Japanese folklore, is often represented with a preposterously exaggerated scrotum. I carved him using his scrotum as an umbrella for protection against the rain.

SIGNED: Masatoshi *tō*.
MATERIAL: ivory.
EYES FOLLOW.
COLOR: *yashadama*; *sumi*—hide, red *nikawa*—mouth.
COMPLETED: October 1978.

275 Weasel
Itachi

Black ebony was my choice of wood to represent the weasel. This agile animal is nocturnal, and its movements are fleeting. Hence, it is infrequently spotted. I tried to convey my impression of the weasel's

streaking mobility by emphasizing its long neck and small head, darting like a snake's.

SIGNED: Masatoshi *tō*.
MATERIAL: ebony.
EYES: carved.
COLOR: natural.
COMPLETED: May 1965.

276 Camel
Rakuda

I designed this piece as a fanciful, comic version of a camel. I am not sure whether I intended the drapery effect over the camel's humps as a stylization of his hide or for weird humor. For additional strength and support I joined the legs to a small stone, which I also used as a reserve for my signature.

SIGNED: Masatoshi.
MATERIAL: boxwood.
EYES: black tortoise shell.
COLOR: *yashadama*.
COMPLETED: May 1961.
ILLUSTRATED: *Arts of Asia*, July/August 1973.

277 Camel
Rakuda

My inspiration for this model was an ancient jade carving.

SIGNED: Masatoshi.
INSCRIPTION: *saikaku* (rhinoceros horn).
MATERIAL: rhinoceros horn.
EYES: black coral.
COLOR: natural.
COMPLETED: October 1975.
ILLUSTRATED: *The Inrō Handbook*, Figure 91.

278 Cat and Lizard
Neko to tokage

The cat thought he had captured the lizard when he pounced on its tail. The lizard nonchalantly left its tail behind, knowing it would grow another, and continued its path across the cat's back. The cat is bewildered.

SIGNED: Masatoshi *tō*.
MATERIAL: boxwood.
EYES: carved.
COLOR: natural except for faint *yashadama*.
COMPLETED: February 1980.

279 Cat and Rat
Neko to nezumi

I imagined the rat unaware of where he had landed and the cat startled. I carved the instant of realization.

The rat cowers in terror and tries to slide back off the cat's back, but the cat, on the other hand, prepares for action. I carved the hair of the animals evenly and raised their whiskers individually.

After carving this one piece, I returned the ivory material to the dealer. I found it too soft and clayey. No matter how patiently I polished it, I could not produce a satisfactory luster.

SIGNED: Masatoshi *tō*.
MATERIAL: ivory.
EYES: black tortoise shell.
COLOR: incense smoke; *sumi* wash.
COMPLETED: February 1972.

280 Scaly Anteater
Senzankō

I saw a scaly anteater stuffed and mounted at an exhibition of Taiwanese products. I carved it standing on an umbrella leaf as it captures a spider.

Generally I avoid using an artificial base as a support, except, as in this case, where the leaf is a natural element of the model.

SIGNED: Masatoshi *tō*.
MATERIAL: ivory.
EYES FOLLOW.
COLOR: incense smoke; *sumi*—markings on scales and leaf.
COMPLETED: January 1967.

281 Otter
Kawauso

At the zoo, I was fascinated by the supple, fluid movements of the otter and the human manner in which it stood erect, using its front paws like hands to manage its food. There was a mechanism by the otters' enclosure for placing a coin in a slot that automatically released a small fish for it to feed on. I began carving my image of the otter that same night.

SIGNED: Masatoshi.
MATERIAL: ebony.
EYES: carved.
COLOR: natural.
COMPLETED: October 1966.

282 Mole
Mogura

A mole once made its home in my garden. It was a nuisance, its digging constantly blocking my water pipes and drains. In an effort to get rid of it, I filled its hole with stones and poured water in, but it had an escape route and eluded me with ease. In some areas farmers call the mole a "potato rat."

I treated the hide of the mole with meticulous hairline engraving (*kebori*) that imparted the silky appearance of fine fur. I carved its whiskers individually in raised relief.

SIGNED: Tokisada.
MATERIAL: ebony.
EYES: ivory and black coral.
COLOR: natural.
COMPLETED: December 1960.

283 Bronze Rhinoceros
Sai no buronzu

I once visited the Tokyo National Museum to see an exhibit of Chinese bronzes. One of the most spectacular pieces was a huge, archaic rhinoceros, a bronze of unbelievable beauty and craftsmanship. I resolved to make a netsuke of the animal, and I decided on ebony as the best material to represent its texture and markings. In order to preserve the massiveness of the original I decided on an outsize netsuke for use by a grand champion *sumō* wrestler (*yokozuna*).

SIGNED: Masatoshi *tō*.
INSCRIPTION: *Sumōtori yō* (for a *sumō* wrestler).
MATERIAL: ebony.
EYES: carved.
COLOR: natural.
COMPLETED: May 1976.
SCALE: nine-tenths life size.

284 Chinese Rhinoceros
Chūgoku no sai

I can't recall for certain whether the original was a bronze or a jade, nor whether I saw it in a museum or a catalogue. I carved it as an eccentric rhinoceros, as it shows some characteristics of the tapir. Its hoofs are three-toed and padded.

SIGNED: Masatoshi *tō*.
INSCRIPTION: *saikaku* (rhinoceros horn).
MATERIAL: rhinoceros horn.
EYES: carved.
COLOR: natural.
COMPLETED: August 1979.

285 Stag
Shika

This stag is a copy of one by the great eighteenth-century *netsuke-shi* Okatomo, but it is a copy only in a very approximate sense of the word. The designs are similar in general outline, but in all else dissimilarities prevail. Okatomo's netsuke is made of wood, very tall, the neck stiff and exaggeratedly elongated, the line of neck and forelegs almost perpendicular, and the antlers flat against the body.

The Okatomo is strong, with interesting distortions. In my copy I separated the antlers from the body, curved the neck, and varied the line running from raised head to forelegs. My version tends toward an emphasis on grace and elegance. I believe the differences in our models represent both gains and losses.

The technique for representing the spots on the deer's hide is simple. I engrave in outline each individual spot, which I then fill in with *sumi* to make it visible. I incise the hairlines of the hide, taking care to avoid scoring the marked spots. After finishing the hairline etching, I apply *sumi* to the entire animal. When I wash away the *sumi*, the spots appear as smooth, white circles, while the etched hide is permanently stained.

SIGNED: Masatoshi *sha*.
MATERIAL: ivory.
EYES: carved; pupils—black tortoise shell.
COLOR: *yashadama*; *sumi*—hairlines.
COMPLETED: March 1974.
ILLUSTRATED: *Netsuke Familiar and Unfamiliar*, Figure 376.
SCALE: nine-tenths life size.

18. Toys and Dolls

286 Ono no Tōfū Inkstone
Ono no Tōfū suzuri

The original is a toy in the form of an inkstone representing the famous Heian Period calligrapher Ono no Tōfū. Every school child knows the story of how Ono no Tōfū learned perseverance from a little frog that tried and tried again and again until it reached the branch for which it was aiming.

I discuss the principles of transfiguring a toy into a netsuke on page 63.

I copied most of the inscriptions which I engraved on netsuke representing toys from the descriptions found in *Unai no tomo* (The Child's Friend).

SIGNED: Tokisada *koku*.
INSCRIPTIONS: *Sagano* (district in Kyoto); *suzuri* (inkstone).
MATERIAL: boxwood.
COLOR: black, green, dark red, and bright red lacquer; gold *nikawa*—pattern on trousers.
COMPLETED: October 1961.

287 Fushimi Ware Calf
Fushimi-yaki koushi

The original is a stylized calf made of unglazed pottery, a product of Fushimi near Kyoto. I chose a rough porous wood, teak, because of its suitability for representing clay pottery. The red lacquer circle on the calf's back conforms with published pictures of the toy, though I can't find an explanation of its significance in the texts.

SIGNED: Tokisada *tō*.
INSCRIPTION: *Fushimi-yaki* (Fushimi ware).
MATERIAL: teak.
EYES: black lacquer.
COLOR: *yashadama*; red lacquer—circle, nostrils.
COMPLETED: October 1961.

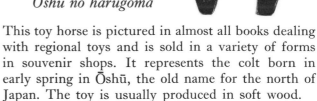

288 Spring Colt of Ōshū
Ōshū no harugoma

This toy horse is pictured in almost all books dealing with regional toys and is sold in a variety of forms in souvenir shops. It represents the colt born in early spring in Ōshū, the old name for the north of Japan. The toy is usually produced in soft wood.

SIGNED: Tokisada *koku*.
INSCRIPTION: *Ōshū no harugoma*.
MATERIAL: boxwood.
COLOR: black and green lacquer; red *nikawa*—ears, mouth, decorations; gold *nikawa*—bridle, decorations.
COMPLETED: October 1961.

289 Barley-Straw Horse
Wara uma

In poor rural areas, children use rice or barley straw to make their toys. The horse is a favorite, and the children weave or bundle the straw in a variety of equine models. I carved a gourd-shaped base to join the legs both for reasons of security and because of the gourd's proverbial association with the horse (see Plate 264). I gave the horse its large member for fun. The design is not that of a regional toy but my own version of a straw horse.

SIGNED: Masatoshi.
MATERIAL: boxwood.
COLOR: potassium permanganate.
COMPLETED: September 1966.
ILLUSTRATED: *Arts of Asia*, July/August 1973.

290 Yakko Kite
Yakko-dako

The *yakko* was a samurai servant, a flunky. When he went to town, he changed into a bully, abusing and intimidating the townsmen, who invariably despised him. A popular design for a kite was a caricature of a blustering *yakko*. The design was also appled as a roly-poly toy. I carved the *yakko-dako* in the design of a kite but rounded the base so that the figure rocks and rotates, though it is not a tumbler.

SIGNED: Tokisada *koku*.
INSCRIPTION: *Ōsaka hyokori yakko* (Ōsaka tumbling *yakko*).
MATERIAL: boxwood.
COLOR: black lacquer—hair, eyebrows, eyes, mustache; red and green *nikawa*—coat; gold *nikawa*—crest.
COMPLETED: October 1961.
ILLUSTRATED: *Horizon*, Autumn 1965.

291 Warty Frog
Ibogaeru

I found the design for this warty frog in one of my illustrated books of regional toys. On page 43 I describe my method of inlaying the warts.

SIGNED: Masatoshi *sha*.
INSCRIPTION: *Seishū Futamigaura no kaeru* (frog of Futamigaura in Sei Province, i.e., Mie Prefecture).
MATERIAL: boxwood.
EYES: ivory and black tortoise shell.
WARTS: black tortoise shell.
COLOR: *yashadama*.
COMPLETED: September 1967.

292 Hollow Badger
Karappo tanuki

In the *Unai no tomo* (The Child's Friend), the hollow badger is described as an earthenware toy of Hakata, a city in Kyūshū. I adapted the toy into a netsuke.

SIGNED: Masatoshi *sha*.
INSCRIPTION: *Chikuzen Hakata no san* (produced in Hakata, Chikuzen, i.e., Fukuoka Prefecture).

MATERIAL: red sandalwood.
EYES: ivory and black coral.
COLOR: natural; red *nikawa*—mouth, ears.
COMPLETED: September 1967.
ILLUSTRATED: *Arts of Asia*, July/August 1973.

293 Galloping Wild Boar
Shissō suru yacho

The galloping wild boar expresses the wonder of a child as the world unfolds before its fresh eyes. It is a world of make-believe—like the snout of the boar, which curves up like the trunk of an elephant.

SIGNED: Tokisada *koku*.
INSCRIPTION: *Fushimi no yacho* (wild boar of Fushimi).
MATERIAL: boxwood.
EYES: black lacquer.
TUSKS: ivory.
COLQR: potassium permanganate; red *nikawa*—ears, base of tusks.
COMPLETED: October 1961.

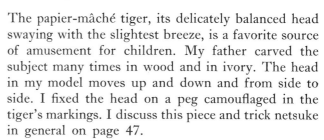

294 Sway-Head Tiger
Kubifuri tora

The papier-mâché tiger, its delicately balanced head swaying with the slightest breeze, is a favorite source of amusement for children. My father carved the subject many times in wood and in ivory. The head in my model moves up and down and from side to side. I fixed the head on a peg camouflaged in the tiger's markings. I discuss this piece and trick netsuke in general on page 47.

SIGNED: Masatoshi *tō*.
MATERIAL: boxwood.
EYES: black coral.
COLOR: potassium nitrate; red *nikawa*—mouth.
COMPLETED: December 1967.

295 Palace Doll
Gosho ningyō

The *gosho* (palace) doll is always a little boy naked or nearly so, his head disproportionately large, with tiny features in a great round face to emphasize his infant charm. I carved the boy holding a fish, though, as a doll, he is invariably holding a toy.

SIGNED: Jikishiin Masatoshi *tō*.
MATERIAL: ivory.
EYES OF BOY: black tortoise shell.
EYES OF FISH: black tortoise shell.
COLOR: incense smoke; *sumi*—hair tufts, eyebrows, eyes, fish scales; gold *nikawa*—hat.
COMPLETED: July 1969.

296 Toy Dog
Koinu

As a toy, the fat, little puppy is a perfect shape for a rounded netsuke. I carved an elevation around his neck to indicate a collar and I colored it with silver nitrate. I also made a hollow and inlaid a bell in translucent tortoise shell.

There are two flaws in the ivory, the nerve channel and a grayish discoloration. I filled in the nerve channel with ivory dust and transparent glue. The grayish discoloration near the inscription is a natural flaw that seldom occurs in ivory.

SIGNED: Masatoshi *sha*.
INSCRIPTION: *Edo gangu* (Edo toy).
MATERIAL: ivory.
EYES: black coral.
BELL: transparent tortoise shell.
COLOR: incense smoke; silver nitrate—collar; red *nikawa*—mouth.
COMPLETED: September 1967.

297 Roly-poly Woman
Okiagari koboshi ningyō

The original toy is made from muddy clay and is weighted like a tumbler. I carved the base with

angular planes so that the netsuke leans forward or backward without falling. The wavy, incised line around the base represents the separation between the weighted bottom and the upper figure.

SIGNED: Masatoshi.
INSCRIPTION: *Sendai no te-asobi gangu* (playtoy of Sendai).
MATERIAL: ivory.
INLAYS: black tortoise shell—eyes and eyebrows; transparent tortoise shell over red *nikawa*—mouth.
COLOR: incense smoke; silver nitrate—hair, arms.
COMPLETED: September 1967.

298a, 298b Owl Whistle
Fukurō-bue

The original is an earthenware whistle in the shape of an owl with prominent ears called *tsuno-fukurō*, the horned owl. I carved the model as a netsuke that can also be used as a whistle. The short lines I cut on the figure are intended to suggest feathers. I used as my medium lignum vitae, a material which I discuss in the description of Plate 201.

SIGNED: Tokisada *tō*.
MATERIAL: lignum vitae.
EYES: black coral.
COLOR: natural.
COMPLETED: June 1964.

299 Earthenware Tiger
Dosei no tora

The original is an earthenware tiger claimed by Kanazawa, a city near the Japan Sea coast, as its traditional product. Except for its vivid stripes, the animal is almost as doggish as it is tigerish.

SIGNED: Masatoshi *sha*.
INSCRIPTION: *Kanazawa no san* (product of Kanazawa).
MATERIAL: ivory.
EYES: black coral.
COLOR: incense smoke; silver nitrate—stripes; red *nikawa*—mouth.
COMPLETED: October 1967.

300 Saga Inari Horse
Saga Inari koma

The original is a pottery toy from Saga in Kyūshū. I decided on a horse design as my first carving of Shōwa 53 (1978) to celebrate the Year of the Horse.

SIGNED: Masatoshi *tō*.
INSCRIPTION: *Saga Inari koma.*
MATERIAL: ivory.
EYES FOLLOW.
COLOR: incense smoke; silver nitrate—mane, bridle, trappings.
COMPLETED: January 1978.

301 Stuffed Monkeys
Kukuri-zaru

The idea for this design came from the Shibamata Taishakuten temple, not far from my home. The toy—made of cloth stuffed with cotton—is sold as a souvenir at the temple, which has long been associated with monkeys. It is called the *kukuri-zaru* (stuffed monkeys). The monkeys are in their traditional grouping of three: one sees no evil, one speaks no evil, and one hears no evil.

The dark areas on the backs of all three monkeys indicate that I carved the piece out of a circumferential slice of the tusk near the tip, where it narrows. Just under the bark the ivory tends to be darker. Besides, this outer rim is more absorbent and darkens more from incense smoke or other coloring (see page 52).

SIGNED: Masatoshi *tō*.
MATERIAL: ivory.
COLOR: incense smoke.
COMPLETED: May 1960.

19. Frogs

302 Frogs and Tadpoles
Kaeru to otamajakushi

My idea for this design came from my daughter's biology textbook, which showed the life cycle of the frog. The group consists of three frogs—one small, one medium sized, and one large—and two tadpoles —one almost all fish, the other almost all frog.

SIGNED: Masatoshi *tō*.
MATERIAL: boxwood.
EYES: black coral.
COLOR: potassium permanganate.
COMPLETED: February 1965.

303 Mitsuhiro Style Frog
Mitsuhiro-fū kaeru

I consider Mitsuhiro's frog in the form of a seal, *Inzai-fū kaeru*, an extraordinary example of simplicity, stylization, and originality. I copied it quite closely—except for the *himotoshi*, which had been drilled through the base, almost certainly by someone who owned the piece at some time or other. The defacement should not be blamed on Mitsuhiro.

SIGNED: Masatoshi *sha*.
INSCRIPTION: *Mitsuhiro genkei* (original).
MATERIAL: ivory.
EYES: carved.
COLOR: incense smoke.
COMPLETED: June 1959.

304 Mitsuhiro Style Frog without Seal Base
Dai nashi Mitsuhiro-fū kaeru

I was spurred by the idea of incorporating Mitsuhiro's design (Plate 303) into a treatment of my own, eliminating the base and providing for a proper *himotoshi*. I had to make other modifications as I carved, since one change necessitates another.

SIGNED: Masatoshi *tō*.
MATERIAL: ivory.
EYES: carved.
COLOR: incense smoke.
COMPLETED: May 1979.

305 Cambodian Bronze Frog
Canbojia seidō-gaeru

I copied this stylized frog from a picture of an ancient Cambodian bronze drum. The frog embellished the drum as a minor decorative element. The legs of the frog project a little, but they are short and do not violate the requirements of a traditional netsuke.

SIGNED: Masatoshi *sha*.
MATERIAL: ivory.
EYES: carved.
COLOR: incense smoke.
COMPLETED: May 1955.

306 Huge Toad of Suō
Suō no ōgama

It is always the snake that ingests the toad. I thought it would be amusing to turn the tables and portray the toad making a repast of the snake. I used an anonymous drawing captioned the "Huge Toad of Suō" as my model. Suō is the name of the old province which is now Yamaguchi Prefecture.

SIGNED: Masatoshi *tō*.
INSCRIPTION: *Suō no ōgama*.
MATERIAL: ivory.
EYES: black coral.
COLOR: incense smoke.
COMPLETED: September 1977.

307 Leopard Frog
Tonosama-gaeru

I carved a leopard frog flicking his deadly tongue to capture a juicy wasp. The frog's tongue is an amazing instrument, narrow at the base but heavy and bulbous at the tip. I did the pimpling on the hind legs and sides of the amphibian in *ukibori*. For amusement I carved the suggestion of a human face among the warts on the back of the frog (see Figure 38).

SIGNED: Masatoshi *tō*.
MATERIAL: boxwood.
EYES: black coral.
COLOR: potassium permanganate.
COMPLETED: August 1975.

308 Chinese Style Frog
Chūgoku-fū kaeru

The model I used was a Chinese bamboo *okimono*. I tried to capture the distinctive weirdness of the Chinese original. I carved the small pimples on the belly and back of the frog in *ukibori*, but I carved the larger warts in raised relief.

SIGNED: Masatoshi *tō*.
MATERIAL: boxwood.
EYES: carved.
COLOR: natural except for faint *yashadama*.
COMPLETED: June 1974.
ILLUSTRATED: *Nestuke Familiar and Unfamiliar*, Figure 382.

309 Weird Frog
Bakegaeru

This frog forms a compact, traditional netsuke with elongated toes well protected. Its skin is completely covered with warts. I designed the body of the frog normally and naturally to emphasize the contrast with its abnormal head. It has a full set of teeth and a phallus for a tongue, both of which characteristics set it apart as a weird frog.

SIGNED: Masatoshi *tō*.
MATERIAL: ebony.
EYES: carved.
COLOR: natural.
COMPLETED: March 1968.

20. Weird Beings

310 Weird Frog with an Itch
Bakegaeru no kayugari

I got the idea for this design from a series of amusing pictures of frogs drawn by an anonymous artist. The frog really is bizarre: he has human arms and legs, a full set of teeth, and a phallus for a tongue. He itches everywhere and scratches vigorously at his navel and back.

The ivory was particularly hard but it polished with an interesting tone.

SIGNED: Masatoshi.
MATERIAL: ivory.
EYES: black coral.
COLOR: gamboge.
COMPLETED: January 1976.
ILLUSTRATED: Catalogue, Raymond Bushell Collection, Tokyo.
The Kotto, No. 3.

311 Sumō Wrestler Frog
Kaeru rikishi

The frog has teeth, laughs heartily, and is three-toed, characteristics which certify him as crazy. He wears a narrow skirt of leaves like the *sumō* wrestler's loincloth (*mawashi*). I carved him in the stance of a *sumō* wrestler (*rikishi*) warming up for a bout.

SIGNED: Masatoshi *tō*.
MATERIAL: boxwood.
EYES: black coral.
COLOR: potassium permanganate.
COMPLETED: November 1968.
ILLUSTRATED: *Collectors' Netsuke*, Figure 354.

312 Weird Being and Grave Marker
Bakemono to tōba

The *bakemono* (weird being) has a forked tongue, showing that he is an inveterate liar. One of his ghoulish activities is stealing *tōba* (grave markers). He clutches one in his grasp. I composed a satirical *kaimyō* (posthumous name), Grudge-bearing Scoundrel, which I engraved on the *tōba*. I also engraved, as is customary, a Sanskrit character, the name of the prayer, and the date, Anei 4 (1775). The *bakemono* wears a straw skirt (*koshimino*).

SIGNED: Masatoshi, with *kakihan*.
MATERIAL: ivory.
EYES: black coral.
COLOR: incense smoke; *sumi*—hair, skirt.
COMPLETED: November 1972.

313 Two-headed Weird Being
Sōtō no bakemono

I found my idea in the *Ehon hyakki yagyō* (Illustrated Book of Nighttime Apparitions) by Toriyama Sekien, who specialized in painting monsters. One head extends a sensuous tongue, the other dozes vacantly.

SIGNED: Masatoshi *tō*.
MATERIAL: ivory.
EYES: black coral.
COLOR: incense smoke; *sumi*—hair, body.
COMPLETED: February 1975.

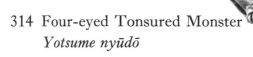

314 Four-eyed Tonsured Monster
Yotsume nyūdō

The story and design are pure invention. The demon (*oni*) ridiculed the monster because of his two extra eyes, one on the top of his head, the other in the middle of his forehead. The monster clenches the demon between his teeth, while he tries to extirpate his abnormal eyes. The demon's life is in the balance, depending on the success of the monster's efforts.

I decorated the monster's breeches with a cloud pattern and the demon's with a leopard-spot pattern.

SIGNED: Masatoshi.
MATERIAL: ivory.
EYES: black tortoise shell.
COLOR: *yashadama*; *sumi*—hair, patterns.
COMPLETED: August 1974.

315 Weird Horse
Bakeuma

It is a mistake to think that all *bakemono* are humanoids. Any animal can be a *bakemono* as long as its characteristics are sufficiently bizarre and unusual. A one-eyed horse that crosses his legs and sits erect is a *bakemono*. It may be that he is imitating his dull-minded groom.

SIGNED: Masatoshi.
MATERIAL: ivory.
EYES: black coral.
COLOR: incense smoke; *sumi*—mane, tail.
COMPLETED: January 1969.
ILLUSTRATED: *Arts of Asia*, July/August 1973.

316 Three-eyed Brat with Endless Tongue
Mitsume no chōzetsu kozō

The little monster is caught in a rainstorm. The irony is that he uses the lotus leaf, the symbol of Buddha, as an umbrella to protect his evil substance.

SIGNED: Masatoshi.
MATERIAL: ivory.
EYES: black coral.
COLOR: incense smoke.
COMPLETED: June 1973.

317 Eight-armed Devilfish
Takohachi

The *bakemono* octopus wears a short coat shredded into eight strips, representing the eight arms of the devilfish. Its long tongue is forked to show that it is double-dealing. One eye looks up, the other down.

SIGNED: Masatoshi *tō*.
INSCRIPTION: *takohachi*.
MATERIAL: stag-antler.
EYES: black coral.
COLOR: incense smoke.
COMPLETED: April 1974.

318 One Hundred Phantoms
Hyaku henge

The monster's name is *Hyaku henge* (literally, One Hundred Phantoms). He can transform himself into a hundred different apparitions, one more horrible than the other. I carved his armless form, a form in which he traditionally wears a belly band (*haramaki*) to keep his stomach warm.

SIGNED: Masatoshi *tō*.
INSCRIPTION: *Hyaku henge*.
MATERIAL: ivory.
EYES: black coral.
COLOR: incense smoke; *sumi*—markings.
COMPLETED: April 1977.

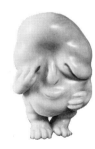

319 *Nupperabō*

Unlike most *bakemono*, the *nupperabō* is neither vicious nor intimidating. He lurks around temples and shrines to discourage those with impure thoughts from entering. His body is a jellylike mass with features in a flux of continuous melting and reforming.

SIGNED: Masatoshi *tō*.
MATERIAL: ivory.
COLOR: gamboge.
COMPLETED: April 1978.

320 Lantern Ghost
Chōchin yūrei

This ghost has no particular identity. In various Kabuki dramas, however, there is a popular scene called *chōchin nuke* (emanations from a lantern). In dark light a half-seen, ghostly apparition emerges from a burning paper-lantern. It is the *chōchin nuke* that I carved here.

SIGNED: Masatoshi *koku*.
MATERIAL: ivory.
EYES: black tortoise shell.
COLOR: *yashadama*; *sumi*—hair; red *nikawa*—tongue.
COMPLETED: July 1952.

321 Long-nosed Monster
Obake hananaga

I found my model in the *Hyakki gadan*, nightmarish phantoms drawn by Kawanabe Gyōsai. The monster manipulates his long prehensile nose like the monkey does his tail.

SIGNED: Masatoshi.
MATERIAL: boxwood.
EYES: black coral.
COLOR: potassium permanganate.
COMPLETED: September 1963.
ILLUSTRATED: *Arts of Asia*, July/August 1973.

322 Monocular Monster
Hitotsume no bakemono

The idea for this one-eyed monster came from a book called *Yume awase* (Interpretation of Dreams). I inscribed the exact words from the book on the letter held by the monster. Translated, they read: "You will be lucky if you dream about this sort of *bakemono*."

SIGNED: Masatoshi *tō*.
INSCRIPTION: *Kono yō na bakemono no yume o mireba ōi ni yoshi.*
MATERIAL: red sandalwood.
EYE: ivory and black tortoise shell.
COLOR: natural.
COMPLETED: March 1974.

323 Drought Monster
Hideri-gami

The Drought Monster manages with a single arm and a single leg. He outruns the wind. Wherever he appears the land suffers a dry spell. If he is sighted in a rainfall, the rain stops.

SIGNED: Masatoshi *tō*.
INSCRIPTION: *Hideri-gami.*
MATERIAL: ebony.
EYES: carved.
COLOR: natural.
COMPLETED: May 1978.
SCALE: life size.

324 Bakemono Bat
Bakemono kōmori

The *bakemono* bat is my invention. It has the wings of a bat, the tail of a rat, and the head of a monster with three eyes. I did not, however, consciously identify the components when I conceived the design. The identifications were an afterthought.

SIGNED: Masatoshi.
MATERIAL: boxwood.
EYES: black tortoise shell.
COLOR: potassium permanganate.
COMPLETED: December 1968.

325 Ghost and Demon
Yūrei to oni

I thought it would be amusing to pair the ghost as the doting mother and the demon as the helpless child. Mother ghosts are often represented beseeching Jizō, the guardian deity of children, to safeguard their orphaned children. Ghosts and *bakemono* are beyond the bounds of human limitations: this bodiless ghost gathers her little demon in her arms for a maternal embrace.

SIGNED: Masatoshi *tō*.
MATERIAL: boxwood.
EYES OF GHOST: carved.
EYES OF DEMON: ivory and black coral.
COLOR: potassium permanganate.
COMPLETED: July 1963.
ILLUSTRATED: *The Wonderful World of Netsuke*, Plate 26.
SCALE: seven-eighths life size.

326 Double-headed Bird
Sōtō no tori

As a *bakemono*, this bird does not require a bo I designed the heads at either end of an elongated neck. *Bakemono* birds do not belong to any particular species, but, in this case, I depicted the heads to resemble those of the pelican and crane.

SIGNED: Jikishiin Masatoshi *tō*.
MATERIAL: hippopotamus tooth.
EYES OF PELICAN FOLLOW.
EYES OF CRANE: black tortoise shell.
COLOR: incense smoke.
COMPLETED: July 1969.

327 Goat-headed Bakemono
Yōtōjin

I have seen dog-headed humanoids in the *Wakan sansai zu-e* and other literature on *bakemono* but never one with a goat's head, so I decided to carve one. Goats feed on grass and other vegetation, but this *bakemono* eats nuts from a proper bowl. I am satisfied with the head but I wish I could have given the body more movement.

SIGNED: Masatoshi *tō*.
MATERIAL: ivory.
EYES: black coral.
COLOR: incense smoke.
COMPLETED: August 1977.
SCALE: seven-eighths life size.

328a, 328b White-robed Kannon Bakemono
Byaku-i no bakemono

One of the forms of Kannon, the goddess of mercy, is that of the White-robed Kannon (Byaku-i Kannon). Even from the rear the familiar curve of her body and the play of her robe identify her as our beloved deity. The idea of a *bakemono* laughing to himself as he parades as Byaku-i Kannon was irresistible—even though sacrilegious.

SIGNED: Masatoshi *tō*.
MATERIAL: ivory.
EYE: black coral.
COLOR: gamboge; *sumi—bakemono*.
COMPLETED: July 1976.
ILLUSTRATED: Catalogue, Raymond Bushell Collection, Tokyo.

329 Melon-headed Bakemono
Meron atama no bakemono

The source for this *bakemono* is an illustration in *Kaiki kusazōshi gafu* (Illustrated Album of Weird Stories). Although there may be a resemblance, I did not intend to carve a caricature of Jurōjin, the god of longevity, or Fukurokuju, the god of wisdom—both of whom are portrayed with an elongated head. The gaps in the teeth, the ridged lips, unequal eyes, and knobs on the cranium are *bakemono* grotesqueries. I shaped the larger of the *himotoshi* as a *bakemono* mouth for bizarreness.

> SIGNED: Masatoshi *tō*.
> MATERIAL: boxwood.
> EYES: black coral.
> COLOR: potassium permanganate.
> COMPLETED: June 1968.
> ILLUSTRATED: *Arts of Asia*, July/August 1973.

330 Macrocephalic Bakemono
Atama dekkachi

I once saw a funny drawing of an apprentice shop boy (*detchi*) in typical costume and hair style of the Edo Period. I exaggerated and caricatured the shop boy still further to the point where he has become a misshapen *bakemono*.

> SIGNED: Masatoshi *tō*.
> MATERIAL: boxwood.
> EYES: black tortoise shell.
> COLOR: natural except for faint *yashadama*.
> COMPLETED: April 1968.
> ILLUSTRATED: *Arts of Asia*, July/August 1973.

331 Ghost
Yūrei

This ghost is an ordinary one; she is not identified as a specific ghost of legend or drama by a lantern, a well bucket, or a fire sieve. "Counterdirectional" eyes and gaps in her teeth, however, are standard characteristics for all ghosts. She balances on her legless extremity. I carved her from a fairly solid branch of the antler.

> SIGNED: Masatoshi *tō*.
> MATERIAL: stag-antler.
> EYES: black tortoise shell.
> COLOR: incense smoke; *sumi*—hair, markings.
> COMPLETED: December 1968.
> ILLUSTRATED: *Arts of Asia*, July/August 1973.

332 Tree Spirit
Hōkō

According to Shintō doctrine, spirits inhabit rocks, rivers, trees, and all of nature. The *hōkō* is the spirit that lives in trees. He melts in and out of the hollow trunks of old decayed trees, sometimes wood, sometimes spirit. I stylized the roots at the base of the trunk. The figure is a male *hōkō*. Someday I intend to carve a female *hōkō*.

> SIGNED: Masatoshi *tō*.
> INSCRIPTION: *hōkō*.
> MATERIAL: ebony.
> EYES: carved.
> COLOR: natural.
> COMPLETED: June 1977.
> SCALE: nine-tenths life size.

333 Cat Monster
Nekomata

The *nekomata* is a cat monster with a forked tail. Children sing a song about the *nekomata* and do a cat dance in which they swirl two tails about. The cat dancer wears a headband. I carved one of the tails alongside the cat's paw so that the netsuke stands securely.

SIGNED: Masatoshi.
INSCRIPTION: *saikaku* (rhinoceros horn).
MATERIAL: rhinoceros horn.
EYES: carved.
COLOR: natural.
COMPLETED: December 1971.

334 "Wet Woman"
Nure onna

The "Wet Woman" lives on desolate rocky shores. She is a serpent with a woman's head. She feeds on seaworms, kelp, and offal thrown up by the sea. Her skin is always damp with a foul slick. I carved her eating a seaworm.

SIGNED: Masatoshi *tō*.
INSCRIPTION: *Nure onna*.
MATERIAL: ebony.
EYES: carved.
COMPLETED: August 1978.

335 Long-tongued Brat
Chōzetsu kozō

The long-tongued brat has, besides the long tongue, a bird's beak and mismatched eyes.

Hippopotamus tooth has a white enamel casing that is extremely hard and dense. The enamel shows on the left hand and elbow of the imp as spots that resisted coloring. I carved the imp as a *sashi* netsuke (see Plate 144 and Diagram E on page 64).

SIGNED: Masatoshi *tō*.
MATERIAL: hippopotamus tooth.
LARGER EYE: transparent tortoise shell and black coral.
SMALLER EYE: black coral.
COLOR: incense smoke; *sumi*—tongue markings.
COMPLETED: August 1971.
SCALE: life size.

336 Nocturnal Bakemono
Yakōsei bakemono

The Nocturnal Bakemono is one of the *bankiōkō*, or Ten Thousand Scampering Ghosts. He hobnobs with rats, which also prefer the darkness of night. He holds one by the tail as it sits on his head.

SIGNED: Masatoshi *tō*.
MATERIAL: ivory.
EYES: black tortoise shell.
COLOR: gamboge; *sumi*—hair, face, rat; faint red *nikawa*—tongue; faint gold *nikawa*—fan.
COMPLETED: January 1976.
SCALE: seven-eighths life size.

337 Jelly-bodied Bakemono
Biron

The *biron* has a soft body like a mass of jelly. He is innocuous and melts when salt is sprinkled where he stands. He is very apprehensive and flees if anyone chants, "*Biro biro*."

SIGNED: Masatoshi *tō*.
MATERIAL: ivory.
EYES: black coral.
COLOR: incense smoke.
COMPLETED: October 1978.
SCALE: seven-eighths life size.

338 Weird Dog
Bakeinu

The figure is a weird dog, a canine *bakemono*. He has the claws of a cat, the fin of a fish, and his tail ends in a loop. He wears the hat of a mountain priest and an expression of annoyance quite unlike anything a dog can manage.

SIGNED: Masatoshi *tō*.
MATERIAL: hippopotamus tooth.
EYES: black tortoise shell.
COLOR: incense smoke; *sumi*—hat, fin, back.
COMPLETED: November 1971.
ILLUSTRATED: *Arts of Asia*, July/August 1973.

339 One-eyed Ogre
Hitotsume ōnyūdō

One of the badger's disguises is to change himself into the One-eyed Ogre. He uses his iron club to make strange noises and frighten humans and holds in his hand an oak leaf, which he can change into money when needed.

SIGNED: Masatoshi *tō*.
MATERIAL: ivory.
EYE FOLLOWS.
COLOR: incense smoke; *sumi*—club.
COMPLETED: February 1979.
SCALE: life size.

340 One-Horn Bakemono
Ikkaku no bakemono

I was once given a *ryūsa* netsuke for a minor repair. The cut-out design was that of a demon of some kind, perhaps a spider demon. It was a provocative design, and I decided to transform it into a carving in-the-round.

SIGNED: Masatoshi *tō*.
MATERIAL: whale-tooth.
EYES: black tortoise shell.
COLOR: incense smoke.
COMPLETED: January 1971.
ILLUSTRATED: Catalogue, Raymond Bushell Collection, Tokyo.

341 Dog with Human Head
Jinshu kenshin

In the *Dai Nihon shi* (Great Japanese History) I read that in the Sixth Month of Kyūju 2 (1155) an animal with something like a human head on a canine body appeared in Kyoto. I carved this *bakemono* from imagination. The body is that of a wild mountain dog.

SIGNED: Masatoshi *tō*.
MATERIAL: ivory.
COLOR: *yashadama*; *sumi*—hair, eyebrow, pupils, mustache.
COMPLETED: October 1979.

342 Tormentor in Hell
Kisotsu

When a human dies, he crosses the Japanese counterpart of the River Styx to hell (*jigoku*), where Enma-Ō, the King of Hell, determines the punishment for the evil acts he has committed on earth and the body in which he will be reborn. Kisotsu is an assistant to the King of Hell, a tormentor. He thrives on the punishments he inflicts on evildoers. I carved Kisotsu as I imagined him. He holds a lotus to direct good souls to the Buddhist paradise (*jōdo*).

SIGNED: Masatoshi *tō*.
INSCRIPTIONS: *Kisotsu*; *saikaku* (rhinoceros horn).
MATERIAL: rhinoceros horn.
EYES: black coral.
COLOR: natural.
COMPLETED: June 1979.
SCALE: seven-eighths life size.

343 Ghost of Concubine
Mekake no yūrei

Concubine and illicit lover committed double suicide. The ghost of the concubine, tormented by her memories of their great love together, cannot rest.

She steals her lover's mortuary tablet from his wife and thus finds respite from her grief. This is the situation as I imagined it for my design. The ribald inscription on the tablet is the husband's posthumous name: *Taiki koji* (Big Tool Buddhist).

SIGNED: Masatoshi *tō*.
MATERIAL: ivory.
EYES: black coral.
COLOR: incense smoke; *sumi*—hair.
COMPLETED: August 1979.
SCALE: seven-eighths life size.

344 Horse-headed Bakemono
Batō no bakemono

One of the principal tormentors in hell is the horse-headed demon, or *mezu*. I had him in mind when I composed this figure.

SIGNED: Masatoshi *tō*.
MATERIAL: ivory.
EYES: black coral.
COLOR: incense smoke; *sumi*—hair, eyebrows, markings.
COMPLETED: October 1979.

345 Haunted Pumpkin
Obake kabocha

There is a scene in the ghost play *Yotsuya kaidan* where a pumpkin breaks apart and a ghost appears. It is that scene I had in mind when I carved the face of a ghost in the contours of the pumpkin. Two rotted holes are the ghost's eyes. The lizard adds to the horror.

SIGNED: Masatoshi *tō*.
INSCRIPTION: *saikaku* (rhinoceros horn).
MATERIAL: rhinoceros horn.
EYES: carved.
COLOR: natural.
COMPLETED: September 1978.

21. Miscellanea

346 Billiken

The billiken doll was popular in Japan many years ago, and we still use the word "billiken" to describe a man with a pointed head.

I used the core section (*shin*) of the ivory (see page 34). The core is the choicest part of the tusk, as it has the smallest grain and the greatest uniformity, but cutting out the core often means wasting a lot of material. "*Shindori*" is the term given to cutting the core out of a tusk. Pipe cases known as *shindori-zutsu* were made from the length of the central core and were extravagantly priced.

SIGNED: Masatoshi *sha*.
MATERIAL: ivory.
EYES: carved.
COLOR: incense smoke.
COMPLETED: September 1960.

347 Kris Handle
Kurisu no e

The Javanese kris handle was heavily patinated and finely carved with a seated, bird-headed god. I adapted it for use as a netsuke by making some minor improvements and adding the *himotoshi*.

The carver who adapts a carved object for use as a netsuke or improves the work of another carver has a choice of three terms to indicate that the basic object is not his own. The words are "*hosoku*," "*hosaku*," and "*hotō*." Were I to perform such steps as repolishing, recoloring, sharpening parts of the design, and adding a pattern or embellishment, I would sign "*hosoku*." Where, as in this case, I modified the length and shape and added *himotoshi*, I signed "*hosaku*." *Hosaku* indicates that a greater amount of carving has been involved than does *hosoku*. *Hotō* is substantially the same as *hosaku* since it indicates the use of a knife (*tō*). *Hosoku* is principally a restoration job, *hosaku* an improvement.

SIGNED: Masatoshi *hosaku*.
MATERIAL: probably Indonesian ironwood.
COLOR: natural.

348 Mother and Son
Haha to musuko

I once attended an exhibition of Mexican art at the Tokyo National Museum. The monumental power of the sculpture was inspiring. I made a pencil sketch as a memory aid of a stone figure of mother and son, which I carved in ivory.

SIGNED: Masatoshi *sha*.
MATERIAL: ivory.
EYES: carved.
COLOR: natural except for faint incense smoke.
COMPLETED: October 1955.

349 Three Beasts
Kemono santō

I paired the horse with the cow as both are beasts of burden on the farm and because of the old protest of farmers in the Edo Period that they were "forced to work like a horse and a cow." The third animal of the group is represented by the material itself. I think it is the tooth of a bear, but I am not sure.

SIGNED: Masatoshi *tō*.
INSCRIPTION: *kemono santō* (three beasts).
MATERIAL: probably bear's tooth.
COLOR: *yashadama*.
COMPLETED: December 1973.
ILLUSTRATED: *Netsuke Familiar and Unfamiliar*, Plate 71.

350 Mother-in-law Daughter-in-law Hell
Ka-ko jigoku

Once a bride enters her husband's household, she is expected to act toward her mother-in-law like a servant. No matter how overbearing and demanding her mother-in-law is, she must be dutiful. Resentment may turn to animosity and animosity to hatred, but smiles must hide her true feelings until the old woman is in her grave. I carved the wife enjoying her revenge in hell, where she twists and tears the hated face to pieces.

SIGNED: Masatoshi *tō*.
MATERIAL: ebony.
EYES: carved.
COLOR: natural.
COMPLETED: December 1975.

351 Sanbasō

This design is a *moji-e*, a design formed from the written character or characters which stand for the subject—for example, a drawing of a bird based on the written character for "bird." My subject here is Sanbasō, the felicitous dance prelude to a traditional theatrical performance. The design (*e*) is based on the characters (*moji*) of the *hiragana* (cursive) syllabary for "Sanbasō."

As the back of the netsuke is plain and level, I decided to carve wide, flat *himotoshi* so that the piece could be used as a netsuke or as an *obidome* (sash fastener).

SIGNED: Masatoshi *tō*.
INSCRIPTION: *Sanbasō*.
MATERIAL: hippopotamus tooth.
EYES: carved.
COLOR: incense smoke and dust; gold *nikawa*—fan design.
COMPLETED: June 1971.

352 Wholeheartedness
Isshin

Like the netsuke in Plate 351, this design is a *moji-e*. It is based on the two characters that together make up the word "*isshin*," wholeheartedness. The figure is a courtier wearing a standing hat (*tate-eboshi*). I balanced the netsuke so that it rocks gently on its base with the characters upright.

SIGNED: Masatoshi *tō*.
INSCRIPTION: *isshin*.
MATERIAL: hippopotamus tooth.
EYES: carved.
COLOR: incense smoke with dust; gold lacquer
—hat.
COMPLETED: June 1971.

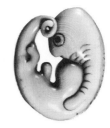

355 Lizard Embryo
Tokage no taiji

I once saw a series of pictures in a popular magazine showing the stages of development of the embryo in a lizard's egg and I was struck by the similarity of the lizard to the human embryo. I fused the series into a single, grotesque design.

I cut out a cross-section of a whale's tooth for my material. The circumference of the embryo was just under the rind and darkened from the incense smoke like a collar.

SIGNED: Masatoshi *tō*.
MATERIAL: whale-tooth.
EYES: black coral.
COLOR: incense smoke.
COMPLETED: February 1970.

353 Circlet Decorated with Bats
Kōmori no kazariwa

The material was a plain circlet when I acquired it. I believe it was a *kuwara*, a kind of brooch for fastening a priest's robes—most likely those of a Chinese priest since the material, stag-antler, is larger and harder than that of the Japanese deer. It is also different from the material out of which I carved the owl shown in Plate 210. That was dry, while this one was quite oily. I engraved a pattern of stylized winged bats.

SIGNED: Masatoshi *tō*.
MATERIAL: stag-antler.
EYES: carved.
COLOR: incense smoke.
COMPLETED: December 1979.
SCALE: seven-eighths life size.

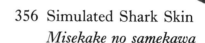

356 Simulated Shark Skin
Misekake no samekawa

The idea for this netsuke came from a shark skin (*samekawa*) *inrō* decorated with metal fish. Thirteen identical fish of no particular species fit the space that was left after I had cut off the base and tip of the narrow whale-tooth I used.

I first carved the fish in relief, lowered the level of the surround, and then carved a pattern of nodules to simulate shark skin. I inlaid the eyes of the fish with the red part of hornbill ivory.

SIGNED: Masatoshi, in a raised oval reserve.
MATERIAL: whale-tooth.
EYES: hornbill ivory.
COLOR: incense smoke; *sumi*—nodules.
COMPLETED: October 1974.

354 Peace and Harmony
Heiwa to chōwa

I made the design simple, as my purpose was to experiment with *ukibori* in ivory. I discuss the method I used on page 48.

The character raised by the *ukibori* technique is "*wa*" standing for "*heiwa*" (peace) and "*chōwa*" (harmony). As mentioned in the text, the fingerprint swirls of ivory do not follow the grain and are not in the ordinary pattern of intersecting arcs. They must result from some hidden property of the ivory. Unlike grain, the swirls go in only one direction.

SIGNED: Masatoshi *tō*.
MATERIAL: ivory.
COLOR: natural.
COMPLETED: December 1969.

Glossary

aisuki: a square chisel; it is flat with the cutting edge perpendicular to the shaft.

Albuquerque, Alfonso de: navigator and adventurer who founded the Portuguese empire in the Orient (1453–1515).

Amakusa Shirō: the popular name of the young Christian samurai who led the Shimabara uprising (1637–1638) in Kyūshū and was killed during the fall of Hara Castle (1621–1638).

Amida Buddha: the Buddha who presides over the Pure Land.

annankiji: see *tōkata*.

arabori: see *arazuki*.

arashi: a technique for roughening surfaces to simulate various materials, such as leather, stone, crepe, and cloth.

arazuki: the rough shaping of a block of material prior to carving.

Asakusa: a district in the heart of old Tokyo.

atari: markings that a carver makes on a block of material to guide him in his design.

bachi-tori: third quarter of the tusk from the tip.

bakemono: a generic term for monsters and goblins of all sorts.

Banko: according to Chinese myth, the first being to emerge from chaos after the creation of the world.

Bashō: Matsuo Bashō; the greatest and most celebrated of *haiku* poets (1644–1694).

bijin: beautiful woman; one of the favorite subjects of *ukiyo-e* artists.

billiken: a doll popular at the beginning of the century; a term used generically to describe a man with a pointed head.

Bizen ware: an unglazed stoneware produced near Okayama.

bokashi: a shading technique in drawing vignettes and tattoos.

bokutō: a wooden sword carried for protection, sometimes used as the insignia of a doctor.

Bugaku: an ancient form of music and dance drama performed with masks.

Bunchō: Ippitsusai Bunchō; illustrator (1727–1796).

Bunraku: Japan's puppet theater; flourished in the Edo Period.

byakudan: white sandalwood; a scented wood often used for incense.

chīku: teak.

chirimen arashi: roughening a surface to simulate the texture of *crêpe de chine*.

Chise: Masatoshi's grandmother, sister of Toshiaki.

chōnin: a member of the merchant or artisan craft inhabiting one of the larger towns or cities in the Edo Period.

chōtsugai: carvings that swing or open on hinges.

chūōban: the central side sections of the turtle's carapace joined to the belly shell.

Daikoku: short for Daikokuten; popularly worshiped as a god of wealth and the guardian of farmers and represented sitting on bales of rice with a big bag slung over his left shoulder and a mallet in his right hand.

daimyō: lords in feudal Japan.

Daruma: short for Bodaidaruma, the name by which the Indian founder of Zen Buddhism in China is known. He sat meditating cross-legged for nine years and, as a result, is represented in popular Japanese art as being limbless and spherical and rolling on a small, flat base.

doriru: spiral drill.

Dutch medicine: the only foreigners allowed in Japan between 1635 and the last years of the Tokugawa regime in the middle of the nineteenth century were the Chinese and the Dutch. Thus, what little the Japanese knew of European civilization was found out from the Dutch and given the epithet "Dutch."

Edo: the name of Tokyo before the Meiji Restoration (1868).

Edo Period: the name of the period from 1603 to 1867, when Japan was ruled by the Tokugawa family; hence, also known as the Tokugawa Period.

Enma-Ō: the King of Hell, of Buddhist origin; he decides the punishment for sinners.

exit hole: the *himotoshi* hole in a netsuke out of which issues the cord.

eyes follow: see *happōnirami*.

Forty-Seven Rōnin, the: the forty-seven former retainers of a feudal lord who was forced to commit ritual suicide in 1702; their quest to avenge their former master ended successfully three years later, but suicide was the price they themselves had to pay for their success. The events of this story have been dramatized and embellished countless times.

Fudō Myō-ō: one of the Go Dai Myō-ō (Five Great Kings of Light); a Buddhist deity originally worshiped as a god of wisdom but also associated with fire. Fudō is normally represented with two attendants and a wreath of flames.

Fukurokuju: also Fukurokujin; like Daikoku and Jurōjin, Fukurokuju is one of the seven gods of good fortune. He is always represented with a very short body and an elongated head, which contains his vast store of wisdom.

Fukusuke: a dwarf with an extremely large head, very popular in the form of a doll; he is famous as a storyteller.

Furisode (Long-Sleeve) Fire: also known as the Great Meireki Fire; in 1657 a great conflagration swept through the new city of Edo, killing a hundred thousand people and destroying half the city. It was three days before the fire was put out.

gagō: art name; also *gō*.

gara: root of an ivory tusk.

genkei: preliminary model, usually made of clay.

Gensō: Chinese name, Xuanzong (Hsüan Tsung); he was the sixth emperor of the Tang Dynasty and ruled from 712 to 756. His increasingly lax hold on government and his infatuation for Yang Guifei led directly to the Anlushan rebellion of 757. (685–762)

Gigaku: a form of Buddhist drama, now rarely performed, which was introduced to Japan from Tibet and India in the seventh century. Gigaku masks are unusually large.

gō: art name; also *gagō*.

Go Dai Myō-ō: The Five Great Kings of Light, Buddhist deities representing the five directions (including the center).

gojitsu nyūmei: a carver's signature added to his work at a subsequent date.

gokuzuihi: fine grit polishing powder.

gosho ningyō: palace dolls; so named because they were first made by courtiers in Kyoto in the first half of the eighteenth century. The dolls are in the shape of naked little boys with an oversized head.

haiku: a type of poem with seventeen syllables, the first and third lines nearly always containing five syllables and the second, seven.

haniwa: clay burial figures that were placed on or around graves in ancient times.

happōnirami: inlaying eyes in a carving so that they follow the viewer.

Harada Naojirō: a painter in the Western style who studied in Germany (1863–1899).

hari: needle; the sort used by netsuke carvers is hard and is made of steel.

Harunobu: Suzuki Harunobu; an artist of the *ukiyo-e* style of woodblock prints, he is particularly famous for his prints of beautiful women (1725–1770).

Hasegawa Tōun: illustrator; active in the latter part of the seventeenth century.

Hashimoto Gahō: a prominent Meiji Era painter who worked in the traditional, Japanese style (1835–1908).

Hashimoto Shingyoku: carver of *okimono*, friend of Masatoshi's father, Kuya.

Heike: another name for the Taira clan, deriving from an alternative reading of the character with which the name is written.

Heike monogatari: the military romance which chronicles the fall of the Taira clan.

hidariba: a triangular knife with the cutting edge on the lefthand side of the apex of the blade's triangle; *hidariba* can be straight, curved, or hooked.

Hidemasa: early nineteenth-century netsuke carver who worked mainly in ivory (exact dates unknown).

himotoshi: the holes and channel in a netsuke for attaching the cords.

hiragana: the more cursive of the two Japanese syllabaries collectively known as *kana*.

Hokusai: Katsushika Hokusai; a prolific artist of the late Edo Period whose drawings are a rich source of ideas for netsuke carvers (1760–1849).

hōnen: the ivory taken from the red and yellow fore part of the cranium of the hornbill bird (also *hōten*).

hō-no-ki: magnolia.

Horikane: the art name of Masatoshi's great-uncle Shimamura Kanetarō, a tattoo artist.

hosaku: a word which, when added to the carver's signature, indicates substantial improvement of another's work (also *hotō*).

hosoku: a reconditioning or minor improvement of another's work.

hōten: see *hōnen*.

hotō: see *hosaku*.

Hōzan: a name Masatoshi used for signing netsuke begun by other carvers.

ibotarō: a wax used for polishing; *ibotarō* is taken from the leaves of the Japanese privet (*Ligustrum ibota*), where it is deposited in the form of a secretion by the male larvae of the wax insect (*Ericerus pela*). It is first melted through the application of heat and then allowed to coagulate in cold water.

ibushi: fumigation, and, specifically, in the case of netsuke, coloring with incense smoke.

Ichikawa Danjūrō: the name of the leading member of a celebrated family of Kabuki actors over a succession of generations; the first Ichikawa Danjūrō, who originated the bravado style of acting called *aragoto*, lived from 1660 to 1704, and the fifth, from 1741 to 1806.

Ii no Hayata: a warrior who, the *Heike monogatari* tells us, along with Minamoto no Yorimasa (1105–1180) killed the beast called *nue*.

Inari: the god of rice, sometimes male but often female; Inari's messenger is a fox and Inari himself is often depicted as a fox.

inoshishi no ha: the tusk of a wild boar.

inrō: a tiered box or case for medicine or a seal, worn hanging by a cord from the sash of a kimono and kept in place by a netsuke acting as a toggle.

irotsuke: coloring or staining.

ishime arashi: a simulation of the surface of stone.

Issai: one of the great early netsuke carvers; he was very popular in his own lifetime. His favorite materials were ivory and whale-tooth. (Latter part of eighteenth century.)

isshi sōden: the tradition among artists and craftsmen of preserving the secrets of their methods by handing them down from father to son.

Ittensai Kuya: an art name used by Masatoshi's father, Kuya.

Ittensai Masatoshi: an art name occasionally used by Masatoshi.

Iwami: the old name for that part of Japan now falling within Shimane Prefecture and part of Yamaguchi Prefecture (*see also* Tomiharu).

Jikishiin Masatoshi: one of Masatoshi's art names, based on his *kaimyō*, or posthumous name.

Jizō: the guardian deity of children, pregnant women, and travelers; Jizō is a compassionate deity, usually represented as a shaven, benevolent-looking priest.

jūkurōmu-san: dichromic acid.

jūniten: the Twelve Gods of Heaven comprise the gods that guard above and below, the sun and the moon, the four directions, and the four intermediary directions.

Jurōjin: one of the seven gods of good fortune, along with Daikoku and Fukurokuju; Jurōjin is the god of longevity and is normally depicted as a scholar and shown in the company of a stag, a crane, or a turtle—all symbols of longevity.

kaba no ha: hippopotamus tooth.

Kaga no Chiyo: the most famous of women *haiku* poets and among the most popular of all poets writing in this form (1703–1775).

kagebori: the carving of baskets and cages.

Kagekiyo: a member of the Taira clan whose adventures form the plot of a Noh drama and a Kabuki play; he tried to assassinate Minamoto no Yoritomo and pulled out his own eyes rather than witness the defeat of the Taira at the hands of the Minamoto (latter part of the twelfth century).

kaibutsu: supernatural animals.

Kaigyokusai: a great netsuke carver who used only the finest quality of ivory and finished his carvings to perfection; he carved *okimono* as well as netsuke (1813–1892).

kaimyō: a posthumous Buddhist name; the religious name by which a person is known after his death.

kajiya: blacksmith.

kakemono: a hanging scroll or picture.

kakihan: an arbitrarily chosen character or design carved with or without the artist's signature for identification.

kamangan-san: potassium permanganate.

kanji: Chinese characters, used for writing Japanese.

Kannon: (Sanskrit, *Avalokitesvara*) a bodhisattva who is revered as the goddess of mercy in Japan and is connected with the Lotus Sutra; there are numerous, varying representations of Kannon.

kappa: water sprites, mythical creatures; they are greenish in color and look something like monkeys with flippers and turtle backs. *Kappa* have an indentation on the top of their heads, which, if emptied of fluid, makes them powerless. They live in rivers and ponds.

katabori: carving in-the-round; also, *marubori*.

kawashibo arashi: a simulation of the texture of leather.

kebori: hairline engraving or etching.

keshifun: the finest grade of gold powder, used for coloring with lacquer and *nikawa*.

kezuri: shaving and carving a netsuke into its final form.

kihō: pores, as found in some woods and stag-antler.

kijidori: the preliminary shaving of a block to be used for carving a netsuke.

Kintarō: the child hero of a famous fairy tale.

kiri: straight drills.

kirin: a mythological Chinese animal commonly found in Japanese art and literature and occasionally identified in translation with the unicorn.

ki-urushi: raw filtered lacquer.

kizu: a bruise, cut, chip, or other form of damage.

knot hole: the *himotoshi* hole in a netsuke which secures the knot tied at the end of the cord.

Kōbō Daishi: also known as Kūkai; he was an early Heian Period propagator of Buddhism whose influence on Japanese religion and literature was second to none. He is the creator of the "native" Japanese syllabaries. (774–835)

kogatana: ordinary flat knife used for shaping handles for tools.

kōguten: dealer in tools and machine parts.

kohaku: amber.

kōki: a kind of red sandalwood.

koku: "carved," a word sometimes added to the carver's signature.

Kokusai: a Meiji Era netsuke carver celebrated for his clever use of stag-antler and whimsical designs (exact dates unknown).

kokusai-bori: a style of carving originated by Kokusai.

kokutan: ebony.

kuchinashi: the gardenia, a plant whose berries produce a dye, known as gamboge, that gives a reddish yellow stain.

kudan: a mythological Chinese beast with the body of a bull and a bearded, goatlike head with horns and numerous eyes.

kujira no ha: whale-tooth, normally from the sperm whale.

Kuniyoshi: Utagawa Kuniyoshi; pupil of Utagawa Toyoharu, he was a skilled landscape artist whose prints show some Western influence (1797–1861).

kurinuki: the carving of perforated and cut-out designs.

kuro-bekkō: black tortoise shell.

kurogaki: black persimmon.

kuwara: a kind of doughnut-shaped brooch worn by priests on the left breast and used as an attachment for the two ends of a priest's robe.

Kuya: art name of Masatoshi's father, Sahara (later Nakamura) Shinzō.

manjū: a type of netsuke named after the round *manjū* bun, which it is said to resemble.

manriki: vise.

marubori: carving in-the-round; three-dimensional carving.

marukami: second quarter of the tusk from the tip.

marunomi: a round chisel; the shaft is concave and the cutting edge curved.

marusaki: the tip of the tusk.

Masakado: *see* Taira no Masakado.

me no arai: coarse textured, heavy grained.

mei: the signature and inscription carved on a netsuke.

migaki: polishing.

migiba: a triangular knife with the cutting edge on the righthand side of the apex of the blade's triangle; *migiba* can be straight, curved, or hooked.

Minamoto no Yoshihira: elder brother of Yoritomo; Yoshihira was famed for his bravery and strength and was nicknamed Akugenta. He died in the Heiji rising against Taira no Kiyomori. (1141–1160)

Minamoto no Yoshitsune: half-brother of Yoritomo; after helping Yoritomo defeat the Taira clan, Yoshitsune fell out with his half-brother, was forced to flee, and eventually committed suicide (1159–1189).

Ming Dynasty: of China, 1368–1644.

Mitsuhiro: one of the most famous of all netsuke craftsmen, especially celebrated for his simple, graceful designs (1810–1875).

Mitsumasa: art name used by Masatoshi at the beginning of his career.

Morita Sōko: a famous netsuke carver, known particularly for his technical mastery (1879–1942).

moyōbori: engraving delicate relief designs, patterns, and textures.

muku (no ki): *Aphananthe aspera*, a tree, member of the elm family, whose leaves, dried, are used in polishing netsuke.

Musōan: art name of Kuya, Masatoshi's father.

Musōan Kuya: art name of Kuya.

Musōin: part of Kuya's posthumous name.

Nakamura: name of family into which Masatoshi's father was adopted.

Nakamura Tokisada: Masatoshi's family name and personal name.

negoro: a red or vermilion lacquer applied on top of a black ground; the red is irregularly polished out to create a pleasing blotched effect.

nemurishin: literally, "sleeping core"; a nerve channel of a tooth or tusk which is solid instead of hollow as a natural result of having become filled with tooth material.

nendo genkei: clay preliminary model.

netsuke: toggle for suspending a purse, tobacco pouch, seal box, or medicine box from the sash of a kimono; especially popular among merchants of the Edo Period.

netsuke-shi: a netsuke carver.

nikawa: a gelatinous fish glue.

nikubori-shi: a tattoo artist.

Niō: the two guardian deities of temples; their images normally stand at temple gates.

nogisu: calipers.

nokogiri: saw.

nokogiri no metate: setting a saw, preparing a saw for use, involving cutting the teeth, sharpening, and polishing.

nue: a tigerlike animal with a monkey's head and a poisonous snake for a tail.

nunome arashi: simulation of the texture of cloth.

obi: the sash worn round the waist with a kimono.

obidome: a clasp for fastening the sash on a kimono.

ojime: a bead, the string fastener for a pouch.

Okatomo: one of the early, great netsuke carvers, famous for his animal subjects (active before 1781).

okimono: decorative objects usually larger than netsuke often placed in the alcove or on cabinet shelves.

okimono-shi: maker of *okimono*.

oni: demons, common in Japanese folklore and art; they are often mischievous and sometimes malicious but are rarely taken seriously. They may have been introduced into Japan from China with Buddhism.

Ono no Tōfū: a great Heian Period calligrapher and statesman; his real name was Michikaze Toyomu (894–966).

Ono Ryōmin: a Meiji Era netsuke carver who worked mainly in ivory.

Otafuku: a name used to describe a particular sort of ugly woman, also used in general to refer mockingly to an ugly woman; also known as Uzume and Okame.

rakan: short for *arakan* (Sanskrit, *arhat*); disciples of Buddha who have reached the highest stage of enlightenment; in Japanese Buddhism, there are sixteen principal *rakan*.

rōnin: masterless samurai.

Ryūjin: the dragon god of the sea; he is normally

portrayed with a fierce expression clutching the Tide Jewel, a jewel with which he controls the ebb and flow of the tide. Storms are a result of his fits of anger.

ryūsa: round, openwork netsuke, similar in shape to *manjū* netsuke, but, unlike *manjū*, they are hollowed out, and the design is executed by perforation. They are named after a carver called Ryūsa who is believed to have originated the form.

ryūsan: sulfuric acid.

sagemono: the collective term for tobacco pouches, purses, and seal and medicine boxes; all such small containers that were suspended from the sash of the kimono.

Sahara Shinzō: the family and "calling name" of Kuya, Masatoshi's father; on his marriage, Kuya adopted his wife's family name, Nakamura (1881–1961).

Sahara Shōzan: Masatoshi's grandfather (d. 1882).

saikaku: rhinoceros horn.

sakame: (cutting) against the grain.

saku: "made" or "carved," sometimes added by a carver to his signature on a netsuke.

sakusan: acetic acid, used as a fixative in coloring.

sankakume: a triangular shape, referring here to the shape of the teeth cut for a saw.

sashi: an elongated type of netsuke, worn thrust inside the sash of a kimono.

seiuchi no ha: walrus tusk.

senkō: incense.

sennin: sages, originally from China and normally associated with Taoism; each *sennin* has a distinctive characteristic, but the feature they hold in common is that they live to a great, old age.

sha: a word meaning "copied" and added to the carver's signature on a netsuke when applicable.

Sharaku: Tōshusai Sharaku; celebrated *ukiyo-e* artist, especially well known for his prints of Kabuki actors (active in the late eighteenth century).

sharime: files for shaping netsuke.

shika no tsuno: stag-antler; also called *kazuno*.

shikakemono: trick netsuke with movable parts, loose heads, extendable tongues, etc.

Shimamura: the name of the family from which Masatoshi traces his lineage.

Shimamura Bunjirō: Masatoshi's great-grandfather.

Shimamura Kanetarō: Masatoshi's great-uncle; he was a tattoo artist and his art name was Horikane.

Shimamura Toshirō: Masatoshi's great-uncle and teacher of Masatoshi's father, Kuya; his art name was Toshiaki.

shin: the core and nerve channel of ivory; or the inner part of whale-tooth.

shindori: the practice of using the core of a tusk for a carving.

shiro-bekkō: literally, "white tortoise shell"; actually, a yellowish color and transparent.

shirochō-gai: a kind of mother-of-pearl; literally, "white butterfly shell."

shishi: the lion of Chinese and Japanese art and folklore; *shishi* sometimes have heads like Pekingese dogs and are often shown with one paw resting on a ball.

shita-e: preliminary drawings and sketches.

shitan: red sandalwood or rosewood.

Shōgitai: a group of die-hard supporters of the Tokugawa regime who rallied on Ueno hill in Edo, where they were routed by forces loyal to the Meiji Emperor in 1868.

shōsangin: silver nitrate.

Shōzan: *see* Sahara Shōzan.

Shunchō: Katsukawa Shunchō; illustrator (died c. 1820).

Shunzan: an art name used by Masatoshi.

Shutendōji: a monster which, according to legend, indulged in rape and plunder in the districts surrounding its mountain abode. It was finally killed by Minamoto no Yorimitsu.

Sosui: a netsuke carver, student of Morita Sōko and contemporary of Masatoshi.

suigyu (no tsuno): water buffalo horn.

Suikoden: (Chinese, *Shuihuzhuan*) translated into English as *All Men Are Brothers* and *Water Margin*; a fourteenth-century Chinese romance set in the Song Dynasty and recounting the adventures of 108 bandit heroes.

sumi: lampblack solidified and shaped into a stick, used for making black ink; also refers to the ink.

sumi-e: a painting in black ink.

sumō: traditional Japanese wrestling involving bouts between two men of great size and strength.

Taira no Kiyomori: general who rose to power at the end of the Heian Period and whose rule came to be characterized by increasing brutality and a growing number of natural calamities; he died four years before the final defeat of the Taira clan at Dannoura (1118–1181).

Taira no Masakado: a member of the Taira clan (Heike) who was a landholder in the east of the country; he led a revolt against the emperor in 935 which ended unsuccessfully in his death five years later (d. 940).

Taira no Shigemori: the favorite son of Taira no Kiyomori; he died before his father, apparently unable to come to terms with his father's brutality (1137–1179).

Takarai Kikaku: most original of the disciples of the great *haiku* master Bashō; his poems are noted for their wit and erudite allusions (1661–1707).

Tang Dynasty: of China, 618–907.

tengu: a mythical goblinlike creature sometimes represented with an eagle's or crow's beak and tiger's claws and sometimes in roughly human form with a very long nose.

tezure: polishing with hands or fingers.

Tide Jewel: *see* Ryūjin.

tō: *tō* means knife, but it is also used after a carver's signature on a netsuke in the same way as "*saku.*"

to-ishi: whetstone for sharpening tools.

tōkata: the finest quality of ivory from the elephants of Southeast Asia.

Tokisada: Masatoshi's personal name and also one of his art names.

Tomiharu: the founder of the Iwami school of carvers, celebrated for their finely detailed representations of insects, for their lengthy inscriptions, and for their skill in using the *ukibori* relief technique (1733–1811).

Tomioka Tessai: a prominent painter in the *nihonga* (traditional Japanese) style of painting (1836–1924).

tonkachi: hammer or mallet.

to-no-ko: very fine polishing powder.

Toriyama Sekien: the teacher of Kitagawa Utamaro; he studied the Kanō style of painting and his book illustrations remain somewhere between traditional work in the Kanō school style and *ukiyo-e* (1712–1788).

Toshiaki: art name of Shimamura Toshirō, Masatoshi's great-uncle and teacher of his father, Kuya.

Toyokuni: Utagawa Toyokuni; an *ukiyo-e* artist famous for his representations of actors (1769–1825).

Toyomasa: an Edo Period carver whose son, Hidari Toyomasa, followed in his footsteps (1773–1856).

tsuge: boxwood.

tsuno-ko: the powder of burnt stag-antler, used for fine polishing.

tsūshō: the "popular" or "calling" name by which a person is known; something like a nickname.

tsuyakeshi: rubbing to reduce the shine of lacquer.

Ueda Akinari: a scholar and writer of stories; he was erudite and versatile, his commentaries on the classics attracting as much interest among scholars as his popular writings did among the general public (1734–1809).

Ueno: one of the oldest districts in Tokyo, the site of the national museum and Tokyo zoo.

Ugetsu monogatari: "Tales of Rain and the Moon," a collection of stories about ghosts and the supernatural, the most famous work of Ueda Akinari.

ukibori: a method of raising surfaces without relief carving.

ukiyo-e: literally, "paintings of the floating world"; *ukiyo-e* constituted a genre art style that flourished from the seventeenth to the nineteenth centuries, *Ukiyo-e* prints depicted themes from the life of common townspeople, landscapes, Kabuki actors, geisha, and suchlike.

umimatsu: literally, "sea pine"; actually, a black or brown coral.

umoregi: lignite, a semifossilized or petrified wood, a form of peat or jet.

urushi-ya: lacquer shop.

waira: a ferocious animal with one daggerlike nail on each paw.

yamai: a natural flaw or diseased condition in whale-tooth, a dentine speck or fleck; blemishes in the form of dentine deposits in the inner part of whale-tooth.

yashabushi: a tree belonging to the same family as the birch.

yashadama: the cone of the *yashabushi* tree used to produce a brown dye; also, the dye itself, sometimes referred to simply as *yasha*.

yasuri: file for shaping tools.

yōkankiji: fine ivory with only a faint grain and appearing grainless.

Yōkihi: Chinese name, Yang Guifei; she was a concubine of the Tang Dynasty emperor Xuanzong and was killed in the Anlushan rebellion (719–756).

yoseki: marquetry, fitting together various woods to make a design.

Yoshitoshi: Tsukioka Yoshitoshi; print artist whose *ukiyo-e* are among the most colorful and dramatic; studied under Kuniyoshi (1839–1892).

Yotsuya: district in Tokyo just west of the imperial palace.

Yūzan: an art name occasionally used by Masatoshi.

zōge: ivory.

Bibliography

I Books which have influenced Masatoshi and which he refers to in the course of his work as a carver of netsuke.

Many of these books were first published during the Edo Period. For ease of reference, therefore, the books are listed alphabetically by title, with an approximate English translation appended in parentheses. Except where indicated, the name which follows is that of the illustrator, with full name in parentheses where applicable. Asterisks appear beside those books mentioned in the text.

Bankō gashiki (Drawings of Various Craftsmen). Illustrator unknown.

Banshoku zukō (Pictorial Studies of Various Occupations). Hokusai (Katsushika Taitō). 1835–1850.

Chūgoku Suikoden gōketsu hyakuhachinin (The Hundred and Eight Heroes of China—illustrations from the Chinese romance *Shuihuzhuan*, "All Men Are Brothers").*

Ehon hōkan (Illustrated Thesaurus—stories and anecdotes from ancient China). Hasegawa Tōun. 6 vols. 1688.*

Ehon hyakki yagyō (Illustrated Book of Nighttime Apparitions). Toriyama Sekien. 3 vols. 1776.*

Eiyō banbutsu hinagata gafū (Miniature Pictures of Many Resplendent Things). Sensai Eitaku.

Hokusai manga (Caricatures by Hokusai). Hokusai (Katsushika Hokusai). 15 vols. 1814–1878.

Hyakki gadan (Drawings and Commentaries on One Hundred Demons). Gyōsai (Kawanabe Gyōsai).*

Japanese Grotesqueries. George Nikolaidis (author). Tokyo: Charles E. Tuttle Co., 1973.*

Kachō sansui zushiki (Drawing Book of Flowers, Birds, Mountains, and Water). Hokusai Isai. Tokyo: Ejima Ihei, 1881.

Kaiki kusazōshi gafū (Illustrated Album of Weird Stories). Ozaki Hisaya.*

Kannon zō kōwa (Discourse on Images of Kannon). Henmi Baiei.

Kirei hyakuchō gafū (Picture Book of One Hundred Attractive Birds).

Nippon dōbutsu zukan (Illustrated Book of Japanese Animals). Uchida Seinosuke (author). Tokyo: Hokuryūkan, 1957.

Obake no zukan (Illustrated Book of Apparitions). Satō Arifumi. Tokyo: K.K. Best Sellers, 1978.*

Sankaikyō (Ghosts and Goblins of China). In *Zusetsu Nippon minzokugaku zenshū*, vol. 3, pp. 185, 186.

Shokkō gafū (Picture Book of Artisans). Inoue Hōshu.

Ukiyo-e to hanga (Pictures of the Floating World and Woodblock Prints). Ōno Shizukata.

Unai no tomo (The Child's Friend—illustrated book on traditional toys). Shimizu Seifū. 10 vols.*

Wakan sansai zu-e (Japanese-Chinese Tripartite Picture Arrangements) 1715.*

Yume awase (Interpretation of Dreams). Matsukawa Hanzan. Osaka: Kawachiya Kihei, 1857.*

Zusetsu Nippon minzokugaku zenshū (Pictorial Encyclopedia of Japanese Folklore). Fujisawa Morihiko (editor). 4 vols. Tokyo: Takahashi Shoten, 1971.*

II Books and articles on netsuke referred to in the text and in the descriptions of the illustrations.

"An Exhibition of Netsuke from the Raymond Bushell Collection." Catalogue of exhibition held at Mikimoto Hall, Tokyo, 1979.

Bushell, Raymond. *An Introduction to Netsuke*. Tokyo: Charles E. Tuttle Co., 1971.

———. *Collectors' Netsuke*. Tokyo: John Weatherhill, Inc., 1971.

———. "Masatoshi: The Last of the Netsuke Artists." *Arts of Asia*. July/August 1973, pp. 22–27.

———. *Netsuke Familiar and Unfamiliar*. Tokyo: John Weatherhill, Inc., 1975.

———. "Netsuke Master." *Orientations*, June 1971, pp. 58–60.

———. *The Inrō Handbook*. Tokyo: John Weatherhill, Inc., 1979.

———. *The Wonderful World of Netsuke*. Tokyo: Charles E. Tuttle Co., 1964.

Masterpieces of Netsuke Art—One Thousand Favorites of Leading Collectors. Compiled by Bernard Hurtig. Tokyo: John Weatherhill, Inc., 1973.

"Netsuke ni tsuite: chisa na karada ni himerareta chōkoku no miryoku." *The Kotto*, April 1980, pp. 51–55 (Yomiuri Shimbun).

III Other books mentioned.

Matsumura Shōfu. *Meijin monogatari* (An Account of Master Artists). 1924.

"Porutogaru no tōhō bōeki" (Portugal's Eastern Trade). *Kinsei sanbyakunen shi* 1(1953): 13.

Tokugawa Mitsukuni, ed. *Dai Nihon shi* (Great Japanese History). 1852.

Index

(Numbers in italics refer to plates)